Aboriginal and Treaty Rights in the Maritimes

· · · · · ·

The *Marshall* Decision and Beyond

D1601566

Purich's Aboriginal Issues Series

Aboriginal and Treaty Rights in the Maritimes

• • • • • •

The *Marshall* Decision and Beyond

Thomas Isaac, B.A., M.A., LL.B., LL.M.

Purich Publishing Ltd.
Saskatoon, Saskatchewan

All enquiries and orders regarding this publication should be addressed to
Purich Publishing Ltd.
Box 23032, Market Mall Postal Outlet
Saskatoon, SK Canada S7J 5H3
Tel: (306) 373-5311
Facsimile: (306) 373-5315
E-mail: purich@sk.sympatico.ca
Web site: www.purichpublishing.com

National Library of Canada Cataloguing in Publication Data
Isaac, Thomas F. (Thomas Francis) 1966-
  Aboriginal and treaty rights in the Maritimes

  (Purich's aboriginal series)
  Includes bibliographical references and index.
  ISBN 1-895830-19-2

  1. Aboriginal title--Maritime Provinces. 2. Indians of North
America--Legal status, laws, etc.--Maritime Provinces. 3. Indians of
North America--Canada--Treaties. 4. Indians of North America--
Canada--Government relations. 5. Indians of North America--
Maritime Provinces. I. Title. II. Series.
KE7709.I82 2001   342.71'0872'09715   C2001-911378-1
KF8205.I82 2001

Editing, design, and layout by Page Wood Publishing Services, Saskatoon
Cover design by NEXT Communications, Inc., Saskatoon
Printed in Canada by Houghton Boston Printers, Saskatoon
Printed on acid-free paper

Readers will note that words like Aboriginal, Native, and Indigenous have been capitalized in this book. In recent years, many Aboriginal people have argued that such words should be capitalized when referring to specific people, in the same manner that European and American are capitalized. I agree; hence the capitalization.
Donald Purich, Publisher

······

Contents

······

Table of Cases

R. v. *Smith,* [1983] 1 S.C.R. 554, [1983] 3 C.N.L.R. 161, 147 D.L.R. (3d) 237, 47 N.R. 132, rev'g [1980] 4 C.N.L.R. 29, 34 N.R. 91, 113 D.L.R. (3d) 522 (F.C.A.); rev'g [1978] C.N.L.B. (No. 4) 121 (F.C.T.D.) 30–31

R. v. *Sparrow,* [1990] 1 S.C.R. 1075, [1990] 3 C.N.L.R. 160, (1990), 46 B.C.L.R. (2d) 1, [1990] 4 W.W.R. 410, 56 C.C.C. (3d) 263, 70 D.L.R. (4th) 385, 111 N.R. 241 (S.C.C.); aff'g [1987] 1 C.N.L.R. 145, 32 C.C.C. (3d) 65, 36 D.L.R. (4th) 246, 9 B.C.L.R. (2d) 300, 2 W.W.R. 577 (B.C.C.A.) 42, 46–47, 51, 56–60, 68–69, 79–80, 85–86, 96, 122–23, 130–31, 133–36, 138–40, 154, 159, 161–63, 166–67

R. v. *Sundown,* [1999] 1 S.C.R. 393, [1999] 2 C.N.L.R. 289, (1999), 170 D.L.R. (4th) 385, 132 C.C.C. (3d) 353, 236 N.R. 251, [1999] 6 W.W.R. 278; aff'g [1997] 4 C.N.L.R. 241, 117 C.C.C. (3d) 140, 158 Sask. R. 53, [1997] 8 W.W.R. 379 (Sask. C.A.); aff'g [1995] 3 C.N.L.R. 152 (Sask. Q.B.); rev'g [1994] 2 C.N.L.R. 174 (Sask. Prov. Ct.) 66–67, 119

R. v. *Syliboy,* [1929] 1 D.L.R. 307, (1928), 50 C.C.C. 389, 4 C.N.L.C. 430 (N.S. Co. Ct.) 50, 52, 170

R. v. *Taylor and Williams,* [1981] 3 C.N.L.R. 114, 62 C.C.C. (2d) 227, 34 O.R. (2d) 360 (Ont. C.A.); aff'g [1980] 1 C.N.L.R. 83 (Ont. Div. Ct.); leave to appeal refused [1981] 2 S.C.R. xi, 1 C.N.L.R. 183n (S.C.C.) 18, 54, 108, 118–19

R. v. *Tomah,* [1999] 3 C.N.L.R. 311, 211 N.B.R. (2d) 59, 539 A.P.R. 59 (N.B.Q.B.) 68, 170

R. v. *Van der Peet,* [1996] 2 S.C.R. 507, [1996] 4 C.N.L.R. 177, 50 C.R. (4th) 1, 109 C.C.C. (3d) 1, 23 B.C.L.R. (3d) 1, [1996] 9 W.W.R. 1, 137 D.L.R. (4th) 289, 200 N.R. 1 (S.C.C.); aff'g [1993] 4 C.N.L.R. 221, 5 W.W.R. 459, 80 B.C.L.R. (2d) 75, 83 C.C.C. (3d) 289 (B.C.C.A.); reconsideration refused January 16, 1997, Doc. 23803 (S.C.C.) 61–63, 75–76, 78, 96, 111, 113, 115, 117, 122, 140

R. v. *Vincent,* [1993] 2 C.N.L.R. 165, 12 O.R. (3d) 427, 80 C.C.C. (3d) 256 (Ont. C.A.); leave to appeal refused 163 N.R. 239n, 15 O.R. (3d) xvin, 83 C.C.C. (3d) viin, [1993] 4 C.N.L.R. vi (S.C.C.) 41

R. v. *Wesley,* [1932] 4 D.L.R. 774, 5 C.N.L.C. 540, 2 W.W.R. 337 (Alta. C.A.) 41

R. v. *White and Bob,* [1965] S.C.R. vi, 6 C.N.L.C. 684, (1965), 52 D.L.R. (2d) 481n (S.C.C.); aff'g 6 C.N.L.C. 629 (1964), 52 W.W.R. 193, 50 D.L.R. (2d) 613 (B.C.C.A.) 40, 51, 53, 112

Re Amendment of the Constitution of Canada (Patriation Case), [1981] 1 S.C.R. 753 80

Re Eskimos, [1939] S.C.R. 104, 5 C.N.L.C. 123, [1939] 2 D.L.R. 417 (S.C.C.) 38

Re R. v. *The Secretary of State for Foreign and Commonwealth Affairs, ex parte the Indian Association of Alberta, Union of New Brunswick Indians, Union of Nova Scotia Indians, Note from Appeal Committee of the House of Lords,* [1982] 3 C.N.L.R. 195, [1982] 2 All E.R. 143 (H.L.); aff'g [1982] 1 Q.B. 892, [1981] 4 C.N.L.R. 86 (C.A.) 31

Re Waters and Water Powers, [1929] S.C.R. 200, [1929] D.L.R. 481 37

R.J.R.-MacDonald Inc. v. *Canada (A.G.),* [1994] 1 S.C.R. 311 144–45

Shubenacadie Indian Band v. *Canada (Human Rights Commission),* [2000] 4 C.N.L.R. 275 (F.C.A.); aff'g [1998] 2 C.N.L.R. 212 (F.C.T.D.); leave to appeal refused, [2001] 1 C.N.L.R. ivn (S.C.C.) 45

Shubenacadie Indian Band v. *Canada (Min. of Fisheries and Oceans),* [2001] 1 C.N.L.R. 282 (F.C.T.D.) 69–70, 143–45, 150, 171

• • • • • •

Selected Bibliography

R. v. Marshall

Barsh, R.L., and J.Y. Henderson, "Marshalling the Rule of Law in Canada: Of Eels and Honour" (Fall 1999) 11 Constitutional Forum 1.

Barss Donham, P., "Lobster Wars" (February 2000) Canadian Dimension 26.

———, "Marshall Decision Book Needs Better Storyteller" (January/February 2001) Canadian Dimension 7.

———, "Lobster Wars: 2001 Edition" (July/August 2001) Canadian Dimension 5.

Bell, C., and K. Buss, "The Promise of *Marshall* on the Prairies: A Framework for Analyzing Unfulfilled Treaty Promises" (2000) 63(2) Sask. L. Rev. 667.

Coates, K., *The Marshall Decision and Native Rights.* Montreal & Kingston: McGill-Queen's University Press, 2000.

Henderson, J.Y., "Constitutional Powers and Treaty Rights" (2000) 63(2) Sask. L. Rev. 719.

Hurlburt, W.H., "Case Comment on *R. v. Marshall*" (2000) 38(2) Alta. L. Rev. 563.

Isaac, T., "The Courts, Government, and Public Policy: The Significance of *R. v. Marshall*" (2000) 63(2) Sask. L. Rev. 701.

———, "Understanding Treaty Rights in Atlantic Canada: *R. v. Marshall*" (2000) 16(3) Solicitor's Journal 15.

———, "The *Marshall* Decision and Governments' Duty to Regulate" (June 2001) 22(5) Policy Options Politiques 53.

Normey, R., "Angling for 'Common Intention': Treaty Interpretation in *R. v. Marshall*" (2000) 63(2) Sask. L. Rev. 645.

Peacock, D., "Burnt Church Affair Needs Closer Look" (January/February 2001) Canadian Dimension 3.

Rotman, L.I., " 'My Hovercraft is Full of Eels': Smoking Out the Message in *R. v. Marshall*" (2000) 63(2) Sask. L. Rev. 617.

Sheffer, W.F., "*R. v. Marshall*: Aboriginal Treaty Rights and Wrongs" (March 2000) 10 Windsor Review of Legal & Social Issues 77.

Maritime Treaties and Aboriginal People

Bartlett, R.H., *Indian Reserves in the Atlantic Provinces of Canada.* Saskatoon, Sask.: University of Saskatchewan Native Law Centre, 1986.

Cumming, P.A., and N.H. Mickenberg, "The Atlantic Provinces" in *Native Rights in Canada,* 2d ed. Toronto: General, 1972, at 93–106 and 295–312.

Patterson, S.E., "Anatomy of a Treaty: Nova Scotia's First Native Treaty in Historical Context" (1999) 48 U.N.B.L.J. 41.

Paul, D.N., *We Were Not the Savages: A Micmac Perspective on the Collision of European and Aboriginal Civilization.* Halifax: Nimbus, 1993.

Upton, L.F.S., *Micmacs and the Colonists, 1713–1867.* Vancouver: University of British Columbia Press, 1979.

Wildsmith, B.H., "Pre-Confederation Treaties" in B.W. Morse, ed., *Aboriginal Peoples and the Law: Indian, Metis and Inuit Rights in Canada.* Ottawa: Carleton University Press, 1985.

General Aboriginal Law

Isaac, T., *Aboriginal Law: Cases, Materials and Commentary*, 2d ed. Saskatoon, Sask.: Purich, 1999.

Imai, S., *The 2000 Annotated Indian Act and Aboriginal Constitutional Provisions.* Toronto: Carswell, 2000.

Woodward, J., *Native Law,* looseleaf. Toronto: Carswell, 1994.

······

Abbreviations

Law Reporters and Journals

Alta. L.R.	Alberta Law Reports
A.R.	Alberta Reports
All. E.R.	All England Law Reports
App. Cas.	Appeal Cases
A.P.R.	Atlantic Provinces Reports
B.C.L.R.	British Columbia Law Reports
C.C.C.	Canadian Criminal Cases
C.E.L.R.	Canadian Environmental Law Reporter
C.N.L.B.	Canadian Native Law Bulletin
C.N.L.C.	Canadian Native Law Cases
C.N.L.R.	Canadian Native Law Reporter
C.R.	Criminal Reports
C.R.R.	Canadian Rights Reporter
C.T.C.	Canadian Tax Cases
D.L.R.	Dominion Law Reports
D.T.C.	Dominion Tax Cases
E.T.R.	Estates and Trusts Reports
F.C.	Federal Court of Canada Reports
N.R.	National Reporter
N.B.R.	New Brunswick Reports
N.S.R.	Nova Scotia Reports
O.R.	Ontario Reports
Q.A.C.	Quebec Appeal Cases

QL	Quick Law
Queen's L.J.	Queen's Law Journal
R.P.R.	Real Property Reports
S.C.R.	Supreme Court Reports
U.B.C. L. Rev.	University of British Columbia Law Review
U.N.B.L.J.	University of New Brunswick Law Journal
W.W.R.	Western Weekly Reports

Courts

App. Div.	Appellate Division
C.A.	Court of Appeal
Co. Ct.	County Court
Ct. J.	Court of Justice
C.S.P.	Cour des Sessions de la paix
Div. Ct.	Divisional Court
F.C.	Federal Court
J.C.P.C.	Judicial Committee of the Privy Council
Prov. Ct.	Provincial Court
Q.B.	Court of Queen's Bench
Sup. Ct.	Superior Court
S.C.	Supreme Court
S.C.C.	Supreme Court of Canada
T.C.C.	Tax Court of Canada
T.D.	Trial Division

Jurisdictions

Alta.	Alberta
B.C.	British Columbia
N.B.	New Brunswick
N.S.	Nova Scotia
N.W.T.	Northwest Territories
Nun.	Nunavut

Ont.	Ontario
P.E.I.	Prince Edward Island
Que.	Quebec
Sask.	Saskatchewan
U.K.	United Kingdom

Statutes

R.S.A.	Revised Statutes of Alberta
R.S.C.	Revised Statutes of Canada
S.N.B.	Statutes of New Brunswick
S.N.S.	Statutes of Nova Scotia
SOR	Statutory Orders and Regulations (Canada)

• • • • • •

Preface

The first question a reader may ask is why a distinct book is needed on Aboriginal and treaty rights in the Maritimes and the 1999 Supreme Court of Canada decision in *R.* v. *Marshall*. There are a number of reasons a focussed text relating to *Marshall* and the Maritimes is useful. First, the extent of public interest in this decision is unparalleled, especially in the Maritimes. Second, *Marshall* represents the culmination of many years of jurisprudence concerning treaty rights in Canada. Third, as a result of *Marshall* and the development of a more active Aboriginal community in the Maritimes, Aboriginal rights issues have been brought to the forefront in the Maritime provinces. Lastly, as a result of these issues being made more public, the issue of Aboriginal title in the Maritimes is being revisited and many new questions are being raised that were once thought not to be relevant to this region of Canada.

Aboriginal issues have been one of the key public-policy and legal issues facing Canada over the past twenty years. Indeed, for the resource sector in Canada—such as the mining, oil, gas, fishing, and forestry industries—this area of the law is becoming increasingly more relevant and pressing. Aboriginal law is changing quickly, and there is a growing demand for information that is accessible and timely. In particular, the vast majority of significant legal developments in this area over the past twenty years have occurred outside the Maritimes. Only recently, particularly with media reports about the living conditions of the Innu in Newfoundland and Labrador and residential school abuse, has any substantive attention been paid to the plight of Aboriginal people on Canada's East Coast. This increased interest culminated in the Supreme Court of Canada's September 17, 1999, decision of *R.* v. *Marshall*.[1] With this single decision from Canada's highest court, legal and other issues affecting the Mi'kmaq and Maliseet were placed in the limelight. Questions began to be raised as to what rights the Mi'kmaq and Maliseet may possess,

---

1   *R.* v. *Marshall,* [1999] 3 S.C.R. 456.

including potential Aboriginal title, and how their interests can be balanced with the interests of non-Aboriginal Maritimers.

Although *Marshall* concerns treaty rights in the Maritimes, it is a decision that affects all of Canada. Particularly important is the approach the Supreme Court used in this case to interpret treaty rights, the impact of this approach in other parts of Canada, and the court's extensive discussion of the duties and (I maintain) the opportunities for public governments, not only in the Maritimes but across Canada. The references throughout the book to the *Marshall* decisions refer not only to the September 17, 1999, decision of the Supreme Court of Canada (referenced throughout as *Marshall No. 1*), but also to the reasons rendered by the Supreme Court on November 17, 1999,[2] regarding the court's refusal to grant a rehearing of the decision (referenced throughout as *Marshall No. 2*).

The term "Aboriginal" is used in this book to describe those persons who come within the meaning of section 35(2) of the *Constitution Act, 1982,* namely the Indian, Inuit, and Métis peoples of Canada. When the term "Indian" is used alone, it refers to those persons identified and registered as Indians within the meaning of the federal *Indian Act.*

Although this book focusses on *Marshall,* it also provides a general overview of the historical and legal context within which Aboriginal and treaty rights are currently understood. It is meant for people who are interested in the legal challenges that lie ahead for both the Maritime provinces and the Aboriginal people living there, and for the rest of Canada and the resource sector generally. Although the book deals with this subject matter in an introductory manner, extensive citations and references have been included for those who are interested in additional commentary and resources.

I wish to acknowledge Don Purich, Karen Bolstad, and Jane Billinghurst for their assistance in the production of this book. I thank Yolande and Gerard Tetrault for their kind hospitality as I finished writing. I also thank Christine Tetrault, my partner and best friend, for her support and assistance. I lovingly dedicate this book to her.

---

2   *R. v. Marshall,* [1999] 3 S.C.R. 533 (rehearing application refused).

Chapter I

••••••

Historical Overview of Aboriginal and Treaty Rights in the Maritimes

Introduction[1]

Prior to 1982, Aboriginal law in Canada was slow to develop and was generally overlooked in the area of public-policy development and decision making. With the enactment of the *Constitution Act, 1982*[2] and its affirmation and recognition of Aboriginal and treaty rights, the rights of Aboriginal people were placed squarely before the courts and the public-policy makers. In the two decades since the *Constitution Act, 1982* came into effect, the changes and developments in Aboriginal law have been dramatic, and they have had an impact in every region of Canada. In 1999, the Maritimes felt the direct impact of these legal developments with the release of the *Marshall* decisions. The Supreme Court of Canada's decisions in this case are two of the many judicial decisions that are redefining the nature of the relationship between Aboriginal people, the courts, and the rest of Canada.

Before discussing the *Marshall* decisions in detail, it is useful to outline the broader context within which the decisions were made. This chapter briefly discusses the early development of Aboriginal and treaty rights law, particularly as it relates to the Maritimes. This chapter also touches on the creation

---

1 Readers should refer to chapter 4 for additional historical and legal context surrounding the development of Aboriginal rights in the Maritimes. There are a number of texts available outlining Aboriginal and treaty rights law in Canada, including T. Isaac, *Aboriginal Law: Cases, Materials and Commentary*, 2d ed. (Saskatoon, Sask.: Purich , 1999), and J. Woodward, *Native Law*, looseleaf (Toronto: Carswell, 1989).

2 *Constitution Act, 1982*, Sched. B. to the *Canada Act 1982* (U.K.), 1982, c. 11, as am. by the *Constitution Amendment Proclamation, 1983*, R.S.C. 1985, App. II, No. 46 [am. ss. 25(b) and add. 35(3), 35(4), 35.1 and 37.1 and 54.1].

of reserves in the Maritimes, the *Royal Proclamation of 1763,* and the social and demographic realities of Aboriginal people in the Maritimes today.

Early Maritime Treaties

At the beginning of the eighteenth century, much of present-day Newfoundland and Labrador, Nova Scotia, New Brunswick, and northern Maine belonged to the French colony of Acadia, which was ceded to the British under the Treaty of Utrecht in 1713. From 1713 to 1763, the Maritimes were central to the struggle between the French and the British over control of North America. The Mi'kmaq and Maliseet (the two First Nations groups presently occupying the Maritimes) were in the middle of this conflict, due in part to British concerns that the Aboriginal people of the region had a stronger political alliance with the French than with the British.

From 1756 to 1763, the Seven Years War raged between European colonial powers intent on consolidating their holdings all over the world. At war's end, Britain emerged as the supreme colonial power and in the 1763 Treaty of Paris, France ceded all its North American possessions except the islands of St. Pierre and Miquelon to Great Britain, bringing Cape Breton and Prince Edward Island under British control. In 1784, the British subdivided Nova Scotia, and the mainland side of the Bay of Fundy became known as New Brunswick. This area included the traditional territory of both the Mi'kmaq[3] (from the Gaspé area to Nova Scotia and the Bay of Fundy) and Maliseet peoples (the Saint John River Valley and Passamaquoddy region).[4]

From 1713, when the British acquired sovereignty over most of the Maritimes, until the proclamations of 1762 and 1763, a series of peace and friendship treaties were signed between the British and the Mi'kmaq[5] and Maliseet. The primary goal of these treaties was to solidify peaceful relations with the Mi'kmaq and Maliseet and to end hostilities between them and the British. The British Crown promised the Mi'kmaq and Maliseet that in return

---

3   For a Mi'kmaq perspective on the interaction between the Mi'kmaq and Europeans and the early treaty negotiations, see D.N. Paul, *We Were Not the Savages: A Micmac Perspective on the Collision of European and Aboriginal Civilization* (Halifax: Nimbus, 1993).

4   See R. Bartlett, *Indian Reserves in the Atlantic Provinces of Canada* (Saskatoon, Sask.: University of Saskatchewan Native Law Centre, 1986) at 14.

5   See W. Wicken, "The Mi'kmaq and Wuastukwiuk Treaties" (1994) 44 U.N.B.L.J. 241, and the Royal Commission on Aboriginal Peoples research paper by W. Wicken and J. Reid, "An Overview of the Eighteenth Century Treaties Signed Between the Mi'kmaq and Wuastukwiuk Peoples and the English Crown, 1693–1928" (Ottawa: Royal Commission on Aboriginal Peoples, 1996).

for agreeing to keep the peace and to respect British law, the Aboriginal peoples could continue to hunt, fish, and trade. These early peace and friendship treaties, unlike later treaties signed in Canada, did not involve the cession of land and, therefore, do not appear to have explicitly extinguished Aboriginal title.[6]

One of the first treaties affecting the Maritimes was the Treaty of Portsmouth in 1713.[7] It was negotiated by the British governor and the chiefs of several Maritime Indian nations. This treaty provided, in part:

> That if any Controversy or Difference at any time hereafter happen to arise betwixt any of the English or Indians, for any real or supposed wrong or injury done on the one side or the other, no Private Revenge shall be taken by the Indians for the same, but proper application shall be made to Her Majesty's Government, upon the place, for remedy thereof, in our Course of Justice, We hereby submitting ourselves to be ruled & Governed by Her Majesty's Laws & desire to have the protection & benefit of the same.[8]

This treaty also ensured that the British would be able to "peaceably & quietly enter upon, improve, & forever enjoy" the lands acquired from the Indians without any fear of "molestation or claims" by any Indians. In return, the Indians were to have their own hunting, fishing, and fowling grounds. This treaty included Indians in the region later designated as New Brunswick, but did not include the Mi'kmaq of Nova Scotia.[9]

The "Submission and Agreement of the Delegates of the Eastern Indians" (Treaty of Boston), which was signed in Boston, Massachusetts, on December 15, 1725, was the treaty that ended the British and Indian War.[10] In it, the Indians acknowledged British jurisdiction and sovereignty over the territories of Nova Scotia, and they agreed to cease all hostilities and use the Crown's courts to settle disputes. Also, the Indians were granted the "priviledge of fishing, hunting, and fowling as formerly." Cumming and Mickenberg noted that the "Treaty was ratified at later dates by the Micmacs and may have been ratified by the Maliseets as well."[11]

---

6 P.A. Cumming and N.H. Mickenberg, *Native Rights in Canada*, 2d ed. (Toronto: General, 1972) at 98; see also chapter 4 in this book.
7 Reproduced in *ibid.* at 296.
8 *Ibid.* at 297.
9 *R. v. Paul*, [1998] 1 C.N.L.R. 209 (N.B.Q.B.) at 219.
10 Cumming and Mickenberg, *supra* note 6 at 95. See *R. v. Perley*, [1982] 2 C.N.L.R. 185 (N.B.Q.B.), and *R. v. Simon*, [1985] 2 S.C.R. 387, upholding the applicability of the treaty.
11 Cumming and Mickenberg, *ibid.* at 95, note 6. The authors cite a useful reference by D.M. Hurley, *Report on Indian Land Rights in the Atlantic Provinces* (Ottawa: National Museum of Canada, 1962).

Most of the early Maritime treaties were signed at British settlements and contain articles relating to relations between the British Crown, the Mi'kmaq, and the Maliseet. Many of the articles in these treaties are similar because they were modelled on the 1725 Treaty of Boston. Most of these treaties contain the following provisions: (1) a recognition of the Crown's jurisdiction and dominion over the territory covered, including Nova Scotia and Acadia, (2) an agreement that conflicts between Indians and settlers would be adjudicated according to British law, (3) an understanding that Indians would not "molest" any English subjects who had already established settlements or who would do so in the future, and (4) an understanding that the English would not "molest" the Indians with respect to their hunting, fishing, planting, and fowling activities.

Treaties signed in 1726, 1749, and 1760 all conferred hunting and fishing rights on the Maliseet.[12] On November 22, 1752, the Mi'kmaq of Nova Scotia signed a peace and friendship treaty with the British, which provided the Indians with "free liberty of hunting and Fishing as usual and that if they shall think a Truck house needful at the River Chibenaccadie, or any other place of their resort they shall have the same built and proper Merchandize."[13] Further treaties signed in 1760 and 1761 covered the Mi'kmaq and Maliseet communities in the Maritimes, and a number of Mi'kmaq and Maliseet First Nations in the Gaspé region of Quebec are also most likely covered by these treaties. A later treaty, signed in 1778, did not guarantee any hunting or fishing rights for the Indians of New Brunswick,[14] but it did note that the Indians would be allies of the British in any hostilities against the United States.[15] In *Marshall No. 1* (1999), the Supreme Court of Canada focussed on treaties signed in 1760 and 1761:

> The 1760-61 treaties were the *culmination* of more than a *decade* of inter-mittent hostilities between the British and the Mi'kmaq. Hostilities with the French were also prevalent in Nova Scotia throughout the 1750s, and the Mi'kmaq were constantly allied with the French against the British. . . . The British wanted peace and a safe environment for their current and future

---

12 *R. v. Paul*, [1981] 2 C.N.L.R. 83 (N.B.C.A.), and *R. v. Paul; R. v. Polchies*, [1988] 4 C.N.L.R. 107 (N.B.Q.B.).

13 Reproduced in Cumming and Mickenberg, *supra* note 6 at 307. See also S. Patterson, "Anatomy of a Treaty: Nova Scotia's First Native Treaty in Historical Context" (1999) 48 U.N.B.L.J. 41.

14 *Paul; Polchies, supra* note 12.

15 *R. v. Polchies*, [1983] 3 C.N.L.R. 131 (N.B.C.A.).

settlers. Despite their recent victories, they did not feel completely secure in Nova Scotia. [Emphasis in original][16]

The court discussed these treaties in detail.[17]

As the settlement of Canada moved west, so did the treaty-making process. For example, in 1850, the Robinson Treaties of Lake Huron and Lake Superior were signed, and between 1871 and 1921, eleven numbered treaties were signed, covering most of the land in northwestern Ontario and the prairie provinces.[18] The Douglas Treaties and part of Treaty No. 8 extend into British Columbia. Treaty No. 11 and part of Treaty No. 8 apply to the Northwest Territories. The legal distinction between pre- and post-Confederation treaties is nominal. Essentially, there was a transfer of responsibility from one crown to another, and treaties made with the British Crown before Confederation are held to be treaties with the Canadian Crown after Confederation.[19]

What is unique about the Maritimes is that the treaties signed there did not acknowledge the cession or release by the First Nations of any rights, including perhaps Aboriginal title, which is discussed in detail in chapter 4. The majority of other historical treaties in Canada involved the Aboriginal people ceding, releasing, and surrendering their rights to land and to their traditional activities in return for specific rights specifically outlined within the terms of the negotiated treaty. In the Maritimes, the potential exists for Aboriginal rights and Aboriginal title to co-exist alongside rights contained in the treaties. At this early stage, it is difficult to ascertain what the effect will be of this unique situation, but no matter what the outcome, the Maritimes will provide an interesting case study of the development of Aboriginal law in Canada.

Whereas governments and the Canadian legal system have tended to view treaties with Aboriginal people from a positivist, literal point of view, many Aboriginal people see treaties as being much more holistic and profound. For Aboriginal people, the historical and modern treaties are significant not only for what they contain, but also for what they represent: namely, solemn agreements and commitments among groups of independent and sovereign peoples. Harold Cardinal, in his ground-breaking work, *The Unjust Society,* wrote:

---

16 *R. v. Marshall (Marshall No. 1),* [1999] 3 S.C.R. 456 at para. 23.

17 *Ibid.* at paras. 3, 15–17, 19–41, 47.

18 A collection of the texts of many treaties can be found in *Consolidated Native Law Statutes, Regulations and Treaties 2000/2001* (Toronto: Carswell, 2000); Treaty Nos. 1 and 2 (1871), 3 (1873), 4 (1874), 5 (1875), 6 (1876), 7 (1877), 8 (1899), 9 (1905), 10 (1906), and 11 (1921).

19 *R. v. Secretary of State,* [1981] 4 C.N.L.R. 86 (Eng. C.A.).

> To the Indians of Canada, the treaties represent an Indian Magna Carta. The
> treaties are important to us, because we entered into these negotiations with
> faith, with hope for a better life with honour. . . . The treaties were the way in
> which the white people legitimized in the eyes of the world their presence in
> our country. It was an attempt to settle the terms of occupancy on a just
> basis, legally and morally to extinguish the legitimate claims of our people
> to title to the lands in our country.[20]

The differences among Aboriginal and non-Aboriginal people regarding the
significance and meaning of treaties have resulted in a novel perspective of
treaties in Canadian law. Courts in Canada have held that treaties are unique
or *sui generis*.[21] Indian treaties are neither international-like agreements between nation-states[22] nor simple contracts.[23] The Supreme Court of Canada
has described Indian treaties in this way: "An Indian treaty is unique; it is an
agreement *sui generis* which is neither created nor terminated by international law."[24]

The treaties depend for their validity on a number of factors. Relying
primarily on *R. v. Simon*[25] and *R. v. Sioui*,[26] Professor Peter Hogg has provided a succinct summary of the characteristics of a valid Indian treaty:

1. Parties: The parties to the treaty must be the Crown, on the one side, and
   an aboriginal nation, on the other side.
2. Agency: The signatories to the treaty must have the authority to bind
   their principals, namely, the Crown and the aboriginal nation.
3. Intention to create legal relations: The parties must intend to create le-
   gally binding obligations.
4. Consideration: The obligations must be assumed by both sides, so that
   the agreement is a bargain.
5. Formality: there must be "a certain measure of solemnity."[27]

---

20 H. Cardinal, *The Unjust Society: The Tragedy of Canada's Indians* (Edmonton:
    Hurtig, 1969) at 28–29.
21 See *R. v. Simon*, [1985] 2 S.C.R. 387 at 404, and *R. v. Sioui*, [1990] 1 S.C.R. 1025
    at 1043.
22 *R. v. Francis*, [1956] S.C.R. 618.
23 *Pawis v. R.*, [1979] 2 C.N.L.R. 52 (F.C.T.D.), and *Hay River v. R.*, [1979] 2
    C.N.L.R. 101 (F.C.T.D.).
24 *Simon, supra* note 21 at 401.
25 *Ibid.*
26 *Sioui, supra* note 21.
27 P. Hogg, *Constitutional Law of Canada*, 4th ed. (Toronto: Carswell, 1997) at
    27.6(c), 691.

To assist in understanding the current situation in the Maritimes and the lack of treaties that either cede land or are modern in nature, a brief examination of the early colonial policy towards Aboriginal people is illuminating. British colonial policy towards Aboriginal people is set out clearly in the *Royal Proclamation of 1763*.

Royal Proclamation of 1763

On October 7, 1763, following the British conquest of New France and its resulting cession to Great Britain in the Treaty of Paris, King George III of Great Britain issued the *Royal Proclamation of 1763*.[28] The *Royal Proclamation* consolidated Great Britain's dominion over North America and set aside a huge tract of land as land reserved to the Indians "as their hunting grounds." It prohibited grants, purchases, or settlement of this land without a licence, and specified that all non-Indians without a licence were to leave the land in question and that a licence was required for all trade with Indians. The *Royal Proclamation* recognized the rights of Indians to unceded lands in their possession and stipulated that the Indians may cede such lands only to the Crown. The *Proclamation* noted that "great Frauds and Abuses have been committed in purchasing Land of the Indians" and it prohibited settlers from purchasing land from the Indians, reserving for itself the sole right to do so.[29]

The *Royal Proclamation of 1763* is a crucial document in that it acknowledges the interests and rights of Aboriginal people. The Supreme Court of Canada has stated that the objectives of the *Proclamation* were

> to provide a solution to the problems created by the greed which hitherto some of the English had all too often demonstrated in buying up Indian land at low prices. The situation was causing dangerous trouble among the Indians and the Royal Proclamation was meant to remedy this.[30]

Thus, the *Proclamation* was an attempt to bring some order to a disorderly situation that was destructive and harmful to many Aboriginal people in North America.

The *Proclamation* described the Indian Territories as those lands lying west of the Appalachians, except those within Quebec, East Florida, West

---

28   *Royal Proclamation of 1763,* R.S.C. 1985, App. II, No. 1.
29   See B. Slattery, *The Land Rights of Indigenous Canadian Peoples as Affected by the Crown's Acquisition of Their Territories* (D.Phil. Thesis, Oxford University; Saskatoon, Sask.: University of Saskatchewan Native Law Centre, 1979) at 191–345.
30   *Sioui, supra* note 21 at 1064.

Florida, and Rupert's Land. These Indian Territories were reserved for the use of the Indians and were closed to settlement "for the present" (that is to say, for now, subject to change). The *Proclamation* required the removal of all persons who had settled within the Indian Territories and "upon any other Lands, which not having been ceded to or purchased by Us, are still reserved for the said Indians." This latter clause clearly covers lands outside the Indian Territories and provides protection to unceded Indian lands claimed by the Crown in North America. Finally, the *Proclamation* referred to the great frauds and abuses that had been committed when Indian lands were purchased. In order to prevent such future frauds and abuses, the *Proclamation* forbade any person from purchasing "any Lands reserved to the said Indians, within those Parts of Our Colonies where, We have thought proper to allow settlement." This crucial provision is not restricted to Indian territories but rather to all colonial lands, thereby reinforcing the interpretation that the *Proclamation* applies broadly throughout North America.

There has been much debate about the geographic application of the *Proclamation*. It does not apply to Rupert's Land[31] or British Columbia,[32] and it has a limited application in Quebec.[33] (In 1774, Quebec passed the *Quebec Act*,[34] which repealed the procedural aspects of the *Royal Proclamation* and reduced the lands reserved, although it did not alter existing rights, titles, or possessions.[35]) Some authorities have suggested that the *Royal Proclamation* does not apply to Nova Scotia or to New Brunswick (which was originally part of Nova Scotia). For instance, in *R. v. Bernard* (2000), Judge Lordon of the New Brunswick Provincial Court stated that there was "never any intent to reserve land for Indians in Nova Scotia . . . nor does it [the *Proclamation*] recognize reserved land unless reserved prior to the Proclamation."[36] Similarly, in *R. v. Jacques* (1978), the *Royal Proclamation* was held not to be applicable to Nova Scotia.[37] However, in *R. v. Smith* (1980),[38] the Federal Court of Appeal concluded that "[the Proclamation's] terms . . . are on the whole broad enough to include the territory that became New Brunswick." Although its decision was reversed on another issue by the Supreme Court of

---

31 *Sigeareak* v. *R.,* [1966] S.C.R. 645 at 650.
32 See Judson J. in *Calder* v. *British Columbia (A.G.),* [1973] S.C.R. 313 at 323.
33 *R.* v. *Côté,* [1994] 3 C.N.L.R. 98 at 106–08 (Que. C.A.); for example, with respect to some existing reserves.
34 *Quebec Act, 1774* (U.K.), c. 83.
35 *Ontario (A.G.)* v. *Bear Island Foundation et al.,* [1989] 2 C.N.L.R. 73 at 85 (Ont. C.A.).
36 *R.* v. *Bernard,* [2000] 3 C.N.L.R. 184 at 217, para. 125.
37 *R.* v. *Jacques* (1978), 20 N.B.R. (2d) 576 (N.B. Prov. Ct.).
38 *R.* v. *Smith,* [1980] 4 C.N.L.R. 29 (F.C.A.); reversed by [1983] 1 S.C.R. 554.

Canada, the court's interpretation of the scope of the *Proclamation* went unchallenged. Further, in *R. v. Sec. of State for Foreign and Commonwealth Affairs* (1982),[39] the English Court of Appeal, in considering the legality of Canada patriating its constitution, agreed with the Nova Scotia Supreme Court in *R. v. Isaac* (1975),[40] where it stated that "the provisions of the Royal Proclamation did and do extend to the provinces of Nova Scotia and New Brunswick." Legal scholar Brian Slattery has suggested that the *Proclamation* applies "to any American territories acquired after 1763 which satisfied the terms of that instrument, so long as it remained in force."[41]

Even though the *Royal Proclamation* may be interpreted as applying to the Maritime provinces, in practice its edicts were often overlooked. In their book *Native Rights in Canada*, P.A. Cumming and N.H. Mickenberg concluded the following regarding the application of the *Royal Proclamation* in the Maritimes:

> [T]here is no indication that any land cession treaties were made nor any compensation paid to the Indians. . . . [T]he conclusion can be drawn that although the Proclamations of 1762 and 1763 applied to the Maritime provinces, the procedures outlined in them were not followed. The reasons for this are not altogether clear. . . . The pressures generated by the influx of settlers combined with the fact that the Indian nations were severely ravaged by disease in the early 19th century, permitted the taking of Indian lands in the Maritimes with little concern for aboriginal rights.[42]

Reserves[43]

As was the case in British Columbia, reserve-creation in the Maritimes did not follow the process laid out by the *Royal Proclamation of 1763*,[44] which affirms that Indian lands are reserved for the Indians until the Indians are

---

39 *Re R. v. The Secretary of State for Foreign and Commonwealth Affairs, ex parte the Indian Association of Alberta, Union of New Brunswick Indians, Union of Nova Scotia Indians, Note from Appeal Committee of the House of Lords,* [1982] 3 C.N.L.R. 195 (H.L.); affirming [1981] 4 C.N.L.R. 86 at 116 (C.A.).

40 *R. v. Isaac* (1975), 13 N.S.R. (2d) 460 at 478 (N.S.C.A.); see also *R. v. Marshall,* [2001] 2 C.N.L.R. 256 (N.S. Prov. Ct.), wherein Curran Prov. Ct. J., at para. 107, agreed that the *Proclamation* applies to Nova Scotia.

41 Slattery (thesis), *supra* note 29 at 361.

42 Cumming and Mickenberg, *supra* note 6 at 105.

43 A historical account of the creation of Indian reserves in Atlantic Canada can be found in Bartlett, *supra* note 4.

44 *R. v. Smith,* [1983] 1 S.C.R. 554 at 568.

inclined to dispose of them. For a variety of reasons, the *Proclamation* was ignored by the governor of Nova Scotia, and in both New Brunswick and Nova Scotia, Indian lands were reserved only upon the request of the Indians. As a result, until a reserve policy was established, settlers or the Crown simply occupied land without regard for the Aboriginal inhabitants. The encroachment by settlers on lands set aside or granted to Indians was so large that the Maritime provinces, and eventually Canada, enacted legislation to protect these lands and make their disposition more orderly.[45]

The *Indian Act* is silent as to how reserves are to be created, but section 18(1) states:

> Subject to this Act, reserves are held by Her Majesty for the use and benefit of the respective bands for which they were set apart; and subject to this Act and to the terms of any treaty or surrender, the Governor in Council may determine whether any purpose for which lands in a reserve are used or are to be used is for the use and benefit of the band.[46]

Reserves in the Maritimes were established by executive orders issuing licences of occupation or by orders-in-council. Although it was the duty of Crown-appointed Indian commissioners to protect Indian lands, the commissioners also had the authority to encroach upon Indian lands and to transfer these lands to settlers if they had the Indians' consent.[47] Indian consent, however, was often ignored, and the reserve-creation process was often imprecise.

Prince Edward Island, for instance, was granted to British owners with no consideration given to the Mi'kmaq; Lennox Island, which was not included in the original survey of Prince Edward Island, was granted to a private landowner in 1772, who permitted the Mi'kmaq to continue living there. The only substantive piece of pre-Confederation legislation concerning Indians and their lands enacted by Prince Edward Island was *An Act relating to the Indians of Prince Edward Island,* which was passed in 1856.[48] This act

---

45 A large number of these statutes are reproduced in T. Isaac, *Pre-1868 Legislation Concerning Indians* (Saskatoon, Sask.: University of Saskatchewan Native Law Centre, 1993).

46 *Indian Act,* R.S.C. 1985, c. I-5.

47 See *An Act to provide for the Instruction and Permanent Settlement of the Indians,* S.N.S. 1842, c. 16, and *An Act to regulate the management and disposal of the Indian Reserves in this Province,* S.N.B. 1844, c. 47, reproduced in Isaac, *supra* note 45 at 28 and 21.

48 *An Act relating to the Indians of Prince Edward Island,* Acts of the Gen. Ass. of P.E.I., 1856, c. 10, reproduced in Isaac, *ibid.* at 39.

provided for the appointment of Indian commissioners to supervise and manage Indian lands. It placed a duty on the commissioners to report all cases of intrusion and sale of Indian reserve lands and allowed the commissioners to establish reserves. Today, there are two Mi'kmaq First Nation communities on Prince Edward Island with a combined population of almost one thousand people, about half of which live on reserve lands.[49] The First Nations have four reserves on the Island, totalling approximately 673 hectares. These four reserves were acquired by purchasing private lands[50] and by the conveyance of Lennox Island to the Indians by a British trust in 1912.[51]

The total amount of reserve lands in New Brunswick has fluctuated dramatically over the last two hundred years, from over 40,450 hectares at the beginning of the nineteenth century to approximately 17,400 hectares at present. The first grant of land to Indians in New Brunswick was made to the Maliseet in 1765 on the St. John River at St. Ann's. This was followed by a licence issued by the governor of Nova Scotia in 1783 to Chief John Julien for the Maliseet to occupy 20,000 acres (8,094 hectares) on both sides of the northwest branch of the Miramichi River. Professor Richard Bartlett has noted that the government of New Brunswick "did not honour the licence issued by its predecessor"[52] and the original grant was never confirmed. From 1789 to 1810, New Brunswick granted to First Nations licences of occupation amounting to almost 40,470 hectares.[53] In 1844, New Brunswick passed legislation concerning the protection of, and dealings related to, Indian reserves.[54] This act permitted the sale or lease of Indian reserve land at auction and provided that any monies arising from the sale or lease of such lands, after expenses, was to be used for the benefit of the Indians. Today, there are nine Mi'kmaq and six Maliseet First Nation communities in New Brunswick with a combined population of approximately 11,000, of which 7,400 reside on reserve lands.[55]

---

49 J. Frideres, *Aboriginal Peoples in Canada: Contemporary Conflicts,* 5th ed. (Scarborough: Prentice Hall, 1998), chap. 5.

50 Cumming and Mickenberg, *supra* note 6 at 233.

51 Bartlett, *supra* note 4 at 6.

52 *Ibid.* at 14; citing L.F.S. Upton, *Micmacs and Colonists* (Vancouver: University of British Columbia Press, 1979) at 99.

53 Bartlett, *ibid.* at 15.

54 *An Act to regulate the management and disposal of the Indian Reserves in this Province,* S.N.B. 1844, c. 47. See also *Of Indian Reserves,* R.S.N.B. 1854, c. 85. Both are reproduced in Isaac, *supra* note 45.

55 For a discussion of the current economic, social, and demographic trends related to New Brunswick First Nations, see D. J. Savoie, *Aboriginal Economic Development in New Brunswick* (Moncton: Canadian Institute for Research on Regional Development, 2000).

Reserve-creation in Nova Scotia began, like it did in New Brunswick, in the form of licences of occupation. The Nova Scotia Indian commissioner noted in his first report, in 1842, that there were just over 22,000 acres (8,904 hectares) of Indian reserve land in Nova Scotia. However, as was the case in New Brunswick, the pressure of encroachment by settlers took its toll and now Nova Scotia Indians are left with about 11,332 hectares of reserve land. In 1842, Nova Scotia passed legislation that allowed the commissioner of Crown Lands to lease or sell Indian reserve land. The legislation was an attempt to protect Indian lands, and it ultimately formed part of the government's reserve policy.[56] Today, there are thirteen Mi'kmaq First Nation communities in Nova Scotia with a combined population of almost 12,000, of which 7,700 reside on the thirty-eight reserves in the province.

Richard Bartlett provides a useful summary of the state of Indian reserves in Atlantic Canada from the time they were set aside until recently:

Indian reserves were established in the Atlantic provinces in order to provide some portion of lands upon which the Indians might settle and possibly commence cultivation. The areas of land were not large but even so were subject to severe encroachment by settlers. Governments in New Brunswick, Nova Scotia, and Prince Edward Island enacted legislation which sought to protect Indian reserves from encroachment and to provide for the disposition of reserves where settlement had already taken place. Immediately after Confederation in 1867 the Government of Canada continued such policy, but usually subject to the requirement that a disposition could only take place upon the obtaining of a surrender from the Indian band.[57]

Professor S.L. Harring has noted:

The legal history of aboriginal rights in Atlantic Canada was one that paralleled that of Ontario. While squatters in New Brunswick, Nova Scotia, and Ontario faced different colonial regimes that had their own unique local practices, none of these regimes could politically afford to resist the push of squatters for more land. . . . [P]olitically, Indian matters in Atlantic Canada were not as important as those in Ontario and, as a result, Indian lands were less protected there and Indian rights perhaps more egregiously ignored.[58]

---

56 *An Act concerning Indian Reserves,* S.N.S. 1859, c. 14; see also *Of Indians,* R.S.N.S. 1859, c. 58 and *Of Indians,* R.S.N.S. 1864, c. 57, all reproduced in Isaac, *supra* note 45.
57 Bartlett, *supra* note 4 at 21.
58 S.L. Harring, *White Man's Law: Native People in Nineteenth-Century Canadian Jurisprudence* (Toronto: University of Toronto Press, 1998) at 185.

Until 1958, Nova Scotia and New Brunswick appeared to hold the title to reserve land within their boundaries. The outstanding issue of the ongoing provincial title in Indian reserve land was eventually settled by negotiated agreements between Nova Scotia, New Brunswick, and Canada.[59] In 1958 the governments of New Brunswick and Canada signed an agreement ensuring the transfer of title from New Brunswick to Canada relating to Indian reserve land.[60] A similar agreement was signed with Nova Scotia in 1959.[61] These agreements transferred all reserve lands, except those lands lying under public highways and minerals, from Nova Scotia and New Brunswick to Canada.

Current Situation in the Maritimes

The plight of Aboriginal people living in the Maritimes is typical of the reality facing Aboriginal people across Canada.[62] As of 1998, the registered Indian population of the Atlantic provinces (including Newfoundland and Labrador) was just over 25,000 (or about 3.9 percent of the general population). Approximately 68 percent of registered Indians live on reserves and 40 percent live in urban areas (both on and off reserve).[63] Aboriginal people experience high unemployment. The Aboriginal participation in the labour force is about 20 percent lower than the national rate. Their participation in the labour force continues "to be on the margins and is not representative of the jobs that characterize modern society."[64] They also experience a litany of public health crises. For example, the death rate for Aboriginal people is double that of the Canadian population generally, with the average age of death for an Aboriginal person being more than twenty years below that of an average non-Aboriginal Canadian. Aboriginal infant mortality is double that of the

---

59 See *Burk* v. *Cormier* (1890), 30 N.B.R. 142 (N.B.C.A.).

60 *An Act to confirm an Agreement between the Government of Canada and the Government of the Province of New Brunswick respecting Indian Reserves,* S.C. 1959, c. 47, and *An Act to confirm an Agreement between Canada and New Brunswick respecting Indian Reserves,* S.N.B. 1958, c. 4; see *R.* v. *Smith,* [1983] 1 S.C.R. 554 at 557 and 558.

61 *An Act to confirm an Agreement between the Government of Canada and the Government of the Province of Nova Scotia respecting Indian Reserves,* S.C. 1959, c. 50.

62 For a good analysis of recent statistical data concerning Aboriginal people across Canada, see Frideres, *supra* note 49, in particular "Profile of Aboriginal Peoples" at 109–195.

63 Canada, "Basic Departmental Data–1999" (Ottawa: DIAND, February 2000).

64 *Ibid.* at 146, 147.

Canadian population as a whole.[65] These problems are compounded by poor housing and quality of life issues, deficiencies in the education system, and general social and economic problems. These pressures, combined with Aboriginal peoples' ongoing struggle to create functional governance regimes and to have their Aboriginal and treaty rights affirmed, have created a situation that offers both promise and concern. Promise because of the forward-moving momentum that rights-based discourse can foster in any "people" and the hope that things can only get better for Aboriginal people in Canada in the current environment. Concern because fundamental change, such as that currently taking place for many Aboriginal people across Canada, takes time; expectations may not be realistic or feasible; and there are competing social, economic, and legal pressures that may be counterproductive to many First Nations' goals.[66] *Marshall* has offered hope to many Aboriginal people in the Maritimes that life may be better with the full recognition of their treaty rights.

Conclusion

None of the early Maritime treaties explicitly acknowledges the cession of land from the Indians to the British Crown. Rather, they deal almost exclusively with the British getting assurances of peaceful relations from the Mi'kmaq and the Maliseet. The *Royal Proclamation of 1763* provides some recognition of Aboriginal rights to land, but its instructions were not followed, particularly with respect to the creation and preservation of Indian reserve land. With their small land base and populations relative to the rest of Canada's First Nations people, Maritime First Nations had to wait until the latter part of the twentieth century before they were able to secure a solid legal basis for their rights in Canadian law, which came in the form of the enactment of section 35 of the *Constitution Act, 1982*. The legislative and constitutional provisions of this act that explicitly reference Aboriginal people and their rights are discussed in chapter 2.

---

65 *Ibid.* at 180.
66 As Frideres has noted: "Health care provided is sometimes countered by social and economic problems such as overcrowding, poor nutrition, chronic unemployment, and community and family violence. . . . [T]he causes of poor mental and physical health are not dealt with." *Supra* note 49 at 180–81.

Chapter 2

• • • • • •

Legislation and Constitutional Provisions Affecting Aboriginal and Treaty Rights

Introduction

In order to understand the significance of Aboriginal and treaty rights developments in the Maritimes, it is helpful to review some of the basic statutory and constitutionally based provisions related to Aboriginal people across Canada. This chapter provides a brief description of the federal *Indian Act,* section 25 of the *Canadian Charter of Rights and Freedoms,* and section 35 of the *Constitution Act, 1982.*[1] A crucial component of this discussion is the division of legislative authority between the provinces and the federal government, with the federal government being primarily responsible for Indians and lands reserved for them. This division has caused a great deal of confusion, but some general rules have been well established, as outlined in the discussion of section 88 of the *Indian Act.*

The *Indian Act*

Section 91(24) of the *Constitution Act, 1867*[2] assigns exclusive legislative authority[3] over "Indians, and Lands reserved for the Indians" to the federal Parliament. Beginning in 1868 with *An Act providing for the organization of the department of the Secretary of State of Canada, and for the management*

---

1   *Constitution Act, 1982,* Sched. B. to the *Canada Act 1982* (U.K.), 1982, c. 11, as am. by the *Constitution Amendment Proclamation, 1983,* R.S.C. 1985, App. II, No. 46 [am. ss. 25(b) and add. 35(3), 35(4), 35.1 and 37.1 and 54.1].
2   *Constitution Act, 1867* (U.K.), 30 & 31 Vict., c. 3 (R.S.C. 1985, App. II, No. 5).
3   See *Re Waters and Water Powers,* [1929] S.C.R. 200.

of Indian and Ordnance Lands[4] and culminating with the present *Indian Act*,[5] Parliament has exercised this authority by enacting legislation dealing specifically with Indians and lands reserved for them.

After the creation of the Dominion of Canada, in 1876, the federal government introduced the first *Indian Act*[6] in an attempt to bring order to the various policies and problems related to Indians across Canada. Much amended over the years,[7] the modern *Indian Act* attempts to govern almost every aspect of Indian life and government on and off reserve. The act defines who is an "Indian" for the purposes of the act and, with a few exceptions,[8] it applies to all registered Indians and band governments across Canada. Although the Inuit are deemed to be "Indian" for the purposes of federal jurisdiction under section 91(24),[9] they are not subject to the *Indian Act,* and the Métis and non-registered Indians are not covered by the act.

The *Indian Act* contains various rights, privileges, and restrictions. It is under this act that reserve lands can be set aside for the use and benefit of Indians. Certain rights are attached to reserve land, such as the tax exemption for property situated on a reserve.[10] In addition, property owned by an Indian and situated on a reserve cannot be seized by a non-Indian.[11] Although this protects Indian property from seizure, it also makes it difficult for Indians to obtain loans because their on-reserve property, including all reserve lands, cannot be used as collateral.

The *Indian Act* as it exists today is a strange mix of paternalism and assimilation. It is considered by many to be an antiquated piece of legislation, and many contemporary discussions of self-government seek to limit its applicability. On April 30, 2001, the federal minister of Indian Affairs and Northern Development launched an initiative that sought to update the *Indian Act,*

---

4   S.C. 1868, c. 42.
5   *Indian Act,* R.S.C. 1985, c. I-5.
6   *Indian Act,* S.C. 1876, c. 18.
7   See S. Venne, ed., *Indian Acts and Amendments 1868–1975: An Indexed Collection* (Saskatoon, Sask.: University of Saskatchewan Native Law Centre, 1981), *The Indian Act and Amendments 1970–1993: An Indexed Collection* (Saskatoon, Sask.: University of Saskatchewan Native Law Centre, 1993), and T. Isaac, *Pre-1868 Legislation Concerning Indians* (Saskatoon, Sask.: University of Saskatchewan Native Law Centre, 1993).
8   Notably those First Nations that have signed modern treaties (and even then the registration provisions of the *Indian Act* continue to apply) and those First Nations governments that have alternative governance arrangements such as the Sechelt Indian Band (*Sechelt Indian Band Self-Government Act,* S.C. 1986, c. 27).
9   *Re Eskimos,* [1939] S.C.R. 104.
10 *Indian Act, supra* note 5, s. 87.
11 *Ibid.* s. 89.

primarily in the areas of governance. In a press release entitled "Communities First: First Nations Governance," the Department of Indian Affairs and Northern Development noted:

> When the *Indian Act* was last amended on these matters in 1951, it gave powers of approval to the Minister and Governor in Council. These authorities should lie within the communities themselves. The *Act* restricts local decision making and undermines the leadership of First Nations themselves. The reality is that the *Act* is still very much a 130-year-old instrument used to provide federal government control over First Nation people and their governments.

Only time will tell if the amendments referred to by the minister will come about and what they will be. However, to date, the response from First Nations to the federal government's plan has not been positive. In May 2001, the Assembly of First Nations chiefs passed a unanimous resolution to boycott all government consultations. The Atlantic Policy Congress of First Nations Chiefs passed a number of resolutions in March and April 2001 rejecting the governance consultation process and called for a parallel process that would have broader objectives.

Even though the notion of more authority and control over their lives is appealing, many First Nations people also feel comfortable with the federal government providing a check on the actions of their chiefs and councils. What is needed is a mechanism by which First Nations can exercise as much control over their lives as possible, in a manner that provides as much accountability as possible, not only to the First Nations people themselves but also to government for the expenditure of public funds.

Section 88, *Indian Act*

Section 91(24) of the *Constitution Act, 1867* assigns exclusive legislative jurisdiction over Indians and Indian lands to the federal Parliament. However, provincial laws that are "provincial in scope"[12] and that do not single out one class of citizens, for example, "Indians,"[13] can apply to Indians of their own effect (*ex proprio vigore*), so long as they do not interfere with the federal Parliament's jurisdiction over Indians and their lands and are not inconsistent with any other federal law, including the *Indian Act*. Motor vehicle legislation is an example of such legislation. The federal government has no legislation governing motor vehicle laws on reserves. In order to ensure that there is

---

12 *R. v. George*, [1966] S.C.R. 267 at 281. Also see discussion in chapter 6.
13 *Kruger and Manuel* v. *R.*, [1978] 1 S.C.R. 104 at 110.

an adequate regulatory regime to cover the operation of motor vehicles on reserves, provincial laws governing motor vehicles are referentially incorporated into federal legislation.

Some provincial legislation, for example, legislation regulating hunting and fishing, does single out Indians from the rest of the population because hunting and fishing are core elements of many Indians' lives. Provincial laws that affect a core of "Indianness" cannot apply to Indians without enabling federal legislation. This is where section 88 comes into play. Section 88 states:

> 88. Subject to the terms of any treaty . . . all laws of general application from time to time in force in any province are applicable to and in respect of Indians in the province[.]

Section 88 of the *Indian Act* allows provincial laws of general application to apply to Indians, even though the federal Parliament has the exclusive power to legislate in regard to "Indians," so long as they are not contrary to the *Indian Act* or any other federal legislation and provided these laws do not conflict with treaty rights.

In *R. v. Dick,* Justice Beetz stated:

> I believe that a distinction can be drawn between two categories of provincial laws. There are, on the one hand, provincial laws which can be applied to Indians without touching their Indianness, like traffic legislation; there are on the other hand, provincial laws which cannot apply to Indians without regulating them *qua* Indians. . . . [I]t is to the laws of the second category that s. 88 refers.[14]

Section 88 does not allow provincial legislatures to stray into federal jurisdiction with respect to Indians and land reserved for Indians unless there is no other federal act that is applicable. By allowing provincial laws of general application to apply to Indians in this way, section 88 ensures that there is no legislative vacuum for Indians. However, section 88 also provides that provincial laws of general application are subject to the terms of any treaty.[15] For example, provincial hunting laws cannot override a treaty right to hunt. Since treaty rights are constitutionally protected under section 35 of the *Constitution Act, 1982,* they are ensured supremacy over provincial laws that infringe on these rights and that cannot otherwise be justified. The justified

---

14 *R. v. Dick,* [1985] 2 S.C.R. 309 at 326, 327. See also *Derrickson* v. *Derrickson,* [1986] 1 S.C.R. 285, and *R. v. Francis,* [1988] 1 S.C.R. 1025.

15 See *R. v. White and Bob* (1965), 52 D.L.R. (2d) 481; *R. v. Simon,* [1985] 2 S.C.R. 387; and *R. v. Sioui,* [1990] 1 S.C.R. 1025.

infringement of Aboriginal and treaty rights—by either federal or provincial jurisdictions—is discussed in chapter 3.

The treaty rights protected under section 88 are not international treaty rights. In *R.* v. *Francis* (1988), the Supreme Court of Canada held that the term "treaty" in section 88 does not include international treaties, like the Jay Treaty (a 1794 treaty between Great Britain and the U.S.A. proposing a duty exemption for Indians who crossed what is now the U.S.-Canada border), but rather refers only to treaties made with Indians.[16] Although the historical treaties are not international treaties and are not formally implemented in Canadian law—except to the extent that they are mentioned in section 88—they are nevertheless enforceable (both before and after 1982).[17] Before 1982, treaties were enforceable by the operation of section 88 and the applicability of provincial legislation. Since 1982, treaties have been enforceable by the operation of section 35(1) of the *Constitution Act, 1982* and the applicability of federal and provincial legislation.

In *R.* v. *Agawa*,[18] the Ontario Court of Appeal held that Indian treaties are not like international treaties, they are *sui generis* and are not self-executing. Treaties acquire the force of law in Canada when they are protected by a statute or by the Constitution. Modern treaties are incorporated into Canadian law by way of complementary legislation. For example, in 2000, Canada enacted the *Nisga'a Final Agreement Act*[19] to bring the Nisga'a Treaty into effect.

Like Aboriginal rights, treaty rights may be extinguished in three ways: (1) by voluntary surrender by Aboriginal people to the Crown;[20] (2) prior to 1982, by federal (not provincial) legislation;[21] and (3) after 1982, by altering section 35 by way of constitutional amendment. Non-exercise of treaty rights

---

16 *R.* v. *Francis,* [1956] S.C.R. 618. For a commentary on *Francis,* see K. Lysyk, "The Unique Constitutional Position of the Canadian Indian" (1967) 45 Can. Bar Rev. 513 at 527–28. The Ontario Court of Appeal held in *R.* v. *Vincent,* [1993] 2 C.N.L.R. 165; leave to appeal refused [1993] 4 C.N.L.R. vi, that the Jay Treaty was not a treaty for the purposes of s. 35(1).

17 See *R.* v. *Wesley,* [1932] 5 C.N.L.C. 540 (Alta. C.A.), and *R.* v. *Prince,* [1964] S.C.R. 81.

18 *R.* v. *Agawa,* [1988] 3 C.N.L.R. 73.

19 *Nisga'a Final Agreement Act,* S.C. 2000, c. 7.

20 In *Sioui, supra* note 15 at 1063, Lamer C.J. stated that prior to 1982 "a treaty cannot be extinguished without the consent of the Indians concerned." This was the case in *R.* v. *Howard,* [1994] 2 S.C.R. 299, where fishing rights were extinguished by treaty.

21 In *Simon, supra* note 15 at 411, Dickson C.J. noted: "It has been held to be within the exclusive power of Parliament under s. 91(24) of the Constitution Act, 1867 to derogate from rights recognized in a treaty agreement made with the Indians."

does not equate with extinguishment.[22] Also, as with Aboriginal rights, a "clear and plain intention" is required to extinguish treaty rights.[23]

Although it is the federal Parliament that has jurisdiction over Indians, provinces do occasionally refer to Indians in their legislation. For example, New Brunswick's *Education Act* states:

> The Minister shall provide and implement programs and services which (a) respond to the unique needs of Micmac and Maliseet children in accordance with any agreement entered into under paragraph 50(2)(b), and (b) foster an understanding of aboriginal history and culture among all pupils.[24]

As a practical matter, however, provinces try to avoid enacting legislation that may affect Indians directly. This is primarily because of the constitutional parameters imposed by section 91(24), but also because of the provincial concern for taking responsibility for a federal head of power: namely, Indians and their lands.

Constitutional Amendments

In October 1980, Prime Minister Pierre Trudeau introduced a proposal to amend the Constitution of Canada by adding a charter of rights and a new amending procedure. These amendments would allow Canada, without Great Britain, to amend its own constitution and to constitutionally protect certain individual and collective rights in Canadian law. Prime Minister Trudeau's proposal contained no reference to Aboriginal and treaty rights. However, through intensive lobbying by Aboriginal people, by the time the Constitution was amended, the *Constitution Act, 1982* included section 25 of the *Charter* and sections 35 and 37, requiring a constitutional conference among the prime minister, premiers, and Aboriginal leaders.[25]

The conference took place in March 1983. It resulted in changes[26] to section 25 of the *Charter*[27] and section 35 of the *Constitution Act, 1982*.[28] In addition, section 35.1 was added to the *Constitution Act, 1982*. This section

---

22 *Sioui, supra* note 15 at 1066.
23 See *R.* v. *Sparrow,* [1990] 1 S.C.R. 1075 at 1099.
24 *Education Act,* R.S.N.B. 1973, c. E-1.12, s. 7.
25 Section 37 was automatically repealed on April 18, 1983, by operation of s. 54 of the *Constitution Act, 1982, supra* note 1.
26 *Constitutional Amendment Proclamation, 1983,* R.S.C. 1983, App. II, No. 46.
27 Section 25 was amended by replacing the phrase "land claims settlement" with "land claims agreements or may be so acquired."
28 Section 35 was amended by adding ss. (3) and (4).

requires that before any constitutional amendment is made to section 91(24) of the *Constitution Act, 1867*, to section 25 of the *Charter*, or to Part II (including section 35) of the *Constitution Act, 1982*, a constitutional conference involving the premiers and the prime minister will be convened and representatives of the Aboriginal peoples of Canada will be invited to participate. Finally, section 37.1 was also added by the 1983 amendments. This section required that at least two additional constitutional conferences be held, with Aboriginal issues to be included on the agenda of each.[29] The remaining constitutional conferences focussed primarily on Aboriginal self-government and failed to produce any amendments.

In March 1987 Prime Minister Brian Mulroney and the ten premiers agreed to the Meech Lake Constitutional Accord,[30] which proposed to recognize Quebec as a distinct society but failed to include any reference to the rights of Aboriginal people. The Meech Lake Accord subsequently failed because it did not receive the consent of the legislatures of Newfoundland and Manitoba. Finally, in 1992 a Canada-wide referendum was held regarding the Charlottetown Accord, which proposed, among other items, that Aboriginal governments comprise a distinct and separate order of government, alongside the federal and provincial governments, and that the inherent right of self-government be constitutionally entrenched.[31] Any future constitutional discussions will undoubtedly include Aboriginal representatives.

Presently, there are a number of constitutional provisions that explicitly refer to Aboriginal people. Section 91(24) of the *Constitution Act, 1867* references federal legislative authority; section 25 of the *Canadian Charter of Rights and Freedoms* protects Aboriginal and treaty rights from interference from other *Charter* rights; and sections 35 and 35.1 of the *Constitution Act, 1982* recognize and affirm Aboriginal and treaty rights.

Section 25, *Canadian Charter of Rights and Freedoms*

With the enactment of the *Constitution Act, 1982* in April 1982 came the *Canadian Charter of Rights and Freedoms*.[32] The *Charter* outlines those rights that individuals (and some groups) possess so as to protect these rights from

---

29 Section 37.1 was repealed on April 18, 1987, by s. 54.1 of the *Constitution Act, 1982, supra* note 1.
30 See P. Hogg, *Meech Lake Constitutional Accord Annotated* (Toronto: Carswell, 1988).
31 See T. Isaac, "The 1992 Charlottetown Accord and First Nations People: Guiding the Future" (1992) 8:2 Native Studies Rev. 109.
32 *Canadian Charter of Rights and Freedoms*, Part I of the *Constitution Act, 1982, supra* note 1.

unjustifiable government infringement. The *Charter* explicitly provides that rights contained in the *Charter* cannot abrogate or derogate from any existing Aboriginal and treaty rights. Section 25 reads as follows:

> The guarantee in this Charter of certain rights and freedoms shall not be construed so as to abrogate or derogate from any aboriginal, treaty or other rights or freedoms that pertain to the aboriginal peoples of Canada including (a) any rights or freedoms that have been recognized by the Royal Proclamation of October 7, 1763; and (b) any rights or freedoms that now exist by way of land claims agreements or may be so acquired.

Professor Bruce Wildsmith has described section 25:

> Section 25 is not a mere canon of interpretation whose force is spent once it is determined that the rights and freedoms in the Charter cannot "be construed so as [not] to abrogate or derogate" from the rights referred to in section 25. Neither does section 25 create substantive rights or in any way enhance or entrench the position of aboriginal peoples. Its purpose and effect are to maintain the special position of Canada's aboriginal peoples unimpaired by the Charter.[33]

Section 25 does not create rights but rather protects Aboriginal rights from being infringed or impaired by *Charter* rights. To date, there has been little judicial commentary on section 25. In *Steinhauer* v. *R.* (1985),[34] the Alberta Court of Queen's Bench held that section 25 acts as "a shield and does not add to Aboriginal rights." In *Corbiere* v. *Canada (Min. of Indian and Northern Affairs)* (1999),[35] the Supreme Court of Canada held that section 77(1) of the *Indian Act,* which provided that only Indians resident on reserve could vote in band elections, violated the equality provisions set out in section 15 of the *Charter.* Writing for the majority, Justice McLachlin (as she then was) stated that the court was not prepared to deal with section 25, since a case for its application in this matter had not been made;[36] however, Justice L'Heureux-Dubé, writing for the minority, outlined some considerations to

---

33 B. Wildsmith, *Aboriginal Peoples and Section 25 of the Canadian Charter of Rights and Freedoms* (Saskatoon, Sask.: University of Saskatchewan Native Law Centre, 1988) at 2; see also W. Pentney, "The Rights of the Aboriginal Peoples of Canada and the *Constitution Act, 1982;* Part I: The Interpretive Prism of Section 25" (1988) 22:1 U.B.C. L. Rev. 21.

34 *Steinhauer* v. *R.,* [1985] 3 C.N.L.R. 187 (Alta. Q.B.) at 191.

35 *Corbiere* v. *Canada (Min. of Indian and Northern Affairs),* [1999] 2 S.C.R. 203.

36 *Ibid.* at para. 20.

be taken into account when examining section 25. She stated that section 25's reference to "other rights and freedoms that pertain to the Aboriginal peoples of Canada" was a reference to more than section 35 rights and could include statutory rights—that is, rights outlined in legislation.[37] She also noted:

> I emphasize, however, that as I will discuss below, the contextual approach to s. 15 requires that the equality analysis of provisions relating to Aboriginal people must always proceed with consideration of and respect for Aboriginal heritage and distinctiveness, recognition of Aboriginal and treaty rights, and with emphasis on the importance for Aboriginal Canadians of their values and history.[38]

In *Shubenacadie Indian Band* v. *Canada (Human Rights Commission)* (2000),[39] the Federal Court of Appeal reaffirmed that section 25 is a shield that "protects the rights mentioned therein from being adversely affected by other *Charter* rights."[40] (This could occur if a *Charter* right were interpreted as superceding an Aboriginal or treaty right.) The Court of Appeal also stated that section 25 can "only be evoked as a defence if it had been found that the Appellant's conduct had violated subsection 15(1) of the *Charter*."[41]

Section 25 represents a mechanism by which the framers of the Constitution wanted to balance the collective rights of Aboriginal people with individual rights and freedoms generally. It is important to note that although section 25 provides strong guidance to constitutional interpretation, it does not stand alone. Rather, section 25 must be read in conjunction with the other sections of the *Charter*. For example, section 1 of the *Charter* provides that "[t]he *Canadian Charter of Rights and Freedoms* guarantees the rights and freedoms set out in it subject only to such reasonable limits prescribed by law as can be demonstrably justified in a free and democratic society." Section 15 guarantees equality rights. Section 28 provides that nothing in the *Charter* affects the rights and freedoms guaranteed in it from being guaranteed equally to male and female persons. Section 25 must also be read with other constitutional provisions, such as section 35 of the *Constitution Act, 1982*. It is, however, unclear what the interplay between section 25 of the *Charter* and section 35 will be.

---

37 *Ibid.* at para. 52.
38 *Ibid.* at paras. 53–54.
39 *Shubenacadie Indian Band* v. *Canada (Human Rights Commission)*, [2000] 4 C.N.L.R. 275 (F.C.A.).
40 *Ibid.* at para. 43.
41 *Ibid.*

Section 35, *Constitution Act, 1982*

Until the explicit recognition and affirmation of Aboriginal and treaty rights in the *Constitution Act, 1982,* their legal status in Canada had been fluid and vulnerable. Although Aboriginal rights existed at common law prior to 1982, they were subject to extensive restriction by the Crown and could be extinguished unilaterally by the federal Crown where a clear and plain intention to do so existed. The law prior to 1982 respecting treaty rights and their vulnerability was succinctly stated by the Supreme Court in *R.* v. *Moosehunter* (1981): "The Government of Canada can alter the rights of Indians granted under treaties (*Sikyea* v. *The Queen* (1965), 2 C.C.C. 129). Provinces cannot."[42]

Section 35(1) of the *Constitution Act, 1982* provides for the substantive recognition and affirmation of existing Aboriginal and treaty rights in Canadian constitutional law. Section 35 of the *Constitution Act, 1982* reads:

(1) The existing aboriginal and treaty rights of the aboriginal peoples of Canada are hereby recognized and affirmed.

(2) In this Act, "aboriginal peoples of Canada" includes the Indian, Inuit and Metis peoples of Canada.

(3) For greater certainty, in subsection (1) "treaty rights" includes rights that now exist by way of land claims agreements or may be so acquired.

(4) Notwithstanding any other provision of this Act, the aboriginal and treaty rights referred to in subsection (1) are guaranteed equally to male and female persons.

The term "existing" means "non-extinguished" or "still in existence" as of April 17, 1982, and does not exclude treaty rights from coming into existence by way of modern treaties. The Supreme Court of Canada has held that "recognized and affirmed" means that Aboriginal and treaty rights are entrenched in the Constitution and protected against further unilateral erosion or extinguishment by the Crown. Section 35(1) also provides a constitutional basis upon which federal, provincial, and territorial laws may be challenged. Prior to section 35(1), federal legislation could restrict or even extinguish Aboriginal rights.[43] Aboriginal and treaty rights are not absolute; rather, they can be limited or infringed in those instances where the Crown can demonstrate justification. The justification test for section 35(1) limitations on Aboriginal rights was first outlined by the Supreme Court of Canada in *R.* v. *Sparrow* (1990)[44] and for treaty rights in *R.* v. *Badger* (1996).[45] Both decisions are discussed in chapter 3.

42 *R.* v. *Moosehunter,* [1981] 1 S.C.R. 282 at 293.

43 *R.* v. *George,* [1966] S.C.R. 267, and *Sikyea* v. *R.,* [1964] S.C.R. 642.

44 *Sparrow, supra* note 23.

45 *R.* v. *Badger,* [1996] 1 S.C.R. 771.

The Nova Scotia Court of Appeal decision in *R. v. Denny* (1990)[46] is a substantive appellate court decision that influenced the Supreme Court's views on the meaning of section 35. In *Denny,* the Nova Scotia Court of Appeal considered the appeal of three Mi'kmaq convicted of offences contrary to the *Fisheries Act*. The Court of Appeal overturned the lower court conviction and acquitted the three Mi'kmaq. The court held that the Mi'kmaq possessed an Aboriginal right to fish for food in the waters of Indian Brook and Afton River. The court also referenced *R. v. Isaac* (1975)[47] in affirming that the right to fish had not been extinguished by treaty, other agreement, or competent legislation. Although the Mi'kmaq claimed a treaty right to fish based on the treaties of 1725 and 1752, the court did not deal with this argument since an Aboriginal right was found to exist already. The court concluded that constitutionally guaranteed Aboriginal rights are not violated by the legislative exercise of reasonable regulation, such as conservation of the fishery. The court ruled, however, that once conservation had been taken into consideration, the Mi'kmaq were entitled to fish to satisfy their food needs.[48] The Supreme Court of Canada affirmed this view of Aboriginal rights and their priority in *Sparrow*[49] and noted *Denny* and *Isaac* with approval in *Marshall No. 1*.[50]

Section 35 is the only provision in the Canadian Constitution that explicitly recognizes and affirms Aboriginal and treaty rights. It does not create new Aboriginal or treaty rights, but it provides constitutional protection for, and entrenchment of, "existing aboriginal and treaty rights." As Brian Slattery has pointed out, these rights are held by Aboriginal people "by reason of the fact that aboriginal peoples were once independent, self-governing entities in possession of most of the lands now making up Canada."[51] By virtue of section 52 of the *Constitution Act, 1982,* section 35 is part of the supreme law of Canada, thereby superseding federal and provincial legislation inconsistent with its provisions.

52(1) The Constitution of Canada is the supreme law of Canada, and any law that is inconsistent with the provisions of the Constitution is, to the extent of the inconsistency, of no force or effect.[52]

Peter Hogg has described the effect of section 52:

---

46 *R. v. Denny,* [1990] 2 C.N.L.R. 115 (N.S.C.A.).
47 *R. v. Isaac* (1975), 13 N.S.R. (2d) 460 (N.S.C.A.).
48 *Denny, supra* note 46 at 133.
49 *Sparrow, supra* note 23 at 1112, 1116–19.
50 *R. v. Marshall (Marshall No. 1),* [1999] 3 S.C.R. 456 at para. 42.
51 B. Slattery, "The Constitutional Guarantee of Aboriginal and Treaty Rights" (1983) 8 Queen's L.J. 232 at 242.
52 *Constitution Act, 1982, supra* note 1, s. 52.

By virtue of s. 52(1), the Constitution of Canada is superior to all other laws in force in Canada, whatever their origin; federal statutes, provincial statutes, pre-confederation statutes, received statutes, imperial statutes and common law; all of these laws must yield to inconsistent provisions of the Constitution of Canada. Section 52(1) provides an explicit basis for judicial review of legislation in Canada, for, whenever a court finds that a law is inconsistent with the Constitution of Canada, the court must hold that law to be invalid ("of no force or effect").[53]

As a result of sections 35 and 52, only constitutional amendment can now alter Aboriginal and treaty rights. Chapter 4 discusses Aboriginal title as a subcategory of Aboriginal rights and the Supreme Court of Canada's decision in *Delgamuukw* v. *British Columbia* (1997),[54] which is the leading decision on Aboriginal title.

Conclusion

In the past twenty years, the status of Aboriginal and treaty rights in Canadian law has been transformed. Rights that at one time could have been unilaterally modified, extinguished, or infringed by the federal Crown are now constitutionally protected and can, depending on the circumstances, override the effects of federal, provincial, and territorial legislation. All this is the result of the "affirmation and recognition" of Aboriginal and treaty rights in section 35 of the *Constitution Act, 1982*. Furthermore, pursuant to section 25 of the *Canadian Charter of Rights and Freedoms,* Aboriginal and treaty rights cannot be abrogated or impaired by *Charter* rights. The net effect of these changes is that governments in Canada are being held to a constitutionally entrenched standard with respect to their legislation and actions as they relate to existing Aboriginal and treaty rights.

For the Maritime provinces, the impact of the constitutional protection of Aboriginal and treaty rights has recently been felt in the *Marshall* decision. Although earlier decisions affected the Maritimes, they did so in a much more limited way. *Marshall* has forever changed the degree of attention that will be paid to the rights of Aboriginal people in the Maritimes.

---

53 P. Hogg, *Constitutional Law of Canada*, 4th ed. (Toronto: Carswell, 1997) at 3.4, p. 53.

54 *Delgamuukw* v. *British Columbia,* [1997] 3 S.C.R. 1010.

Chapter 3

······

Judicial Decisions Affecting Aboriginal and Treaty Rights

Introduction

An understanding of what is developing in the Maritimes regarding Aboriginal and treaty rights must be founded upon a basic understanding of the key developments in this area of the law. This chapter provides the context for *Marshall* by briefly highlighting key judicial decisions that form the basis of Aboriginal law in Canada. Over time, courts in Canada have grown increasingly more flexible and liberal in their interpretation of treaty rights. Restrictive, narrow views of these rights are being replaced by flexible and accommodating interpretations. However, it is also important to point out that the Supreme Court has not given *absolute* expression to existing treaty rights but, rather, those rights must be *balanced* with the legislative authority of the federal and provincial governments and with the interests of other Canadians. It is against this backdrop that the *Marshall* decision is discussed and that *Marshall*'s significance to Maritime circumstances is underscored. It is appropriate that the first decision to be discussed (*Syliboy*) comes from the Maritimes.

Pre-1982 Decisions

Judicial decisions made prior to 1982 illustrate the limited view of Aboriginal and treaty rights that once prevailed in Canadian law. Prior to the enactment of the *Constitution Act, 1982,* much of the case law with respect to Aboriginal and treaty rights did little to affirm the existence or legitimacy of these rights. Although this was in part due to the dubious and unclear status of these rights in Canadian law, it was also the result of paternalistic and negative attitudes towards Aboriginal people.

In *R.* v. *Syliboy* (1928),[1] the Nova Scotia County Court considered the appeal of the grand chief of the Mi'kmaq, who had been convicted of unlawfully possessing furs. The Treaty of 1752 was used a defence since it provided Indians with the right to hunt and trap at all times. The court concluded that the Treaty of 1752 made with the Mi'kmaq of Nova Scotia was not a real treaty because it had not been made between competent contracting parties. That is to say, it had not been made with the Mi'kmaq Nation as a whole, but with a smaller group of Mi'kmaq who were not associated with the accused. Therefore, the court held, the accused could not appeal to this treaty to uphold a general right for any Mi'kmaq to hunt and trap at all times. The court also held that the treaty did not extend to Cape Breton and that, based on the court's reading of the *Proclamation,* the *Royal Proclamation of 1763* did not apply to Nova Scotia.

Syliboy is a clear example of the narrow approach employed by courts in the early part of the twentieth century and demonstrates the attitudes many had towards Aboriginal people; namely, that they could not be a "competent contracting party." This, of course, changed dramatically when section 35 was included in the Constitution and Aboriginal and treaty rights received constitutional protection. With constitutional protection and a general change in attitude politically and judicially, the stage was being set for a more liberal approach to interpreting the meaning of Aboriginal and treaty rights.

In *R.* v. *Simon* (1958),[2] the New Brunswick Court of Appeal considered an appeal from a Mi'kmaq convicted of illegally setting a net contrary to the New Brunswick Fishery Regulations made under the federal *Fisheries Act.* The appellant claimed immunity by virtue of the Boston Treaty of 1725 and the Treaty of 1752. Using reasoning similar to that employed by the Nova Scotia court in *Syliboy,* the New Brunswick court held that there was no connection between the appellant and those who signed the Treaties of 1725 and 1752. *Simon* is another Maritime example of the narrow approach many courts took with respect to Aboriginal and treaty rights prior to the enactment of section 35.

In *R.* v. *Sikyea* (1964),[3] the Supreme Court of Canada considered an appeal by a Treaty No. 11 Indian who had been charged with unlawfully killing a migrating bird during a closed season. The Indian claimed hunting rights under the treaty. The court affirmed the Northwest Territories Court of Appeal decision upholding the conviction and held that federal legislation could prevail over treaty rights. This result was later affirmed by the Supreme Court in *R.* v. *George* (1966)[4] and in *Daniels* v. *White* (1968).[5] Of course, this result

---

1   *R.* v. *Syliboy,* [1929] 1 D.L.R. 307 (N.S. Co. Ct.).
2   *R.* v. *Simon* (1958), 124 C.C.C. 110 (N.B.S.C., App. Div.).
3   *Sikyea* v. *R.,* [1964] S.C.R. 642.
4   *R.* v. *George,* [1966] S.C.R. 267.
5   *Daniels* v. *White,* [1968] S.C.R. 517.

was significantly altered in 1982. Since 1982, federal legislation and provincial legislation have been subject to existing treaty rights.

R. v. *White and Bob* (1965)[6] is an early example of a broad and liberal approach to treaty interpretation. The decision concerned two members of a Vancouver Island First Nation who had been charged with possessing game during the closed season without a valid licence, contrary to provincial regulations. In this case, the Supreme Court of Canada affirmed a British Columbia Court of Appeal decision and held that provincial game laws could be superseded by treaty provisions, however vague, by virtue of section 88 of the *Indian Act.* Thus, *White and Bob* affirmed the legal status of treaties in Canadian law. It also illustrates the origins of a broad and liberal approach to the rules governing whether a document is, in fact, a treaty. Justice Norris of the British Columbia Court of Appeal stated:

> In the section [what is now s. 88, *Indian Act*] "treaty" is not a word of art and in my respectful opinion, it embraces all such engagements made by persons in authority as may be brought within the term "the words of the white man" the sanctity of which was, at the time of British exploration and settlement, the most important means of obtaining the goodwill and co-operation of the native tribes and ensuring that the colonists would be protected from death and destruction. On such assurance the Indians relied.[7]

As Justice Norris's remarks make clear, the case also emphasized the importance of the honour of the Crown. The "honour of the Crown" was referenced in *R.* v. *Sparrow*[8] in the context of valid legislative objectives required to justify an infringement of Aboriginal and treaty rights. Chief Justice Dickson wrote:

> The way in which a legislative objective is to be attained must uphold the honour of the Crown and must be in keeping with the unique contemporary relationship, grounded in history and policy, between the Crown and Canada's aboriginal peoples.

In *R.* v. *Francis* (1969),[9] the courts reverted, once again, to a narrower interpretation of Aboriginal and treaty rights. In this case, the New Brunswick Court of Appeal upheld the conviction of a Mi'kmaq in the Richibucto area

---

6   *R.* v. *White and Bob,* [1965] S.C.R. vi; affirming (1964), 50 D.L.R. (2d) 613 (B.C.C.A.).

7   *Ibid.* at 649.

8   *R.* v. *Sparrow,* [1990] 1 S.C.R. 1075 at 1110; also see *R.* v. *Marshall (Marshall No. 1),* [1999] 3 S.C.R. 456 at para. 4.

9   *R.* v. *Francis* (1969), 10 D.L.R. (3d) 189 (N.B.S.C. App. Div.).

who had been charged with fishing for salmon without a licence. The court adopted the reasoning in *Syliboy* in stating that the Treaty of 1752 was not made with the Mi'kmaq Nation as a whole but only with a smaller group of Mi'kmaq. The court also referenced *R.* v. *Simon,* which held that the Treaties of 1725 and 1752 could not provide a defence since it could not be shown that the treaties applied to the appellant. The court held that the Treaty of 1779 did apply to the Mi'kmaq in the Richibucto area; however, it also held that any rights to fish contained in the 1779 treaty were overridden by the New Brunswick Fishery Regulations under the federal *Fisheries Act.* The court also cited *Sikyea* v. *R.*[10] as authority that laws made by the Parliament of Canada are not qualified or made unenforceable in any way by treaty rights.

Gradually, the broad and liberal interpretative approach of Aboriginal and treaty rights became more common. In *R.* v. *Isaac* (1975),[11] the Nova Scotia Court of Appeal quashed a conviction of a Mi'kmaq charged with illegally possessing a firearm on Indian reserve lands contrary to provincial legislation. The court noted that the provincial legislation did not apply to Indians on reserve lands. In coming to this decision, the court noted the Aboriginal hunting and fishing rights of the Mi'kmaq and that no Nova Scotia treaty "has been found whereby Indians ceded land to the Crown, whereby their rights on any land were specifically extinguished."[12] The Supreme Court of Canada in *Marshall No. 1* referenced *Isaac* approvingly when it noted that peace and friendship treaties with the Mi'kmaq did not extinguish Aboriginal hunting and fishing rights.[13] Nova Scotia Court of Appeal chief justice MacKeigan also noted:

> I have been unable to find any record of any treaty, agreement or arrange-
> ment after 1780 extinguishing, modifying or confirming the Indian right to
> hunt and fish, or any other record of any cession or release of rights or lands
> by the Indians.[14]

Another narrow application of treaty rights can be found in *R.* v. *Cope* (1981),[15] where the Nova Scotia Court of Appeal considered the appeal of a Mi'kmaq who had been convicted under the federal *Fisheries Act.* Mr. Cope contended that he was not subject to the fishery regulations because the Treaty of 1752 was equivalent to a royal grant and conferred a vested property right to fish and hunt on all Mi'kmaq in Nova Scotia. The court held that even if

---

10 *Sikyea, supra* note 3.

11 *R.* v. *Isaac* (1975), 13 N.S.R. (2d) 460 (N.S.C.A.).

12 *Ibid.* at 479.

13 *Marshall No. 1, supra* note 8 at para. 42.

14 *Isaac, supra* note 11 at 483.

15 *R.* v. *Cope,* [1982] 1 C.N.L.R. 23 (N.S.C.A.).

the Treaty of 1752 conferred the special rights that the Mi'kmaq claimed, those rights could be extinguished by federal legislation. The court continued by stating that the treaty did not grant the Mi'kmaq a special right but merely affirmed their Aboriginal right to hunt and fish. Finally, the court held that the treaty was not made with the Mi'kmaq Nation as a whole but only with a small group of Mi'kmaq inhabiting the eastern part of what is now Nova Scotia. The Supreme Court of Canada refused to hear the appeal on the basis that this issue had already been decided in *R. v. Derrickson* (1976).[16] In *Derrickson,* the Supreme Court of Canada held that Aboriginal rights to fish are subject to regulation as set out in the federal *Fisheries Act.* The Supreme Court of Canada in *Marshall No. 1* referenced *Cope* approvingly when it noted that peace and friendship treaties with the Mi'kmaq did not extinguish Aboriginal hunting and fishing rights.[17]

The 1981 Ontario Court of Appeal decision of *R. v. Taylor and Williams* (1981)[18] was significant because it brought together a number of critical factors to be considered when interpreting treaties. The decision dealt with a treaty signed in 1818 and charges laid against a number of Chippewa who had taken bullfrogs during the closed season contrary to provincial legislation. In order to determine whether the Chippewa continued to possess hunting and fishing rights based on oral promises made at the signing of the treaty, the court examined the broader context under which the treaty had been negotiated and signed.

Although fishing and hunting rights were not guaranteed by the written terms of the treaty, the minutes from the negotiation of the treaty revealed that these rights had been discussed, and the court held that these oral portions of the treaty were as much part of the treaty as the written portions. The court stated that the history and oral traditions of the tribes concerned were important to consider. Treaties should be interpreted in a manner that upholds the honour of the Crown and avoids the appearance of "sharp dealings," resolves any ambiguity in favour of the Indians, and considers the parties' understanding of the terms of the treaty when it was signed. In *Marshall No. 1,*[19] the Supreme Court of Canada reaffirmed these important interpretative principles.

As illustrated above, prior to 1982, judicial decisions affecting treaty rights in Canada generally limited the impact of treaty rights on Canadian law. Although some earlier and lower court decisions such as *White and Bob* (1965)[20]

---

16   *R. v. Derrickson,* [1976] 2 S.C.R. v.

17   *Marshall No. 1, supra* note 8 at para. 42.

18   *R. v. Taylor and Williams,* [1981] 3 C.N.L.R. 114 (Ont. C.A.).

19   *Marshall No. 1, supra* note 8 at para. 51; see also para. 14.

20   *White and Bob, supra* note 6.

and *Taylor and Williams* (1981)[21] were helpful in expanding the interpretative regime for treaty rights, generally treaty rights were at the mercy of the federal Crown and its legislation. The Maritimes were no different from the rest of Canada in this regard, as the decisions discussed above clearly demonstrate. It is important to recognize that the early judicial reasoning was a product of the times and was influenced by prevailing misunderstandings and misconceptions about Aboriginal people. This perception ultimately changed and culminated in the 1982 constitutional amendments. The impact and effect of Aboriginal and treaty rights, and indeed attitudes, to some extent, changed dramatically with the constitutional protection afforded to Aboriginal and treaty rights in the *Constitution Act, 1982.*

Post-1982 Decisions

R. v. Simon (1985)

R. v. Simon[22] is the leading decision from the Supreme Court of Canada regarding early Maritime treaties. The case concerned Mr. Simon, a member of the Shubenacadie Indian Brook Band in Nova Scotia, who had been charged with illegally possessing a rifle during the closed season, contrary to provincial legislation. In this case, the Supreme Court considered the Treaty of 1752 and held that it was validly created by competent parties and that it had not been terminated by section 88 of the *Indian Act.* Chief Justice Dickson wrote:

> In my view, Parliament intended to include within the operation of s. 88 all agreements concluded by the Crown with the Indians, that would otherwise be enforceable treaties, whether land was ceded or not.[23]

In other words, "treaties" are to be given a broad interpretation and include all agreements between the Crown and Indians. The court also held that Mr. Simon, who was a Mi'kmaq, was covered by the terms of the treaty, even though the treaty had been signed by a small group of Mi'kmaq and not by the Mi'kmaq Nation as a whole.

The case is important because the Supreme Court recognized that a treaty of peace and friendship is a treaty even though the cession of land by Indians was not involved. The court emphasized that treaties are *sui generis* and must be interpreted in a manner that is evolutionary and not static. They must be given meaning in a modern contemporary context. The decision affirms that

---

21 *Taylor and Williams, supra* note 18.
22 *R. v. Simon*, [1985] 2 S.C.R. 387.
23 *Ibid.* at 410.

provincial laws are subject to treaties by way of section 88 of *Indian Act*. Prior to 1982, the federal Parliament under section 91(24) of the *Constitution Act, 1867*[24] had the authority to derogate from rights recognized by a treaty. *Simon* confirmed that section 35 changed this and that the status of treaties in Canadian law had been elevated.

Simon is significant because it reverses earlier interpretations that substantially limited the effect of the Treaty of 1752, and it affirms the court's liberal approach to interpreting treaty rights.[25] The decision affirmed the *sui generis* nature of treaty rights, particularly those affecting the Maritimes. The decision did not go into detail, however, on the scope of the analysis required when examining treaty rights, extinguishment, and treaty interpretation generally. Finally, the court held that treaties that did not cede land were nevertheless treaties, capable of possessing substantive rights. This became a key element in subsequent decisions and has now opened the door—nudged further open by *Marshall*—to the concept that the Maritime treaties need to be revisited to determine what rights they protect. Like *Sioui, Simon* was a forerunner of *Marshall*.

R. v. Sioui (1990)

In *R. v. Sioui*,[26] the Supreme Court of Canada considered the rights of the Hurons under a treaty made in 1760 to exercise their cultural and traditional activities within the boundaries of Jacques-Cartier Park in Quebec. The decision concerned a number of Hurons who had been charged with making fires, cutting trees, and camping in a provincial park, contrary to the provincial regulations of Quebec. In their defence against the charges, the Hurons made reference to a number of short documents dated September 5, 1760. The defendants argued that the clause that the Hurons were to be "allowed the free Exercise of their Religion, their Customs, and Liberty with the English," which appeared in one of the documents,[27] allowed them to undertake the actions for which they were charged.

As with *Simon,* the Supreme Court affirmed that treaties are *sui generis* and that they demand a liberal, generous interpretative approach in favour of the Aboriginal people concerned. The court held that section 88 of the *Indian Act* affirmed the validity of the treaty in question to exempt the Hurons from the application of provincial park regulations. The court also affirmed that

---

24 *Constitution Act, 1867* (U.K.), 30 & 31 Vict., c. 3 (R.S.C. 1985, App. II, No. 5); s. 91(24) assigns exclusive legislative authority to the federal Parliament over "Indians, and Lands reserved for the Indians."

25 *Marshall No. 1, supra* note 8, referenced *Simon* at paras. 14, 16, 20, 44, and 53.

26 *R. v. Sioui*, [1990] 1 S.C.R. 1025.

27 *Ibid*. at 1031.

when the treaty was made, the Indian nations were regarded by the Europeans as "independent nations" capable of making treaties. The court made it clear that treaty rights are in addition to rights recognized by the *Royal Proclamation of 1763*[28] and other like instruments, and that they cannot be extinguished merely because they have not been utilized or invoked for a long period of time. Thus, although the document was very brief and signed only by the governor of Quebec, it was nevertheless deemed to be a treaty on the grounds that it contained certain assurances and promises made to the Hurons.[29]

Sioui interprets treaty rights in a liberal manner by expanding the notion of what a treaty may include. That is, it does not have to have the word "treaty" printed on it, but rather the intention of the parties is one of a number of relevant factors to be taken into consideration. Building on *Simon, Sioui* was a precursor of what was to come from the Supreme Court, particularly with regard to the *Marshall* decision and its liberal interpretation of what constitutes a treaty right or promise and how the intention of the parties is to be ascertained.

R. v. *Sparrow* (1990)

In 1990, the Supreme Court of Canada rendered its decision in *R. v. Sparrow*.[30] This decision remains one of the most important and illuminating decisions regarding the meaning of section 35. In *Marshall No. 2,* the Supreme Court of Canada stated that the *Sparrow* decision was the first of a series of important decisions that affirmed that constitutionally protected Aboriginal and treaty rights are subject to regulation that can be justified on the basis of conservation or other grounds of public importance.[31]

Mr. Sparrow, a member of the Musqueam Indian Band of British Columbia, had been charged and convicted under section 61(1) of the *Fisheries Act*[32] for fishing with a drift net that was longer than that permitted under the

---

28 *Royal Proclamation of 1763,* R.S.C. 1985, App. II, No. 1.

29 *Marshall No. 1, supra* note 8 referenced *Sioui* at paras. 11, 13, 14, 19, 39, 44, and 46.

30 *R. v. Sparrow, supra* note 8. For commentary on *Sparrow,* see W.I.C. Binnie, "The Sparrow Doctrine: Beginning of the End or End of the Beginning?" (1991) 15 Queen's L.J. 217; T. Isaac, "The Honour of the Crown: Aboriginal Rights and the *Constitution Act, 1982*; The Significance of *R. v. Sparrow*" (1992) 13:1 Policy Options Politiques 22; D.W. Elliot, "In the Wake of *Sparrow*" (1991) 40 U.N.B.L.J. 23; and M. Asch and P. Macklem, "Aboriginal Rights and Canadian Sovereignty: An Essay on *R. v. Sparrow*" (1991) 26:2 Alta. L. Rev. 502.

31 *R. v. Marshall ((Marshall No. 2),* [1999] 3 S.C.R. 533 (reconsideration refused) at para. 6.

32 *Fisheries Act,* R.S.C. 1970, c. F-14, ss. 34, 61(1), now R.S.C. 1985, c. F-14, ss. 43, 79.

band's food-fishing licence. Sparrow admitted that the facts constituted an offence, but defended his action on the basis that he was exercising an existing Aboriginal right to fish and that the drift-net length restriction was inconsistent with section 35(1) of the *Constitution Act, 1982* and, therefore, invalid.

In *Sparrow,* the Supreme Court held that legal problems regarding Aboriginal people require "sensitivity to and respect for the rights of aboriginal peoples on behalf of the government, courts and indeed all Canadians."[33] It also held that section 35 constitutionally protects existing Aboriginal and treaty rights and prevents the extinguishment of Aboriginal rights that existed as of April 17, 1982. The Supreme Court held that "existing" refers to the rights that were in existence when the *Constitution Act, 1982* came into effect. The court also stated that "existing" means unextinguished[34] and that "existing aboriginal rights" require an interpretation that is flexible so as "to permit their [aboriginal rights] evolution over time."[35] The court adopted the language of Brian Slattery in noting that "existing" means that rights are "affirmed in a contemporary form rather than in their primeval simplicity and vigour."[36]

The court's discussion of "recognized and affirmed" is the most substantive portion of the decision. On the issue of Crown sovereignty and legislative power and Aboriginal title, the court wrote: "[T]here was from the outset never any doubt that sovereignty and legislative power, and indeed the underlying title, to such lands vested in the Crown." The court noted that the interpretation of "recognized and affirmed" is derived from "general principles of constitutional interpretation"[37] and that section 35 shall be interpreted in a "purposive way." That is, it shall be given a "generous, liberal interpretation."[38] The court then cited its earlier decision of *R.* v. *Nowegijick,*[39] wherein it stated that "treaties and statutes relating to Indians should be liberally construed and doubtful expressions resolved in favour of the Indians."[40]

Sparrow is an important decision that outlined, for the first time, the scope and nature of section 35(1). In doing so, however, the court made it clear that although Aboriginal and treaty rights may be given a liberal interpretation,

---

33 *Sparrow, supra* note 8 at 1119.

34 *Ibid.* at 1092.

35 *Ibid.* at 1093.

36 B. Slattery, "Understanding Aboriginal Rights" (1988) 66 Can. Bar Rev. 782, as cited in *Sparrow, supra* note 8 at 1093.

37 *Ibid.* at 1106.

38 *Ibid.*

39 *R.* v. *Nowegijick,* [1983] 1 S.C.R. 29.

40 *Ibid.* at 36.

these rights are not absolute. Rather, Aboriginal rights may be limited in their application where government can demonstrate that it is justified in interfering with the exercise of these rights. *Sparrow* sets out the test for interfering with existing Aboriginal rights and the justification of such interference.[41] The justification analysis comprises a series of questions. The first question to be asked is whether the legislation in question has the effect of interfering with an existing Aboriginal right; if it does have such an effect, it represents a *prima facie* infringement of section 35(1). The second question to be asked is whether the *prima facie* infringement, if it is found to exist, is justified.

The inquiry with respect to interference begins with a reference to the characteristics or incidents of the right at issue. For example, fishing rights are not traditional property rights; they are rights held by a collective and are in keeping with the culture and existence of the affected group. Traditional property rights are individual and are contractual in nature, and they do not necessarily rely on an individual's culture for their meaning. The test then moves to a determination of whether the fishing rights have been interfered with such as to constitute a *prima facie* infringement. First, is the limitation on the right unreasonable? Second, does the regulation impose undue hardship? Third, does the regulation deny the holders of the right their preferred means of exercising that right?

The onus of proving a *prima facie* infringement lies with the individual or group challenging the legislation. In the case of *Sparrow,* the regulation would be found to be a *prima facie* interference if it were found to be an adverse restriction on the Musqueam exercise of the right to fish for food. The court noted that the issue did not merely require looking at whether the fish catch had been reduced below that needed for the reasonable food and ceremonial needs of the Musqueam. Rather, the test involved asking whether either the purpose or the effect of the restriction on net length unnecessarily infringed the interest protected by the fishing right.

Under the *Sparrow* test, if a *prima facie* interference is found, the analysis moves to the issue of justification. In other words, does the *prima facie* interference constitute a legitimate regulation of a constitutional Aboriginal right? This part of the analysis shifts the onus of demonstrating justification onto the Crown. The justification analysis comprises two main steps, and it proceeds as follows. The first step of the justification process is to establish whether the regulation in question meets a valid legislative objective. Here, the court would inquire whether the objective of Parliament in authorizing the fisheries department to enact regulations regarding fisheries is valid. An

---

41 This test was reaffirmed, in the context of treaty rights, in *Marshall No. 1, supra* note 8 at para. 64.

objective aimed at preserving section 35(1) rights by conserving and managing a natural resource, for example, would be valid. Also valid would be objectives purporting to prevent the exercise of section 35 rights that would cause harm to the general populace or to Aboriginal people themselves. There are a number of other objectives that would be found to be compelling and substantial. In *Sparrow*, the court rejected the "public interest" justification because it was so vague as to provide no meaningful guidance and so broad as to be unworkable.

If a valid legislative objective is found, the analysis proceeds to the second step of the justification test: the honour of the Crown. The special trust relationship and the responsibility of the government vis-à-vis Aboriginal people must be the first consideration in determining whether legislation or the action in question can be justified. For example, if the objective pertains to conservation, the conservation plan would be scrutinized to assess priorities. The court acknowledged that the justificatory standard to be met may place a heavy burden on the Crown. However, government policy with respect to the British Columbia fishery regardless of section 35 already dictates that in allocating the right to take fish, Indian food fishing is to be given priority over the interest of all other user groups. This objective is to guarantee that those plans treat Aboriginal people in a way that ensures that their rights are taken seriously.

There are other questions to be asked within the justification analysis, and these will depend on the circumstances of the inquiry. Examples include whether there has been as little infringement as possible in order to effect the desired result; whether, in a situation of expropriation, fair compensation is available; and whether the Aboriginal group in question has been consulted with respect to the conservation measures being implemented. (The requirement of consultation by the Crown to justify an infringement of an Aboriginal right is discussed in chapter 4.)

Sparrow contains several important principles in understanding Aboriginal rights and therefore assists in understanding the relationship between Aboriginal rights and a right of self-government. For example, the court spoke of a "flexible interpretation" of Aboriginal rights so as to permit their "evolution." The court noted, however, that sovereignty and underlying title to the land vests in the Crown.[42] However, the issue of underlying title may not necessarily rule out a favourable interpretation on internal Aboriginal sovereignty in the future from the Supreme Court. The court has offered more favourable comments in other cases. In *R. v. Sioui*,[43] the Supreme Court stated:

---

42 *Sparrow, supra* note 8.
43 *Sioui, supra* note 26.

The British Crown recognized that the Indians had certain ownership rights over their land. . . . . It also allowed them autonomy in their internal affairs, intervening . . . as little as possible.[44]

The Supreme Court briefly considered the proposition that a right of self-government may be contained within section 35(1) in its 1996 decision of *R. v. Pamajewon* (1996).[45] The court affirmed a number of principles to be used when exploring how courts may interpret a right of self-government, including that the test for proving a right of self-government would be no different from a test for other Aboriginal rights and would come within the legal framework set out in *Sparrow* (1990), *Van der Peet* (1996), and other decisions. Additionally, the court emphasized the need for specificity when claiming a right. *Pamajewon* concerned a number of Aboriginal people appealing convictions related to illegal gaming activities. They claimed they possessed a "broad right" to manage their lands. This right was not considered specific enough.

Where the debate over self-government will go in the future is uncertain, but it does have significant implications for the Maritimes, particularly for those First Nations claiming a right to self-regulate the fishery and other resources to which they possess rights. *Sparrow* is a crucial decision to the future development and understanding of what rights Aboriginal people possess in the Maritimes and the degree to which governments may justifiably infringe those rights. This is so because *Sparrow* provides the initial analysis of what section 35 means, the framework within which it is to be interpreted, and how it affects governmental authority.

R. v. Horseman (1990)

In *R. v. Horseman*,[46] the Supreme Court of Canada affirmed that the onus to prove the extinguishment of a treaty right rests with the Crown and that ambiguities in treaties must be resolved in favour of the Indians. The decision concerned a Treaty No. 8 Indian who had been charged with illegally hunting a grizzly bear, contrary to Alberta's *Wildlife Act*.[47] In this case, Mr. Horseman's original acquittal was restored. The court ruled that relevant provisions of the *Wildlife Act* were applicable to Treaty No. 8 Indians only to the extent that the Indian engaged in sport or commercial hunting. The court also acknowledged that, prior to the enactment of the *Constitution Act, 1982,* the federal government had the exclusive authority to modify treaty rights without the consent of the Indians affected. The court cited as evidence the *Constitution Act,*

---

44   *Ibid*. at 1055.

45   *R. v. Pamajewon,* [1996] 2 S.C.R. 821.

46   *R. v. Horseman,* [1990] 1 S.C.R. 901.

47   *Wildlife Act,* R.S.A. 1980, c. W-9, s. 1(s), 42.

1930[48] (Natural Resources Transfer Agreement or NRTA), in which the federal government unilaterally "merged and consolidated" Treaty No. 8 rights to hunt by moving the Treaty No. 8 right to hunt from Treaty No. 8 to the NRTA. This agreement not only dealt with hunting rights, but also recognized that the federal government may need provincial land in order to fulfil its legal obligations to provide land to Indians under the treaties. Like the later *Marshall* decisions, *Horseman* noted the non-absolute nature of treaty rights: "[T]he hunting rights granted by the 1899 Treaty were not unlimited. Rather they were subject to governmental regulation."[49]

Although dealing with western treaty issues, *Horseman,* like the other decisions referenced in this section, adds significantly to the understanding and meaning of treaty rights protection under Canadian law. It reiterates that treaty rights are not absolute and can be subject to regulation, and it clearly places the onus for proving the extinguishment of a treaty right on the Crown. These same messages were reaffirmed in *Marshall.*

R. v. Van der Peet (1996)

In *R. v. Van der Peet,*[50] the Supreme Court of Canada considered an appeal dealing with Ms. Van der Peet, a member of the Stolo First Nation in British Columbia, who had been charged under the federal *Fisheries Act* for selling salmon caught with a food-fishing license. The court held that in this case, fishing for food and ceremonial purposes was integral to the Stolo culture, but the exchange of fish was merely incidental and therefore not protected by section 35(1). Chief Justice Lamer stated that "[i]n order to be an Aboriginal right an activity must be an element of a practice, custom or tradition integral to the distinctive culture of the Aboriginal group claiming the right."[51] He set out ten factors that must be considered to establish Aboriginal rights.

1. Courts must consider the perspective of Aboriginal peoples themselves.
2. Courts must identify precisely the nature of the claim being made in determining whether an Aboriginal claimant has demonstrated the existence of an Aboriginal right.
3. In order to be integral, a practice, custom, or tradition must be of central significance to the Aboriginal society in question.
4. The practices, customs, and traditions that constitute Aboriginal rights are those which have continuity with the traditions, customs, and practices that existed *prior* to contact.

---

48 *Constitution Act, 1930,* R.S.C. 1985, App. II, No. 26.
49 *Horseman, supra* note 46 at 936.
50 *R. v. Van der Peet,* [1996] 2 S.C.R. 507.
51 *Ibid.* at para. 46.

5. Courts must approach the rules of evidence in light of the evidentiary difficulties inherent in adjudicating Aboriginal claims.
6. Claims to Aboriginal rights must be adjudicated on a specific rather than general basis.
7. For a practice, tradition, or custom to constitute an Aboriginal right, it must be of independent significance to the Aboriginal culture in which it exists.
8. The integral-to-distinctive-culture test requires that a practice, custom, or tradition be distinctive; it does not require that the practice, custom, or tradition be distinct.
9. The influence of European culture will be relevant to the inquiry only if it is demonstrated that the practice, custom, or tradition is integral only because of that influence.
10. Courts must take into account both the relationship of Aboriginal people to the land and the distinctive societies and cultures of Aboriginal people.

In *Van der Peet*, a two-stage process was used to determine whether Aboriginal rights existed. First, the court had to identify the precise nature of the claim for recognition of an Aboriginal right. Second, the court had to answer the following question: Was the practice of exchanging fish for money or other goods an integral part of the specific distinctive culture of the Sto:lo prior to contact with Europeans? It is important to note that the *Van der Peet* test is not dependent upon land-based rights. Perhaps this is why the court emphasized that Aboriginal title comes from Aboriginal rights and not vice versa.

The *Van der Peet* analysis will be crucial when examining the continued existence of Aboriginal rights in the Maritimes. Unlike other parts of Canada where treaties have been signed, the Maritimes is unique in that Aboriginal rights may co-exist alongside treaty rights, since Aboriginal rights were not ceded by way of treaty (that is, in the Maritimes, a treaty right to fish and an Aboriginal right to fish may co-exist). The same holds true for treaty rights co-existing alongside Aboriginal title. The possibility of having Aboriginal rights, title, and treaty rights co-existing in some form or another is extremely interesting and raises many questions. If Aboriginal rights and title are found to continue to exist in the Maritimes, it will only underscore the necessity for negotiations.

R. v. Adams (1996)

In *R. v. Adams,*[52] the Supreme Court of Canada applied the *Van der Peet* test regarding activities that are integral to the distinctive culture of the Aborigi-

---

52 *R. v. Adams,* [1996] 3 S.C.R. 101.

nal group claiming Aboriginal rights. In *Adams,* the Supreme Court of Canada considered the appeal of Mr. Adams, a Mohawk who had been convicted under the *Quebec Fishery Regulations* and the *Fisheries Act* for fishing for food without a proper licence. The court considered whether the *Quebec Fishery Regulations* were of no force or effect because of Aboriginal rights possessed by Mr. Adams under section 35(1). The question centered around whether a claim to an Aboriginal right to fish must rest on a claim to Aboriginal title to the area where the fishing occurred.

In applying the *Van der Peet* test, the court held that the licence requirement infringed the appellant's Aboriginal right to fish for food and that the regulatory scheme was dependant upon ministerial discretion that had no criteria attached to its application. Using *Van der Peet,* the court determined that although the Mohawks' claim to occupancy over the area in question was weak, the claim with respect to their use of the lands and waters in question, that is their distinct practices in the area, was strong. Thus, although a link to land may be crucial to support Aboriginal rights, a link to a particular piece of land and associated Aboriginal title is not necessary for a claim of Aboriginal rights. In *Marshall No. 1,*[53] the Supreme Court referenced with approval the *Van der Peet* test outlined in *Adams* as it applied to licensing schemes. In *Adams* the court stated:

> In light of the Crown's unique judiciary obligations towards Aboriginal peoples, Parliament may not simply adopt an unstructured discretionary administrative regime which risks infringing Aboriginal rights in a substantial number of applications in the absence of some explicit guidance. If a statute confers an administrative discretion which may carry significant consequences for the exercise of an Aboriginal right, the statute or its delegate regulations must outline specific criteria for the granting or refusal of that discretion which seek to accommodate the existence of Aboriginal rights. In the absence of such specific guidance, the statute will fail to provide representatives of the Crown with sufficient directives to fulfil their fiduciary duties, and the statute will be found to represent an infringement of Aboriginal rights under the *Sparrow* test.[54]

Adams underscores one of the central themes of the *Marshall* decision and strikes at the heart of an important practical issue affecting the Maritimes. The court in *Marshall* spends considerable time dealing with the need for ministerial discretionary authority to be clear and for it to be sensitive to the

---

53 *Marshall No. 1, supra* note 8 at para. 64.
54 *Adams, supra* note 52 at para. 54.

rights of Aboriginal people. This aspect of *Marshall* is based directly on the court's decision in *Adams*. Practically speaking, discretionary and regulatory authorities go to the heart of the current problems facing the East Coast fishery, and the solutions to those problems lie exclusively with government.

R. v. *Badger* (1996)

The interpretative regime within which treaty rights are to be analyzed was made clearer with the 1996 Supreme Court of Canada's decision in *R. v. Badger*.[55] *Badger* concerned Treaty No. 8 and whether registered Indians possess the right to hunt on privately owned land within the treaty's territory, whether treaty hunting rights were extinguished or modified by the Natural Resources Transfer Agreement (1930) (NRTA), and the degree to which legislation requiring hunting licences applies to registered Indians. Although the court held that the treaty right to hunt for food was not extinguished by the NRTA, the right was limited geographically by using the concept of "visible incompatible land use." This concept requires a case-by-case analysis and means that if privately owned land is occupied or put to a visible use, Indians do not have a right to access. If the land is unoccupied and not being put to visible use, Indians will have a right to access, pursuant to Treaty No. 8. The court held that, in this case, the requirement of licences was a *prima facie* infringement of treaty rights that had to be justified. A new trial was ordered for one of the appellants to deal with the issue of justification, while the other two appellants' claims were dismissed because they were hunting on occupied land.

Badger is significant because it provides a useful summary of the principles of interpretation to be used when adjudicating cases involving treaty rights.[56] These principles are as follows.

1. A treaty represents an exchange of solemn promises between the Crown and Indian nations and the nature of this agreement is sacred.
2. The honour of the Crown is always at stake when dealing with Indian people, and it is always to be assumed that the Crown intends to fulfil its promises. The integrity of the Crown must be maintained when interpreting statutes or treaties that affect Aboriginal and treaty rights. The appearance of "sharp dealing" is not to be sanctioned.
3. When interpreting a treaty or document, any ambiguities or doubtful expressions in the wording must be resolved in favour of the Indians. Any limitations that restrict Indian treaty rights must be narrowly construed.

---

55 *R. v. Badger*, [1996] 1 S.C.R. 771.
56 *Ibid.* at para. 41.

4. The onus of proving the extinguishment of a treaty right lies with the
    Crown. Strict proof of the extinguishment is required, as is a clear and
    plain intention to do so.

Badger also affirmed that the *Sparrow* justificatory analysis—which is
used to determine whether government infringement of section 35(1) rights
may be justified—is to be applied in cases concerning treaty rights. Justice
Cory noted:

> [J]ustification of provincial regulations enacted pursuant to the NRTA should
> meet the same test for justification set out in *Sparrow*. The reason for this is
> obvious. The effect of paragraph 12 of the NRTA is to place the provincial
> government in exactly the same position as formerly occupied by the federal
> Crown. Thus the provincial government has the same duty not to infringe
> unjustifiably the hunting right provided by Treaty No. 8 as modified by the
> NRTA. Paragraph 12 of the NRTA provides that the province may make laws
> for a conservation purpose, subject to the Indian right to hunt and fish for
> food. Accordingly, there is a need for a means to assess which conservation
> laws will be justifiable even if they infringe that right. The *Sparrow* analysis
> provides a reasonable, flexible and current method of assessing conservation
> regulations and enactments.[57]

Badger applied the principle of co-existence on Crown lands, developed
in *Sioui,* to private lands, thereby underscoring the significance of the decision. *Badger* also used oral history as a basis for interpreting treaty rights and
stressed the importance of such history in understanding the context surrounding the signing of a treaty.[58] The *Badger* approach to unoccupied land was
applied in the Saskatchewan Court of Appeal decision of *R. v. Peeace.*[59] In
Peeace, the court held that Treaty No. 4 hunting rights can be exercised when
private land can be shown to be abandoned and "unoccupied," using a case-
by-case analysis. Land that is visibly put to use as agricultural land is not
unoccupied and, therefore, Treaty No. 4 hunting rights do not apply.

Badger forms a key component to understanding the existing state of
treaty rights law in Canada. Although it dealt with a western numbered treaty,
it nevertheless outlined the Supreme Court's interpretative approach to treaty

---

57 *Badger, ibid.* at para. 96; also reaffirmed in *Marshall No. 1, supra* note 8 at para.
    7, and *Marshall No. 2, supra* note 31 at para. 14.
58 *Badger, ibid.* paras. 45 and 52; also reaffirmed in *Marshall No. 1, ibid.* at para.
    14.
59 *R. v. Peeace,* [2000] 2 C.N.L.R. 228 (Sask. C.A.).

rights, which was affirmed and found to be applicable in the Maritime situation in *Marshall*.

Delgamuukw v. British Columbia (1997)

Although *Delgamuukw* v. *British Columbia*[60] is discussed in detail in chapter 4, no outline of major Canadian decisions dealing with Aboriginal people would be complete without it. *Delgamuukw* is the leading Canadian decision concerning Aboriginal title, and it will undoubtedly play a major role in any litigation regarding Aboriginal title in the Maritimes. The decision concerned the Gitksan and Wet'suwet'en First Nations, who sought a declaration affirming their ownership, jurisdiction, and Aboriginal rights over a large portion of land in northern British Columbia. *Delgamuukw* affirmed that Aboriginal title exists under Canadian law and that its legal recognition depends on a case-by-case analysis.

R. v. Sundown (1999)

In *R.* v. *Sundown*,[61] the Supreme Court of Canada considered the Crown's appeal of the quashing of Mr. Sundown's conviction for constructing a structure within a provincial park, contrary to provincial regulations. Mr. Sundown was a Treaty No. 6 Cree, and the shelter constructed was part of a long-standing tradition of the respondent's First Nation when hunting or fishing. The court held that

> [a] hunting cabin is, in these circumstances, reasonably incidental to this First Nation's right to hunt in their traditional expeditionary style. . . . A reasonable person apprised of the traditional expeditionary method of hunting would conclude that for this First Nation the treaty right encompasses the right to build shelters as a reasonable incident to that right. . . . It has evolved to the small log cabin, which is an appropriate shelter for expeditionary hunting in today's society.[62]

Sundown is an interesting decision in light of the "reasonably incidental" analysis it outlines. *Sundown* provides First Nations with a potentially useful tool regarding a liberal and expansive approach to treaty interpretation. This may be particularly interesting in the Maritime context, where the treaty rights in written form are vague, thus leaving room for a fairly broad approach to the rights themselves, let alone what rights may be incidental to them. In-

---

60 *Delgamuukw* v. *British Columbia*, [1997] 3 S.C.R. 1010.
61 *R.* v. *Sundown*, [1999] 1 S.C.R. 393.
62 *Ibid.* at para. 33.

deed, this may be the case with the facts in *Marshall*. What other rights exist that are incidental to the right to hunt, fish, gather, and trade for necessaries?

Maritime-Specific Decisions Post-1982

The following is a summary of some of the more influential and noteworthy decisions post-1982 affecting Aboriginal and treaty rights in the Maritimes.

In *R. v. Johnson* (1993),[63] the Nova Scotia Court of Appeal considered the Treaty of 1752 and held that nothing in that treaty exempts Indians from complying with Nova Scotia's tobacco-tax legislation. In this case, Mr. Johnson, a Nova Scotia Mi'kmaq, had been charged with possessing tobacco not purchased from an authorized wholesale vendor, contrary to provincial regulation.[64] The conviction was upheld since the accused could not claim any protection from either the *Indian Act* or the Treaty of 1752.

In *R. v. Paul* (1994),[65] the New Brunswick Court of Appeal ordered a new trial of three Maliseet who had been charged with unlawfully possessing deer meat. The Crown argued that the deer had been shot in an unsafe manner since the accused were hunting on private lands near a highway. The accused claimed they possessed a right to hunt in an unfettered manner according to the Treaty of 1725. The court held that the trial judge's conclusion—that the Maliseet possessed a right to hunt anywhere in New Brunswick at any time—could not be supported. Treaty rights must be exercised with regard to the safety of others and each case must be considered on its own merits. In another decision relating to the Treaty of 1725, the New Brunswick Provincial Court held that Maliseet who are not registered under the federal *Indian Act* are entitled to benefits under the treaty.[66]

In *R. v. McCoy* (1993),[67] the New Brunswick Court of Appeal considered the Crown's appeal of Mr. McCoy, a Maliseet who had been acquitted of unlawfully hunting wildlife with the aid of a light. Mr. McCoy claimed that he possessed a treaty right to hunt pursuant to the Treaty of 1725 and the Articles of Submission of 1726. The court held that the Treaty of 1725 does guarantee a right to hunt; however, it ruled that the right is not absolute and must be exercised in a safe manner.

63 *R. v. Johnson* (1996), 156 N.S.R. (2d) 71 (N.S.C.A.); leave to appeal refused (1997), 162 N.S.R. (2d) 80n (S.C.C.); see also *R. v. Johnson,* [1994] 1 C.N.L.R. 129 (N.S.C.A.).

64 *Tobacco Tax Act,* R.S.N.S. 1989, c. 470, ss. 25(1)(b), (2), 40.

65 *R. v. Paul,* [1994] 2 C.N.L.R. 167 (N.B.C.A.).

66 *R. v. Fowler,* [1993] 3 C.N.L.R. 178 (N.B. Prov. Ct.).

67 *R. v. McCoy,* [1994] 2 C.N.L.R. 129 (N.B.C.A.); see also *R. v. Paul; R. v. Polchies,* [1988] 4 C.N.L.R. 107 (N.B.Q.B.).

A 1998 New Brunswick Court of Queen's Bench decision[68] affirmed that, based on a number of eighteenth-century treaties (for example, the Treaty of 1725) affecting the Mi'kmaq and Maliseet of eastern Canada, trees on Crown land belong to the Indians. Mr. Paul had been charged under New Brunswick's *Crown Lands and Forest Act*[69] for unlawfully removing timber from Crown lands. Although Mr. Paul admitted that he had removed the timber, he relied on a number of documents dated between 1725 and 1762 to support his claim that he possessed a treaty right to harvest and sell timber. Obviously, the impact of this decision in a province where logging is prevalent is significant. Justice Turnbull referred to the Indians' interest in the trees as one of "ownership." He wrote:

> I believe there are several ways one could describe the status of rights in Crown land. A legally correct way would be to consider Crown lands as reserved for Indians. Not exclusively, but their rights to them are protected by treaty. The trees on Crown land are Indian trees. Not exclusively, but their rights are protected by treaty. The Crown has jurisdiction and dominion over all land. Undoubtedly the Legislature and Parliament can enact laws which affect Indian treaty rights in New Brunswick. Governments must accept that Dummer's Treaty was understood to protect Indian land and recognize the Indians' primacy when enacting legislation if it intends to enact laws affecting treaty rights. At the present time Indians have the right to cut trees on all Crown land. If this provision in the Crown Lands and Forests Act (supra) had met the guidelines set out in *R. v. Sparrow* [1990] 1 S.C.R. 1075 the law would apply to Mr. Paul. Such a license to Stone Consolidated Inc. would in my opinion be considered an exclusive license. My rationale is that the Act is not applicable to the Indians of New Brunswick. Considerable argument was advanced before me that one must slash a maple tree to first determine if it is bird's eye. This is indeed deplorable, but an owner is legally entitled to do so.[70]

The New Brunswick Court of Appeal allowed an appeal by the Crown on the basis that the defendant did not produce sufficient evidence to demonstrate possession of an Aboriginal right to harvest and sell timber. Leave to appeal to the Supreme Court of Canada was refused.

In *R. v. Tomah* (1999),[71] an appeal by two Maliseet who had been charged with unlawfully fishing was dismissed. The New Brunswick Court of Queen's

---

68   *Peter Paul v. R.,* [1998] 1 C.N.L.R. 209 (N.B.Q.B.); revised by [1998] 3 C.N.L.R.
     221 (N.B.C.A.); leave to appeal to S.C.C. refused.
69   *Crown Lands and Forest Act,* S.N.B. 1980, c. 381, s. 67(2).
70   *Ibid.* at para. 71.
71   *R. v. Tomah,* [1999] 3 C.N.L.R. 311 (N.B.Q.B.).

Bench held that there was no evidence that fishing on the Miramichi River for food was a tradition, custom, or practice of the Maliseet people. Following the *Sparrow* test, the burden for proving a right rests with those who claim that they possess the right. Justice Riordon concluded:

> There is no evidence whatsoever that fishing in the Miramichi River for food was a tradition, custom or practice of the Maliseets. There was no evidence presented at trial that any treaty conferred a right to fish the Miramichi River to the Maliseets. No treaty was introduced into evidence. . . . The appellants . . . have the burden of proving that they have the right to fish by any such Treaty.[72]

In *R. v. Bernard* (2000),[73] Judge Lordon of the New Brunswick Provincial Court held that the Mi'kmaq of the Miramichi in New Brunswick do not possess a treaty right under treaties made in 1761 and 1779 to commercially harvest wood. (This is the same trade clause that would later be analyzed in *Marshall.*) Judge Lordon stated that

> to interpret the right to "gather" as a right to participate in the wholesale uncontrolled exploitation of natural resources would "alter the terms of the treaty" and "wholly transform" the rights therein confirmed.[74]

The court also stated that the *Royal Proclamation of 1763* did not reserve lands in Nova Scotia (including what is now New Brunswick).[75] The Court of Queen's Bench upheld the trial court's decision.

In *Shubenacadie Indian Band v. Canada (Min. of Fisheries and Oceans)* (2000),[76] Justice Pelletier of the Federal Court, Trial Division considered an application by the Shubenacadie Indian Band for an interlocutory injunction enjoining the minister of Fisheries and Oceans from seizing from the band and its members lobster traps, fishing vessels, equipment used to harvest lobsters, and lobsters harvested by them, and from otherwise impeding or interfering with their lobster fishing and lobster sales. The band made reference to the *Marshall* decision as evidence of the Mi'kmaq right to engage in a livelihood fishery as opposed to a commercial fishery. Justice Pelletier concluded:

---

72 *Ibid.* at para. 16.
73 *R. v. Bernard,* [2000] 3 C.N.L.R. 184 (N.B. Prov. Ct.); affirmed by [2001] N.B.J. No. 259 (N.B.Q.B.); see also chapter 4.
74 *Ibid.* at 206.
75 *Ibid.* at 217.
76 *Shubenacadie Indian Band v. Canada (Min. of Fisheries and Oceans),* [2001] 1 C.N.L.R. 282 (F.C.T.D.); see also chapter 6.

[T]he public interest is against creating a vacuum of authority with respect
to the fishery resource until the necessary negotiations and consultations
have taken place. To grant this injunction to this Band is to grant it to every
other Band which is entitled to claim the benefit of the Peace and Friendship
treaties. It may be that this is exactly what will happen once the issue is
decided on its merits. If that is what the law requires, it shall be done. But
such a determination can only be made after all the issues are fully canvassed, including the issue of justification.[77]

The "vacuum of authority" to which Justice Pelletier refers concerns granting
an injunction against the Crown regarding the East Coast lobster fishery,
thereby creating an unregulated fishery.

Conclusion

The number of decisions affecting Aboriginal and treaty rights in the Maritimes
and Canada continues to grow. What was once an area of the law that received relatively little judicial scrutiny has become not only a focus of judicial attention, but also an issue that strikes at the heart of how Canada defines
itself. Nowhere is this new judicial activism and public-policy focus more
needed and so little understood than in the Maritimes. Although relatively
small by way of demographics, the Maritime First Nations are using the courts
to explore the meaning and content of their Aboriginal and treaty rights. The
next chapter explores Aboriginal title and its potential impact on the Maritimes.

---

77 *Ibid.* at para. 75.

Chapter 4

• • • • • •

Aboriginal Title and the Maritimes

Introduction[1]

Although this book focusses on Aboriginal and treaty rights within the context of the *Marshall* decisions, no discussion of the current state of Aboriginal-Crown relations in the Maritimes would be complete without commenting on the outstanding matter of Aboriginal title. This chapter outlines the current state of law in Canada regarding Aboriginal title. It pays particular attention to the Supreme Court of Canada's decision in *Delgamuukw* v. *British Columbia* (1997)[2] and outlines some recent case law concerning governments' duty to consult with Aboriginal people when their rights may be affected by a governmental decision or act. It ends by providing some thoughts on the existence and impact of Aboriginal title in the Maritime provinces. Although *Delgamuukw* is a British Columbia–based decision, it is the most extensive discussion of Aboriginal title from the Supreme Court to date, and it will have a significant impact on any Aboriginal title claims in the Maritimes.

Aboriginal Title in General

Aboriginal title is the special legal interest that Aboriginal people possess in lands, based on their historical occupation of and relationship to those lands. Land lies at the core of how many Aboriginal people define themselves. It is therefore not surprising that for Aboriginal people, the link between the land and their rights is strong. Justice Judson of the Supreme Court of Canada stated, in *Calder* v. *British Columbia (A.G.)* (1973), that "the fact is that when

---

1   See P.A. Cumming and N.H. Mickenberg, *Native Rights in Canada*, 2d ed. (Toronto: General, 1972) at 93–106. See also chap. 1 of T. Isaac, *Aboriginal Law: Cases, Materials and Commentary*, 2d ed. (Saskatoon, Sask.: Purich, 1999) at 1–114.

2   *Delgamuukw* v. *British Columbia*, [1997] 3 S.C.R. 1010.

the settlers came, the Indians were there, organized in societies and occupying the land as their forefathers had done for centuries. This is what Indian title means."[3]

Although the connection many Aboriginal people make with the land is important, the courts have made a key legal distinction to the benefit of Aboriginal people. That is, Aboriginal and treaty rights can exist independent of Aboriginal title. This means that Aboriginal title is not essential to proving the existence of Aboriginal rights.[4] In *R.* v. *Adams* (1996),[5] the Supreme Court of Canada noted the following, based on its analysis of the *Van der Peet* (1996)[6] decision:

> [W]hile claims to Aboriginal title fall within the conceptual framework of Aboriginal rights, Aboriginal rights do not exist solely where a claim to Aboriginal title has been made out. Where an Aboriginal group has shown that a particular activity, custom or tradition taking place on the land was integral to the distinctive culture of that group then, *even if they have not shown that their occupation and use of the land was sufficient to support a claim of title to the land,* they will have demonstrated that they have an Aboriginal right to engage in that practice, custom or tradition. . . . To understand why Aboriginal rights cannot be inexorably linked to Aboriginal title it is only necessary to recall that some Aboriginal peoples were nomadic. [Emphasis in original][7]

The Supreme Court of Canada affirmed the existence of Aboriginal title in Canadian law in *Calder*,[8] reaffirmed it in *R.* v. *Guerin*,[9] and extensively expanded the understanding of it in *Delgamuukw* v. *British Columbia*.[10] In *Calder*,[11] the Supreme Court of Canada dealt with an application from the Nisga'a of the Nass Valley in British Columbia for a declaration that the Aboriginal title to their asserted traditional lands had not been not extinguished. The Nisga'a had previously been unsuccessful in the lower courts. The Supreme Court of Canada held four to three that the Nisga'as' Aboriginal rights

---

3   *Calder* v. *British Columbia (A.G.)*, [1973] S.C.R. 313 at 328.
4   *Delgamuukw, supra* note 2 at paras. 137–39, and *R.* v. *Côté*, [1996] 3 S.C.R. 139 at para. 41.
5   *R.* v. *Adams*, [1996] 3 S.C.R. 101.
6   *R.* v. *Van der Peet*, [1996] 2 S.C.R. 507; see para. 74.
7   *Adams, supra* note 5 at paras. 26–27.
8   *Calder, supra* note 3.
9   *R.* v. *Guerin*, [1984] 2 S.C.R. 335.
10 *Delgamuukw, supra* note 2.
11 *Calder, supra* note 3.

with respect to their traditional lands had been extinguished. Justice Pigeon (among the four) decided against the Nisga'a claim for procedural reasons. Thus, the court was split three to three on the substantive issue.

The majority judgement of Justices Pigeon, Judson, Martland, and Ritchie, and the minority judgement of Justices Hall, Spence, and Laskin elaborated on the origins, recognition, and nature of Aboriginal rights to land in British Columbia. Both judgements held that Aboriginal title did not originate with the *Royal Proclamation of 1763*.[12] The majority decision, given by Justice Judson, held that the *Proclamation* was not applicable to British Columbia;[13] whereas the minority decision, given by Justice Hall, held that it was.[14] Justice Judson, for the majority, defined Aboriginal title as follows:

> [I]t is clear that Indian title in British Columbia cannot owe its origin to the Proclamation of 1763, the fact is that when the settlers came, the Indians were there, organized in societies and occupying the land as their forefathers had done for centuries.[15]

Justice Hall, for the minority, described the nature of the Nisga'as' Aboriginal title as follows:

> The exact nature and extent of the Indian right or title does not need to be precisely stated in this litigation. . . . This is not a claim to a title in fee but it is in the nature of an equitable title or interest . . . a usufructuary right and a right to occupy the lands and to enjoy the fruits of the soil, the forest and of the rivers and streams which does not in any way deny the Crown's paramount title. . . . Possession is of itself at common law proof of ownership. . . . Unchallenged possession is admitted here.[16]

Calder stated that Aboriginal rights in respect of land are not dependent on the *Royal Proclamation of 1763* or any other instrument for its existence. Aboriginal title and ownership of the lands is a common law right. Common law is that system of jurisprudence based on judicial precedent rather than on legislation, and it depends upon the recognition of courts for its authority. Justice Judson, for the majority, defined Aboriginal title in terms of the Nisga'as' centuries-long use and occupancy of the lands at issue and thus embodied Aboriginal title in the communal structure of Nisga'a society; Justice

---

12 *Ibid.* at 395; *Royal Proclamation of 1763*, R.S.C. 1985, App. II, No. 1.
13 *Calder, ibid.* at 323.
14 *Ibid.* at 395.
15 *Ibid.* at 328.
16 *Ibid.* at 352 and 368.

Hall, for the minority, defined Aboriginal title as a usufructuary[17] right based in the common law.

The Supreme Court of Canada also dealt with the nature of Aboriginal rights respecting land in *R* v. *Guerin* (1984).[18] In October 1957, the Musqueam Indian Band of British Columbia surrendered 162 acres (approximately 66 hectares) of reserve land situated in the City of Vancouver to the federal Crown pursuant to sections 37 to 41 of the *Indian Act*.[19] The surrender enabled the band to secure a lease with a golf club. The terms and conditions of the lease were not part of the surrender but, rather, were discussed between federal officials and the band at band meetings. The Crown executed the lease on terms less favourable than the terms originally agreed upon orally. The Crown did not receive the band's permission to change the terms of the lease, nor did it provide a copy of the lease to the band until 1970. The band instituted a suit against the Crown for breach of trust.

The Supreme Court of Canada's judgement consisted of three separate opinions of the eight justices taking part. Seven of the eight judges held that the Crown has a fiduciary duty respecting Indians lands. Justice Dickson wrote:

> [T]he nature of Indian title and the framework of the statutory scheme established for disposing of Indian land places upon the Crown an equitable obligation, enforceable by the courts, to deal with the land for the benefit of the Indians. This obligation does not amount to a trust in the private law sense. It is rather a fiduciary duty. If, however, the Crown breaches this fiduciary duty it will be liable to the Indians in the same way and to the same extent as if such a trust were in effect.[20]

Justice Dickson held that Indian title comes from two sources: Indians' historical occupation and possession of their lands, and the *Royal Proclamation of October 7, 1763*.[21] Aboriginal title is *sui generis* or unique. The nature of this right was described by Justice Dickson in *Guerin* as follows:

> Indians have a legal right to occupy and possess certain lands, the ultimate title to which is in the Crown. While their interest does not, strictly speaking, amount to beneficial ownership, neither is its nature completely exhausted by the concept of a personal right. It is true that the *sui generis* interest which the Indians have in the land is personal in the sense that it cannot be

17 "Usufructuary" refers to rights to enjoy and use benefits attached to land without ownership of the land.
18 *Guerin, supra* note 9.
19 *Indian Act,* R.S.C. 1952, c. 149; now R.S.C. 1985, c. I-5.
20 *Guerin, supra* note 9 at 376.
21 *Ibid.* at 377.

transferred to a grantee, but it is also true, as will presently appear, that the interest gives rise upon surrender to a distinctive fiduciary obligation on the part of the Crown to deal with the land for the benefit of the surrendering Indians. . . . The nature of the Indians' interest is therefore best characterized by its general inalienability, coupled with that fact that the Crown is under an obligation to deal with the land on the Indians' behalf when the interest is surrendered. Any description of Indian title which goes beyond these two features is both unnecessary and potentially misleading.[22]

This statement by Justice Dickson illustrates the difficulty that the courts have had in trying to put into words what Aboriginal title means. Justice Dickson described Aboriginal title by way of its characteristics. The Supreme Court, however, changed much of the uncertainty surrounding the meaning of Aboriginal title in 1997 in *Delgamuukw*.

Delgamuukw v. *British Columbia* (1997)

The December 1997 Supreme Court of Canada decision in *Delgamuukw* v. *British Columbia*[23] is a landmark decision for its treatment of oral histories as meeting the evidentiary rules of court, for Aboriginal title generally, and for the importance of negotiated settlements in the development of Aboriginal jurisprudence.[24] *Delgamuukw* reaffirmed the Supreme Court's discussion of the rules of evidence in *Van der Peet*.[25] Specifically, trial courts must consider evidentiary rules in light of the special nature of Aboriginal claims and in keeping with the *sui generis* nature of Aboriginal rights.[26] In *Van der Peet*, the Supreme Court stated that when courts adjudicate Aboriginal rights cases, they should approach the rules of evidence, and interpret the evidence that exists, with a consciousness of the special nature of Aboriginal claims and of the evidentiary difficulties in proving a right that originated in times when there were no written records of Aboriginal practices, customs, and traditions. The courts must not undervalue the evidence presented by Aboriginal claimants simply because that evidence does not conform precisely to the evidentiary standards that would be applied in, for example, a torts case.[27]

---

22 *Ibid.* at 382.
23 *Delgamuukw, supra* note 2.
24 A study of the history of Aboriginal title in British Columbia, especially within the context of *Delgamuukw*, can be found in D. Culhane, *The Pleasure of the Crown: Anthropology, Law and First Nations* (Burnaby, B.C.: Talon Books, 1998).
25 *Van der Peet, supra* note 6 at paras. 42, 49, 50, and 68.
26 *Delgamuukw, supra* note 2 at para. 82.
27 *Van der Peet, supra* note 6 at para. 68.

Delgamuukw affirms that oral histories, rejected by the trial court judge in this case, must be considered in Aboriginal rights decisions. The laws of evidence must accommodate Aboriginal oral history and place it "on an equal footing with the types of historical evidence that courts are familiar with."[28] This decision on the admissibility of oral histories is not simply a procedural matter; it is crucial to the interpretation of Aboriginal rights. Given that the trial judge in *Delgamuukw* rejected the argument that the Gitksan and Wet'suwet'en people had the required extent of occupation necessary for ownership of the lands in question and given that, to a large degree, the oral history evidence presented dealt with the historical nature of the use and occupation of the lands in question, the finding that this important evidence is now admissible and must be considered should prove useful for all Aboriginal people in litigation.

In *Delgamuukw*, Chief Justice Lamer also discussed the *sui generis* nature of Aboriginal title and its various dimensions: namely, that it is inalienable, that it arises from the prior occupation of Canada by Aboriginal people, and that it is held communally.[29] Aboriginal title includes the right to exclusive use and occupation of the land for an array of purposes, not limited to Aboriginal practices, customs, and traditions integral to distinct Aboriginal cultures. As well, Aboriginal title imposes on the lands in question a limit, in that the use of the land cannot be irreconcilable with the Aboriginal occupation of the land and it is the relationship that the Aboriginal group in question has with the land that gives rise to the Aboriginal title in the first place.[30] Aboriginal rights are activities that must be an element of a practice, custom, or tradition integral to the distinctive culture of the Aboriginal people claiming the right.[31] Aboriginal title is a distinct variation of Aboriginal rights, which are recognized and affirmed in section 35(1) of the *Constitution Act, 1982.*[32]

Delgamuukw affirmed that Aboriginal title is a right in land. It conferred the right to use land for a variety of activities, some of which are aspects of practices, customs, and traditions that are integral to the distinctive cultures of the Aboriginal people concerned and some of which are not. Those activities that are not integral aspects of practices, customs, and traditions are "para-

---

28 *Delgamuukw, supra* note 2 at para. 87.
29 *Ibid.* at paras. 113–15.
30 *Ibid.* at paras. 117 and 128.
31 *Ibid.* at para. 140; *Van der Peet, supra* note 6 at para. 46.
32 *Delgamuukw, ibid.* at para 2; *Constitution Act, 1982,* Sched. B. to the *Canada Act 1982* (U.K.), 1982, c. 11, as am. by the *Constitution Amendment Proclamation, 1983,* R.S.C. 1985, App. II, No. 46 [am.ss. 25(b) and add. 35(3), 35(4), 35.1 and 37.1 and 54.1].

sitic to the underlying Aboriginal title."[33] Aboriginal title includes mineral rights and the right to exploit the land for oil and gas.[34] However, these rights are not absolute. They must be balanced with and are limited by the special nature of the Aboriginal title to the land in question. For example, they must be balanced with the inherent limitation that the lands must not be used in a manner irreconcilable with the intent of Aboriginal title. In practical terms, a complete understanding of the scope of Aboriginal rights and title is uncertain.[35] In *Delgamuukw,* the court described the content of Aboriginal title as a "*sui generis* interest that is distinct from normal proprietary interests, most notably fee simple."[36]

Proof of Aboriginal Title

Common law Aboriginal title is protected in its complete form by section 35(1) of the *Constitution Act, 1982,* but how does a First Nation prove Aboriginal title? Issues to consider include whether Aboriginal rights and Aboriginal title apply only to those activities that are land based. That is, are Aboriginal rights restricted solely to the use, occupation, enjoyment, and possession of traditional lands, or can they apply beyond the land base? Examples of issues that do not necessarily require a land base but yet have been claimed as being Aboriginal rights are gambling and gaming, non-application of the *Criminal Code,*[37] and the jurisdiction of Aboriginal governments over those Aboriginal persons not living on an Aboriginal land base, such as an Indian reserve.

In practice, it seems that Aboriginal rights protected by section 35(1) fall along a spectrum. At one end of the spectrum are those Aboriginal rights that are practices, customs, and traditions integral to the distinctive culture of the group claiming a right. However, the occupation and use of the land where the activities are occurring is not sufficient to support a claim to title of the land. Nevertheless, these activities have constitutional protection. In the middle of the spectrum there are activities that, out of necessity, take place on land and, indeed, might be intimately related to a particular piece of land. Even though an Aboriginal group may not be able to prove title to this land, it may be able to prove a site-specific right to engage in a particular activity. At the other end of spectrum, there is Aboriginal title itself.[38]

---

33 *Delgamuukw, ibid.* at para. 111.
34 See also *Blueberry River Indian Band* v. *Canada,* [1995] 4 S.C.R. 344.
35 *Delgamuukw, supra* note 2 at para. 128.
36 *Ibid.* at para. 125
37 *Criminal Code of Canada*, R.S.C. 1985, c. C-46.
38 *Delgamuukw, supra* note 2 at para. 138.

Proving Aboriginal title is becoming more difficult for Aboriginal people, primarily because of the Eurocentric definitions attributed to concepts such as "title," "ownership," and "beneficial interest." Prior to *Delgamuukw,* the test used by Canadian courts to determine the existence of Aboriginal title was that set out in *Hamlet of Baker Lake* v. *Min. of Indian Affairs and Northern Development* (1979).[39] This decision was modified and refined by the *Delgamuukw* decision.

In *Delgamuukw,* Chief Justice Lamer laid out three criteria required to make a claim for Aboriginal title.[40] These criteria are (1) prior to the British assertion of sovereignty, the land must have been occupied by the ancestors of the Aboriginal group claiming title, (2) continuity between existing and pre-sovereignty occupation must be demonstrated when existing occupation of the lands in question is being offered as proof of pre-sovereignty occupation, and (3) at the time of sovereignty, the occupation by the Aboriginal group must have been exclusive.[41] The exclusivity of the occupation does not mean that other Aboriginal groups were not present, but rather must take into account the context of the Aboriginal society at sovereignty. Lack of exclusivity, however, does not prevent the Aboriginal group from claiming, and indeed establishing, Aboriginal rights. The court stated that exclusive occupation can be shown even though other Aboriginal groups were present or frequented the lands in question. In those circumstances, the exclusivity could be established by demonstrating that the group claiming title had the intent and capacity for exclusive control.[42] Noticeably missing from this listing is *Baker Lake*'s reference to the need for an "organized society." This may be an implicit recognition by the court not to judge the nature of pre-contact Aboriginal governance structures. Occupation, continuity, and exclusivity are enough to make an Aboriginal title claim. The court relied on Australia's *Mabo*[43] decision to conclude that the "substantial maintenance of the connection" between the people and the land is a crucial relationship when proving Aboriginal title.[44] Also noteworthy is the court's reference to pre-sovereignty occupation as opposed to pre-contact occupation, as was used by the court in *Van der Peet*[45] to prove Aboriginal rights. Proof of Aboriginal title seems to have a lower threshold than Aboriginal rights generally.

---

39 *Hamlet of Baker Lake* v. *Min. of Indian Affairs and Northern Development,* [1979] 3 C.N.L.R. 17 (F.C.T.D.). For a more thorough discussion see Isaac, *supra* note 1 at 10–11 and 97–105.
40 *Delgamuukw, supra* note 2 at paras. 140–59.
41 *Ibid.* at para. 143.
42 *Ibid.* at para. 156.
43 *Mabo* v. *Queensland,* [1992] 5 C.N.L.R. 1 (High Ct. of Aust.).
44 *Delgamuukw, supra* note 2 at para. 153.
45 *Van der Peet, supra* note 6 at para. 60.

As noted below in this chapter, the issue for Maritime First Nations will be to meet this standard of proof. Proof of occupation and continuity may not be so difficult. However, it is unclear to date what the standard will be when analyzing exclusivity.

Justifying an Infringement of Aboriginal Title

An infringement of Aboriginal title, like an infringement of Aboriginal rights generally, must be justified. In *Delgamuukw,* Chief Justice Lamer summarized the law in this regard. First, the infringement of an Aboriginal right must be in pursuit of a legislative objective that is compelling and substantive. Chief Justice Lamer cited agricultural development, forestry, mining, hydroelectric development, economic development generally, protection of the environment and of endangered species, and infrastructure development as objectives consistent with a valid legislative objective capable of infringing Aboriginal title.[46] In *Gladstone* (1996),[47] the Supreme Court noted that compelling and substantial objectives are those that strike at the purposes behind the recognition and affirmation of Aboriginal rights in section 35(1). These purposes are "the recognition of the prior occupation of North America by aboriginal peoples or . . . the reconciliation of aboriginal prior occupation with the assertion of sovereignty of the Crown."[48] The list of valid legislative objectives capable of infringing Aboriginal title is so long that the meaning of *Delgamuukw* generally is questionable; the court did note, however, that a case-by-case analysis is required in order to understand the meaning of Aboriginal title.

The second element of the test to justify an infringement of Aboriginal title is a determination if the infringement is in keeping with the Crown's fiduciary relationship with Aboriginal people. The nature of this relationship depends on the "legal and factual context" of each particular case.[49] Although the *Sparrow* justification test applies to Aboriginal title cases, a number of other factors peculiar to Aboriginal title are relevant: namely, (1) Aboriginal title is a right to the exclusive use and occupation of land, (2) Aboriginal title provides to the holders of the title the right to choose how the land may be used, subject to the land not being used for purposes that would destroy the land for future generations of Aboriginal people, and (3) the lands to which Aboriginal title apply invariably have an economic element integral to them.

Chief Justice Lamer's conclusions to his majority judgement in *Delgamuukw* are revealing in that he reaffirmed that litigation is not necessarily the

---

46 *Delgamuukw,* supra note 2 at para. 165.
47 *R. v. Gladstone,* [1996] 2 S.C.R. 723.
48 *Ibid.* at para. 72, as cited in *Delgamuukw, supra* note 2 at para. 161.
49 *Ibid.* at para. 56, as cited in *Delgamuukw, ibid.* at para. 162.

best route to finding solutions to such broad issues as how Aboriginal and non-Aboriginal peoples are to live together in Canada. He wrote:

> By ordering a new trial, I do not necessarily encourage the parties to proceed to litigation. . . . [U]ltimately, it is through negotiated settlements, with good faith and give and take on all sides, reinforced by judgments of this Court, that we will achieve . . . a basic purpose of s. 35(1)—"the reconciliation of the pre-existence of aboriginal societies with the sovereignty of the Crown". Let us face it, we are all here to stay.[50]

The chief justice's conclusion is quite telling in its purpose and is consistent with the court's approach to those matters of a particularly political and public-policy nature. For example, see *Re Amendment of the Constitution of Canada (Patriation case),* whereby the Supreme Court balanced constitutional convention with strict jurisprudence and recommended a more conciliatory approach to federal-provincial relations, resulting in the *Constitution Act, 1982.*[51] In *Delgamuukw,* as in *Sparrow,* the court placed section 35(1) into a much broader political and public-policy realm by suggesting that it "at the least, provides a solid constitutional base upon which subsequent negotiations can take place."[52] Negotiated settlements will become all that much more important in provinces such as New Brunswick, Nova Scotia, and British Columbia, where the issue of Aboriginal rights and title remains outstanding.

Consultation

The duty of the Crown to consult Aboriginal people when activities or decisions of the Crown have an impact on Aboriginal and treaty rights has been an issue of great confusion and difficulty for both public and Aboriginal governments. Starting with *Sparrow* (1990)[53] and culminating with *Delgamuukw,* the onus on government to justify its actions and decisions has resulted in, and continues to demand, a fundamental change in the way government interacts with Aboriginal people. Because of the influence of *Delgamuukw,* some governments have attempted to enhance their mechanisms for consultation. The need for consultation is equally applicable to the justification of

---

50 *Delgamuukw, ibid.* at para. 186.
51 *Re Amendment of the Constitution of Canada (Patriation case),* [1981] 1 S.C.R. 753.
52 *R. v. Sparrow,* [1990] 1 S.C.R. 1075 at 1105.
53 *Ibid.* at 1113. The justification analysis should also include whether the Aboriginal group in question has been consulted regarding the regulation of their rights. See also *Guerin, supra* note 9.

Aboriginal rights infringements generally. What is becoming clear is that Aboriginal and public governments are in a Catch-22 situation when it comes to consultation. It is the Aboriginal or treaty right that gives rise to the duty to consult and yet, the duty arises only when the Aboriginal right is proven to exist. The right generally cannot be proven to exist until there is an infringement of the right.

In the Maritimes, an understanding of governments' duty to consult will be crucial to achieving a lasting harmony between Aboriginal people and government. This is particularly true when scarce resources, such as fish, certain wildlife, and timber, are involved. This challenge of changing the way governments do business, and how they consult with Aboriginal people, is particularly pressing on Maritime governments who, until recently, have not had to focus much of their attention or resources on these types of concerns.

Delgamuukw stressed the importance of consultation[54] by the Crown with First Nations regarding decisions and actions that may infringe Aboriginal title. Chief Justice Lamer, for the majority, noted:

> There is always a duty of consultation. . . . The nature and scope of the duty of consultation will vary with the circumstances. In occasional cases, when the breach is less serious or relatively minor, it will be no more than a duty to discuss important decisions that will be taken with respect to lands held pursuant to Aboriginal title. Of course, even in these rare cases when the minimum acceptable standard is consultation, this consultation must be in good faith, and with the intention of substantially addressing the concerns of the Aboriginal peoples whose lands are at issue. In most cases, it will be significantly deeper than mere discussion. Some cases may even require the full consent of an Aboriginal nation, particularly when provinces enact hunting and fishing regulations in relation to Aboriginal lands.[55]

Additionally, it has been held that there is a duty of procedural fairness[56] when decisions are made that may affect claimed Aboriginal rights.[57]

Three basic categories of consultation appear to be emerging. First, there is the occasional or rare mere consultation that must occur to address the

---

54 See S. Lawrence and P. Macklem, "From Consultation to Reconciliation: Aboriginal Rights and the Crown's Duty to Consult" (2000) 70 Can. Bar Rev. 252.

55 *Delgamuukw, supra* note 2 at para. 168.

56 "Procedural fairness" refers to the body of law governing basic safeguards in administrative adjudication, such as having all the relevant information made available to all parties in a conflict.

57 *Westbank First Nation v. British Columbia (Min. of Forests),* [2001] 1 C.N.L.R. 361 (B.C.S.C.).

concerns of Aboriginal people over the lands in question. This may involve some discussion between government and the First Nation affected, with the Crown responding to Aboriginal concerns. Second, in most cases something significantly deeper than mere consultation will be required. Little guidance is provided by the Supreme Court on what this category means. Although it involves participation in the decision-making process, it most likely does not extend to the upper reaches of consultation, which include consent. Finally, at the end of the consultation spectrum is consultation amounting to the required consent of the First Nation involved, which may be tantamount to a veto.

Marshall No. 2 reaffirmed the importance of consultation in the context of treaty rights:

> The Court has emphasized the importance in the justification context of consultations with Aboriginal peoples. . . .This special trust relationship includes the right of the treaty beneficiaries to be consulted about restrictions on their rights, although, as stated in *Delgamuukw, supra,* at para. 168: "The nature and scope of the duty of consultation will vary with the circumstances." This variation may reflect such factors as the seriousness and duration of the proposed restriction, and whether or not the Minister is required to act in response to unforeseen or urgent circumstances. As stated, if the consultation does not produce an agreement, the adequacy of the justification of the government's initiative will have to be litigated in the courts.[58]

The question for governments in the Maritimes will be just how far they need to go to satisfy their consultation requirements under the many treaties that are applicable. This will not be an easy task, but can, in part, be ameliorated by putting into place consistent, thorough standards and policies regarding consultation that apply to both federal and provincial levels of government. However, it is the nature of these issues that they require a case-by-case analysis and, in many respects, a subjective approach as to what does, and does not, require consultation and to what degree.

In *Halfway River First Nation* v. *British Columbia (Min. of Forests)* (1999),[59] the British Columbia Court of Appeal considered the duty owed by the Ministry of Forests to consult with the Halfway River First Nation over various cutting decisions made by the ministry. Although dealing with Treaty No. 8, the court nevertheless provided substantive comments regarding the nature of the Crown's duty to consult. The court affirmed that the ministry

---

58 *R. v. Marshall (Marshall No. 2)*, [1999] 3 S.C.R. 533 at para. 43.
59 *Halfway River First Nation* v. *British Columbia (Min. of Forests)*, [1999] 4 C.N.L.R. 1 (B.C.C.A.).

had a duty to consult the First Nation prior to making decisions that might affect Aboriginal and treaty rights. It noted that the ministry failed to take all reasonable efforts to consult with, and inform itself about, the Halfway River First Nation.

The court also noted that the ministry failed to give the First Nation relevant information relating to decisions being made. While relevant information must be provided to First Nations in a timely manner and their representations must be taken seriously by government, First Nations also have a duty not to frustrate or obstruct the consultation process by refusing to participate in it or by placing unreasonable conditions on government. The Court of Appeal noted:

> The fact that adequate notice of an intended decision may have been given, does not mean that the requirement for adequate consultation has also been met. The Crown's duty to consult imposes on it a positive obligation to reasonably ensure that Aboriginal peoples are provided with all necessary information in a timely way so that they have an opportunity to express their interests and concerns, and to ensure that their representations are seriously considered and, wherever possible, demonstrably integrated into the proposed plan of action. . . . There is a reciprocal duty on Aboriginal peoples to express their interests and concerns once they have had an opportunity to consider the information provided by the Crown, and to consult in good faith by whatever means are available to them. They cannot frustrate the consultation process by refusing to meet or participate, or by imposing unreasonable conditions.[60]

This statement is interesting in that it clearly places a duty not only on government, but also on First Nations. Maritime First Nations, in becoming attuned to what rights they possess by way of treaty—Aboriginal title or otherwise—must also be attuned to their corresponding duties. Thus, like governments, and certainly like their First Nations counterparts in British Columbia and other parts of Canada, Maritime First Nations will have to develop processes by which they manage the consultations in which governments have, and will want, to become engaged. Establishing the appropriate administrative, legal, and other mechanisms necessary to fully respond to governments' requests for consultation can be a daunting task for many First Nations that do not have adequate resources.

---

60 *Ibid.* at 44. The Ontario Court of Appeal felt that this onus on First Nations not to frustrate the consultation process as enunciated in *Halfway River* had "considerable merit"; see *Ontario (Min. of Municipal Affairs and Housing)* v. *Trans-Canada Pipelines Ltd.,* [2000] 3 C.N.L.R. 153 at 181, para. 123 (Ont. C.A.).

Kelly Lake First Nation v. *British Columbia (Min. of Energy and Mines)* (1999)[61] is interesting because in that case, the Crown did not have an obligation to consult and if there was such an obligation, it was met when the Kelly Lake First Nation failed to provide any response to the Crown's letter following discussions between the Crown and the First Nation. The court also noted that the decision-maker for government in this case took into consideration potential Aboriginal and treaty rights that might be affected.

Cheslatta Carrier Nation v. *British Columbia* (1998)[62] provides a useful example of where government failed to meet its duty to consult. The decision concerned petitions made by the First Nation for judicial review of decisions made by provincial ministers of the Crown regarding the approval and review of a copper mine project. Insufficient information was possessed by the British Columbia government to adequately assess the potential impact on Aboriginal rights, and therefore the government did not allow the First Nation to mount a proper defence to the proposed action. The court's decision in this case was based primarily on a statutory duty to consult outlined in the *Environmental Assessment Act*.

In *Ontario (Min. of Municipal Affairs and Housing)* v. *Trans-Canada Pipelines Ltd.* (2000),[63] the Ontario Court of Appeal considered an order made by a commission under the Ontario *Municipality Act* to amalgamate a number of townships into a single municipality. A number of First Nations sought a declaration that the order infringed hunting, fishing, and trapping rights guaranteed in Treaty No. 9 and could impede future land claims negotiations. The lower court allowed the applications for judicial review. The Court of Appeal allowed the appeal, thereby confirming the original order creating a single municipality. One argument upon which the lower court rested its decision, and which the Court of Appeal addressed in considerable detail, concerned the issue of whether the Crown failed to consult with the First Nations. The Court of Appeal held that the commission did not lose its jurisdiction when it failed to consult with the relevant First Nations as the *Municipality Act* places no obligation on the commission to consult. The Court of Appeal stated:

> [O'Driscoll J.] elevated the Crown's duty to consult with First Nations from merely being one, of several, justificatory requirements to be met by the Crown when a challenge is mounted to a law, or government action, on the ground that it unduly interferes with Aboriginal rights or treaty rights . . . to

---

61   *Kelly Lake First Nation* v. *British Columbia (Min. of Energy and Mines)*, [1999] 3 C.N.L.R. 126 (B.C.S.C.).
62   *Cheslatta Carrier Nation* v. *British Columbia*, [1998] 3 C.N.L.R. 1 (B.C.S.C.).
63   *Trans-Canada Pipelines Ltd., supra* note 60.

an independent ground on which such a law, or a government action, may be challenged.[64]

This interpretation appears more consistent with earlier and superior court decisions regarding consultation. That is, consultation is not an independent right held by First Nations but rather, it attaches to already existing rights. Thus, in commenting on *R. v. Sparrow* (1990),[65] *R. v. Badger* (1996),[66] and *Delgamuukw* (1997),[67] the Court of Appeal noted:

> [W]hat these cases decide is that the duty of the Crown to consult with First Nations is a legal requirement that assists the court in determining whether the Crown is constitutionally justified in engaging in a particular action that has been found to *prima facie* infringe an existing Aboriginal or treaty right of a First Nation. It is only after the First Nation has established such infringement through an appropriate hearing that the duty of the Crown to consult with First Nations becomes engaged as a factor for the court to consider in the justificatory phase of the proceeding. [68]

In *Liidlii Kue First Nation v. Canada* (2000),[69] the Federal Court, Trial Division considered an application by the First Nation, which was seeking a declaration that the Crown (through its land-use administrator) had breached its fiduciary duty to consult the First Nation prior to issuing a land-use permit for test drilling. The court refused to grant the declaratory relief, but it did send the matter back to a different land-use administrator for reconsideration. The court confirmed that there exists a constitutional duty to consult with those exercising the Treaty No. 11 rights to hunt, trap, and fish on unoccupied Crown lands. The court also affirmed that the duty to consult, and the standard required, varies from case to case.

Thus, in order to support the justification of a governmental infringement of an Aboriginal or treaty right, consultation is not required to produce an agreement, but it must be "adequate" considering the circumstances. Indeed, the court contemplates that litigation may well be the only means by which the parties involved can conclude whether or not the level of consultation in a particular case was "adequate." Consultation is a crucial component for any government conducting its business and especially when this business may

---

64   *Ibid.* at para. 112.
65   *Sparrow, supra* note 52.
66   *R. v. Badger,* [1996] 1 S.C.R. 771.
67   *Delgamuukw, supra* note 2.
68   *Trans-Canada Pipelines Ltd., supra* note 60 at para. 119.
69   *Liidlii Kue First Nation v. Canada,* [2000] 4 C.N.L.R. 123 (F.C.T.D.).

infringe the rights of Aboriginal people. Consultation is also a key component for any government seeking to justify an infringement of Aboriginal
rights. *Marshall No. 1* and *No. 2* affirmed that the *Sparrow* test (as expanded
upon in *Delgamuukw*) applies to treaty rights cases: "[T]reaty rights within
the meaning of s. 35 . . . are subject to regulations that can be justified under
the *Badger* test."[70] However, even with these decisions, there continues to be
no clear and consistent definition of what "adequate" consultation means.
Rather, the determination of what is adequate consultation depends on a case-
by-case analysis.

The another important aspect to the consultation issue is that the duty to consult (which is tied to the "honour of the Crown" and its fiduciary obligation)
rests with the federal or provincial Crown and not with private interests, such
as development or logging companies, or with municipal governments. In the
end, it rests with the Crown and its respective governments to be diligent in
ensuring that their decisions and activities adequately account for and consider Aboriginal interests that may be affected. This consideration and ac-
counting must be done in good faith and transparently.

The duty to consult extends beyond Aboriginal title issues and directly
affects all decisions and activities of the Crown as they may have an impact
on Aboriginal and treaty rights. Governments in the Maritimes should be re-
visiting regulations that may affect Aboriginal and treaty rights to ensure that
these regulations provide for sufficient consultation and consideration. Although the detail may be lacking, in part because relatively few post-1982
superior court decisions concern Aboriginal and treaty rights specifically in
the Maritimes, *Marshall* and other decisions clearly point out the direction in
which the courts are heading. Although consultation may not head off all
potential impasses and problems, adequate consultation measures by government can mitigate the current state of uncertainty.

Extinguishment of Aboriginal Title

The precise means by which Aboriginal title can be extinguished, other than
by express means on the part of Aboriginal people or the federal Crown,
remain unclear. As the *Royal Proclamation of 1763* bears witness, Indians'
interest in their lands cannot be extinguished without their "consent." Namely,
Indian lands are reserved for Indians until the Indians "should be inclined to
dispose of the said lands."[71] The Judicial Committee of the Privy Council in
St. Catherine's Milling and Lumber Co. v. *R.* (1888) makes it clear that Ab-

---

70 *R.* v. *Marshall (Marshall No. 1),* [1999] 3 S.C.R. 456 at para. 7. See also *Marshall
    No. 2, supra* note 58 at para. 32, and *Badger, supra* note 54 at paras. 96–97.
71 *Royal Proclamation of 1763, supra* note 12.

original title is "dependent upon the goodwill of the Sovereign."[72] Justice Steele of the Ontario High Court adopted this reasoning in the *Bear Island* decision, when he wrote that Aboriginal title "exists solely at the pleasure of the Crown."[73] In *R. v. Howard* (1994),[74] the Supreme Court of Canada held that a treaty (other than an international treaty)[75] is one way the Crown can extinguish Aboriginal title. An international treaty, however, cannot serve to restrict or extinguish rights protected under section 35.

The distinction between extinguishing Aboriginal title and extinguishing Aboriginal rights was exemplified in the Supreme Court of Canada decision of *R. v. Adams* (1996).[76] In that case, the Government of Quebec argued that since it had flooded a key fishing area to create a canal in 1845 and since the Mohawks had surrendered the lands around the area in 1888, their Aboriginal right to fish had been extinguished. In response, Chief Justice Lamer stated:

> While these events may be adequate to demonstrate a clear and plain intention in the Crown to extinguish any Aboriginal *title to the lands* of the fishing area, neither is sufficient to demonstrate that the Crown had the clear and plain intention of extinguishing the appellant's Aboriginal *right to fish for food* in the fishing area. . . . The surrender of lands, because of the fact that title to land is distinct from the right to fish in the waters adjacent to those lands, equally does not demonstrate a clear and plain intention to extinguish a right. [Emphasis in original][77]

This important statement underscores the necessity for a careful examination of the facts and intentions of the parties when making a claim for or defending a claim of extinguishment of Aboriginal title or Aboriginal rights.

In *Delgamuukw,* Chief Justice Lamer, writing for the majority of the Supreme Court of Canada, considered the issue of whether the Province of British Columbia had the power to extinguish Aboriginal rights after 1871, either by way of its own jurisdiction or by the application of section 88 of the *Indian Act.*[78] Chief Justice Lamer made it clear that the federal government has

---

72 *St. Catherine's Milling and Lumber Co. v. R.* (1889), 2 C.N.L.C. 541 at 549 (J.C.P.C.).
73 *Ontario (A.G.) v. Bear Island Foundation et al.,* [1985] 1 C.N.L.R. 1 at 28 (Ont. S.C.).
74 *R. v. Howard,* [1994] 2 S.C.R. 299.
75 *Mitchell v. Canada (Min. of National Revenue),* [1999] 1 C.N.L.R. 112 (F.C.A.) at 116; reversed on other grounds by [2001] S.C.C. 33 (S.C.C.).
76 *Adams, supra* note 5.
77 *Ibid.* at 30.
78 *Delgamuukw, supra* note 2 at paras. 172–82.

the exclusive jurisdiction to legislate with respect to "Indians and lands reserved for Indians" pursuant to section 91(24) of the *Constitution Act, 1867,*
and within that authority is the exclusive power to extinguish Aboriginal title
and Aboriginal rights.[79] It is noteworthy that Chief Justice Lamer dealt only
with British Columbia's authority to extinguish Aboriginal rights after 1871,
when it joined Canada. The issue of whether British Columbia had the authority, as a colonial power, prior to 1871, was not explicitly considered. This
does, however, beg the question of how a provincial law could be justified
over an area (in this case, Aboriginal title) that is at the core of "Indianness,"
within the meaning of the federal government's authority under section
91(24).[80] For Maritime First Nations, as discussed below, there appears to be
little evidence of extinguishment ever occurring. Indeed, the treaties that were
signed in the Maritimes did not cede land or acknowledge the relinquishment
of title or other interests.

Related Maritime Decisions

There are a limited number of cases that deal specifically with Aboriginal
rights and title in the Maritimes. The following are a few of the lower court
decisions that have dealt with these issues. Although they do not necessarily
reflect the current state of the law, they are helpful from both a historical and
a legal perspective in understanding the progress that has occurred and the
potential for further developments.

In *Warman v. Francis* (1958),[81] the New Brunswick Supreme Court considered the application of Aboriginal title to New Brunswick. Although the
court found that the Mi'kmaq were prevented from entering a neighbouring
farmer's property, in part because they could not show any Aboriginal title,
the decision is interesting. First, the court concluded that the *Royal Proclamation of 1763* applied to the Atlantic provinces. Second, the court noted that
the Mi'kmaq never surrendered their Aboriginal rights in the Maritimes, adding, however, that there are "no proprietary rights in our law in the circumstances."[82] We now know this latter statement to be inaccurate, considering
the numerous decisions of the past twenty years concerning Aboriginal title
in Canada, most notably *Delgamuukw*.

Commenting on the status of the cession of Indian land, Chief Justice
MacKeigan of the Nova Scotia Court of Appeal stated in *R. v. Isaac* (1975):

---

79   *Ibid.* at para. 173.
80   K. McNeil, "Aboriginal Title and the Division of Powers: Rethinking Federal and
     Provincial Jurisdiction" (1998) 61:2 Sask. L. Rev. 431.
81   *Warman v. Francis* (1958), 20 D.L.R. (2d) 627 (N.B.S.C.).
82   *Ibid.* at 630.

No Nova Scotia treaty has been found whereby Indians ceded land to the Crown, whereby their rights on any land were specifically extinguished, or whereby they agreed to accept and retire to specified reserves.[83]

He also commented that "neither the French nor British had extinguished the Indian rights in Nova Scotia."[84]

In *Peter Paul v. R.* (1998),[85] the New Brunswick Court of Appeal considered an appeal from the Crown regarding Mr. Paul, a registered Indian and member of the Mi'kmaq Nation, who had been charged with unlawfully removing timber from Crown lands without a license contrary to the New Brunswick *Crown Lands and Forests Act*.[86] The question at trial was whether the act had been done unlawfully. Mr. Paul argued that he was exempt from the requirement of obtaining a license because he had a treaty right, granted by a treaty signed in 1726, to harvest timber on Crown lands. He also advanced an argument based on Aboriginal title.

At trial, Justice Arsenault had held that Mr. Paul's activities were within the terms of a 1726 treaty concluded at Annapolis Royal with the tribes inhabiting the Province of Nova Scotia, which included Indians in territories in modern New Brunswick. Justice Arsenault had held that small-scale harvesting of timber for commercial purposes was a "lawful occasion" within the terms of the treaty, which provided, in part, that "[t]he said Indians shall not be molested in their persons hunting, fishing and shooting and planting on their planting ground nor on any other their lawful occasions."[87] The Court of Queen's Bench upheld Justice Arsenault's decision. The Court of Appeal, however, overturned the lower court's decision. The Appeal Court concluded that since the arguments of counsel and the evidence tendered were not directed to the issue of Aboriginal title, this was not a case in which a court could properly assess any claim of Aboriginal title to Crown lands in New Brunswick. The Appeal Court rejected Justice Arsenault's interpretation of the treaty provision on the ground that there was insufficient historical evidence presented at trial regarding the intentions of the parties to the treaty and, in particular, there was no evidence to support the conclusion that commercial tree harvesting was "a lawful occasion" contemplated by the treaty. Leave to appeal to the Supreme Court was denied.

Peter Paul is important in that it recognizes that although Aboriginal and

---

83 *R. v. Isaac* (1975), 13 N.S.R. (2d) 460 at 479 (N.S.C.A.).
84 *Ibid.* at 482.
85 *Peter Paul v. R.,* [1998] 3 C.N.L.R. 221 (N.B.C.A.); leave to appeal to the Supreme Court refused.
86 *Crown Lands and Forests Act,* S.N.B. 1980, c-38.1.
87 See Treaty of 1726.

treaty rights are distinct, the line between the two is not always clear. The
Appeal Court was correct in stating that Aboriginal title in New Brunswick is
a complex issue; however, the court seemed to go against its own reasoning
when it stated that it did not want to deal with Aboriginal title but nevertheless made the following statement:

> Mascarene's Treaty [of 1726] does not create or acknowledge an Aboriginal
> title to land. Indeed, by it, Mr. Peter Paul's ancestors acknowledge not only
> the Crown's jurisdiction and dominion over the lands, but also the Crown's
> title and rightful possession to the lands.[88]

The Appeal Court erred by connecting the Crown's jurisdiction and dominion over the lands to Aboriginal title. There is no direct link between the two;
sovereign jurisdiction and dominion can co-exist with Aboriginal title.

Because of the continuing uncertainty over the status of Aboriginal and
treaty rights in the Maritimes, Aboriginal title will most likely become a domi-
nant public-policy issue in the region. Commenting on a partial defence of
Aboriginal title to support a claim of treaty rights to commercially harvest
forest products in *R.* v. *Bernard,* Provincial Court judge Lordon wrote:

> There was no evidence of capacity to retain exclusive control and, given the
> vast area of land and the small population they did not have the capacity to
> exercise exclusive control. . . . [A]ccording to the evidence of Chief Augus-
> tine, the Mi'kmaq had neither the intent nor the desire to exercise exclusive
> control, which, in my opinion, is fatal to the claim for Aboriginal title.[89]

When this case was appealed to Court of Queen's Bench, Justice Savoie
concurred with the Provincial Court judge's reasoning:

> The trial judge in his well reasoned ruling on the matter of occupation came
> to the conclusion that the Mi'kmaqs did not have exclusive occupation of the
> Sevogle area at the time of sovereignty in 1759 and have not had it since
> then. That conclusion was not unreasonable. On a review of the evidence, I
> agree with him.[90]

Like the rest of Canada, where comprehensive treaties that deal with the
question of Aboriginal title have been negotiated, New Brunswick and Nova
Scotia would do well to examine their options and develop their policy frame-

---

88 *Ibid.* at para. 27.
89 *R.* v. *Bernard,* [2000] 3 C.N.L.R. 184 at 213 (N.B. Prov. Ct.).
90 *R.* v. *Bernard,* [2001] N.B.J. No. 259 at para. 39 (N.B.Q.B.).

works in this regard. Brian Slattery has written:

> [T]he question of aboriginal title in New Brunswick and Nova Scotia is very
> much alive and will continue to preoccupy the courts of those provinces for
> some years to come. Perhaps the governments of New Brunswick and Nova
> Scotia would be wise to read the judicial writing on the wall and take steps
> to resolve the matter by timely negotiations.[91]

Although the issue of negotiations is dealt with in chapter 7, it should be
noted here that negotiations will undoubtedly help resolve the question of
Aboriginal title in the Maritimes. Whether or not Aboriginal title is found to
exist, it is clear that Aboriginal and non-Aboriginal peoples, and their respective governments, must arrive at better ways to communicate and interact
with one another. Assuming Aboriginal title were to exist, negotiations would
be essential. Because a case-by-case analysis is required, without a negotiated settlement, either government or First Nations would have to use the
courts extensively to ascertain the precise scope and meaning of title to a
particular area of a province.

A case-by-case analysis is precisely what Provincial Court judge Curran
considered in *R. v. Marshall* (Stephen Marshall) (2001).[92] This *Marshall* decision concerned thirty-five Mi'kmaq who had been charged with cutting timber on, and removing timber from, Crown land without authorization, contrary
to Nova Scotia's *Crown Lands Act*. The Mi'kmaq offered as a defence that
they possessed Aboriginal title to all Nova Scotia and that their treaties of
1760–61 include a right to harvest forest products for sale. In adjudicating
this case, Judge Curran extensively reviewed the history of the Mi'kmaq, but
spent little time analyzing the Aboriginal title claim according to the test outlined
in *Delgamuukw*.[93] Nevertheless, he came to some interesting conclusions:

1. The Mi'kmaq of the eighteenth century were moderately nomadic and
   maintained communities generally in the same area on mainland Nova
   Scotia.
2. The Mi'kmaq historically used bays, rivers, and nearby hunting grounds
   intensively. However, there was no evidence to deduce precisely where
   this use occurred. It did not encompass all mainland Nova Scotia but was
   site specific.
3. There was no evidence to conclude that the Mi'kmaq occupied Cape
   Breton to the extent required to prove Aboriginal title.

---

91 B. Slattery, "Some Thoughts on Aboriginal Title" (1999) 48 U.N.B.L.J. 19 at 40.
92 *R. v. Marshall,* [2001] 2 C.N.L.R. 256 (N.S. Prov. Ct.).
93 *Ibid.,* see paras. 136–42.

4. The Mi'kmaq of the eighteenth century probably had Aboriginal title to specific sites on mainland Nova Scotia, particularly around their local communities.[94]

The weakness in the trial judge's analysis is that he did not submit the evidence provided to the *Delgamuukw* test. Although considerable evidence was presented at trial, relatively little time was spent linking this evidence directly and explicitly to the trial judge's conclusions. The trial judge also concluded that the Treaties of 1760–61 and Belcher's Proclamation of May 4, 1762, do not provide a basis for claiming a right to harvest wood. The trial judge used both *Marshall No. 1* and *Marshall No. 2* in coming to this conclusion.[95] He dismissed using the Treaties of 1760–61 as a defence, stating that there was "no evidence the Mi'kmaq sold or traded timber up to the time of the treaties and no reason to believe they did."[96] The trial judge dismissed using Belcher's Proclamation as the source for a treaty right to log since the proclamation did not apply to the cutting sites in question. Finally, the trial judge agreed with the conclusion noted earlier in this book that the *Royal Proclamation of 1763* applies to Nova Scotia.[97]

Although this decision is from a lower court, it is noteworthy because it is the first post-*Marshall* decision to deal directly with Aboriginal title, and it suggests, as does this book, that Aboriginal title is a live issue in the Maritimes. It also underscores the immense evidentiary burden on First Nations attempting to prove Aboriginal title, and the corresponding burden on the courts to consider that evidence carefully and refer to it appropriately when considering the merits of a case.

The Maritimes and Aboriginal Title

It is clear that Aboriginal title is a pressing issue for the Maritime provinces. The following discussion attempts to apply the relevant principles regarding Aboriginal title to the circumstances that exist in the Maritimes. There are three main reference points that suggest that Aboriginal title remains outstanding in the Maritimes: *The Royal Proclamation of 1763,* proving Aboriginal title, and the Mi'kmaq peace and friendship treaties.

The first reference point is the *Royal Proclamation of 1763.* Although Aboriginal title does not find its source in the *Proclamation,* the *Proclamation* is nevertheless a powerful piece of evidence supporting Aboriginal title.

---

94 *Ibid.* at paras. 142–43.
95 *Ibid.* at paras. 90, 93–95.
96 *Ibid.* at para. 92.
97 *Ibid.* at para. 107.

The *Proclamation,* which applies to the Maritimes, reserves land for the Indians and clearly provides that lands that were not ceded or purchased by the Crown continue to be reserved for the Indians. Thus, the *Proclamation* confirms the existence of Aboriginal title in the Maritimes.

The second reference point is the question of proving Aboriginal title. In *Delgamuukw,* the Supreme Court of Canada laid out the three criteria required to make a claim for Aboriginal title. The first criterion is that prior to the British assertion of sovereignty, the land must have been occupied by the ancestors of the Aboriginal group claiming title. Although the onus of proving Aboriginal title rests with those making the claim, it is clear that the Mi'kmaq and Maliseet have occupied various parts of the Maritimes for generations. When the Europeans arrived, there were Mi'kmaq in what is now New Brunswick, Nova Scotia, and Prince Edward Island, and Maliseet in New Brunswick. The second criterion is that when the existing occupation of the lands in question is being offered as proof of pre-sovereignty occupation, continuity between existing and pre-sovereignty occupation must be demonstrated. The Supreme Court of Canada considered this matter to some extent in *R.* v. *Simon* (1985), concerning the Treaty of 1752 and whether or not the present-day Mi'kmaq could possess rights signed by their ancestors. The court said they could.[98] The third criterion is that at the time of sovereignty, the occupation by the Aboriginal group must have been exclusive. As previously noted, the exclusivity that is required is not necessarily the exclusion of other Aboriginal groups in the area, but rather requires a case-by-case analysis of the particular Aboriginal group making the claim for title; that is, the extent to which they used and/or occupied a particular area of land. How this will be applied has yet to be seen.

The requirement that the group claiming Aboriginal title bears the onus of proving the existence of Aboriginal title is a significant burden on First Nations. Proving such a claim requires a First Nation to undertake immense research and enter into litigation, as a result of which it may—or may not— prove its title to a very restricted geographical area. It is important to bear this burden in mind when considering how British Columbia's First Nations reacted when the Supreme Court released its decision in *Delgamuukw.* Initially, and to some extent rightly, there was significant jubilation on the part of British Columbia's First Nations over *Delgamuukw,* while governments and industry were, in some circles, shocked at the content and potential impact of the decision. Nevertheless, First Nations face an onerous process and burden of proving Aboriginal title.

Delgamuukw expanded and clarified the meaning of Aboriginal title in Canadian law. The decision made clear that the existence of Aboriginal title

---

98 *R.* v. *Simon,* [1985] 2 S.C.R. 387 at 407.

requires a case-by-case analysis, is a matter of fact to be determined at trial, and may be justifiably infringed. Although the precise limitations on the government's authority to regulate areas in which Aboriginal title exist arc not clear, as *Marshall* demonstrates, in *Delgamuukw*, the Supreme Court of Canada provided an extensive array of tools that the Crown can utilize to regulate lands covered by Aboriginal title.

An additional perspective was put forward in *Delgamuukw* by Justice LaForest (with Justice L'Heureux-Dubé concurring). Justice LaForest adopted the same standards for proving Aboriginal title as the majority but added some flexibility. He suggested that in some circumstances, Aboriginal title could be acquired after sovereignty. He wrote:

> I am also of the view that the date of sovereignty may not be the only relevant moment to consider. For instance, there may have been Aboriginal settlements in one area of the province but, after the assertion of sovereignty, the Aboriginal peoples may have all moved to another area where they remained from the date of sovereignty until the present. This relocation may have been due to natural causes, such as the flooding of villages, or to clashes with European settlers. In these circumstances, I would not deny the existence of "Aboriginal title" in that area merely because the relocation occurred post-sovereignty.[99]

Needless to say, this widens the geographical scope of an Aboriginal title case and may be particularly helpful to Maritime First Nations that were relocated or had their traditional lands settled or severely encroached upon. Given the history of the Maritimes, the possible use of encroachment as evidence to support an Aboriginal title claim may be appropriate. The understanding of Aboriginal title, while assisted greatly by the *Delgamuukw* decision, is not complete. *Delgamuukw* leaves the room for more novel or flexible approaches to the interpretation of Aboriginal and treaty rights. This can only assist First Nations in the Maritimes who are attempting to prove the continued existence of Aboriginal title in their traditional lands.

The third reference point concerning the continued existence of Aboriginal title in the Maritimes is the eighteenth-century peace and friendship treaties. As these treaties do not include the cession of land and some of the corresponding rights associated with it, there is the potential that, in the Maritimes, treaty rights co-exist with Aboriginal title. If this were found to be the case, this situation would be unique in Canada. Although the broad and liberal interpretation that the *Marshall* decision gave to the Treaties of 1760–61 does not by itself prove the existence of Aboriginal title in the Maritimes,

---

99 *Delgamuukw, supra* note 2 at para. 197.

it is not far-fetched to presume that this interpretation could be an important piece of evidence supporting the continued existence of Aboriginal title in the region.

What, then, would be the implications for the Maritimes if Aboriginal title were deemed to continue to exist? The first practical implication would be that both sides, the First Nations and the Crown, would have a strong incentive to negotiate comprehensive treaties. This mode of determining the content and meaning of Aboriginal rights and title is strongly supported by the Supreme Court of Canada. Negotiations in this area have to deal with complex legal, governance, and resource-management issues, the historical rights of Aboriginal people, and the constitutional legislative authority of the federal and provincial governments. If British Columbia is anything to go by, and I suggest that in this case it would be, then the negotiations will not be easy.

In the absence of negotiated settlements, it is clear—as reaffirmed by *Marshall* and other decisions—that government must change the way it regulates activities that affect Aboriginal and treaty rights. Writing on this subject elsewhere, I have stated:

> [T]he one thing that is becoming apparent is that whatever form Aboriginal rights take, either as treaty rights or title issues or as subsistence activities, governments have been delivered an extremely clear message—change the way you have traditionally conducted your actions with respect to Aboriginal peoples and their inherent interest in their tribal lands. Dealing with Aboriginal peoples and their interests is simply a cost of doing business in Canada. . . . Governments have an obligation to ensure that their mechanisms for consultation and engagement are appropriately resourced and that they are given a clear message to engage at a substantive level appropriate to the situation at hand.[100]

Assuming negotiations do not reach a settlement in the near future, governments should take, indeed they have a duty to take, a proactive stance with respect to regulating resources and activities affecting Aboriginal and treaty rights. This regulation must be sensitive to, and consistent with, the existence of Aboriginal and treaty rights. It is clear that governments across Canada are having a difficult time understanding what this new legal regime means for their regulatory and legislative authority. As noted earlier in this book, the *Marshall* decision provides an extremely helpful and clear articulation of the extent to which governments may justifiably regulate Aboriginal and treaty rights, including Aboriginal title. This was further evidenced and supported

---

100 Isaac, *supra* note 1 at xi.

by the Supreme Court of Canada decisions in *Delgamuukw, Sparrow, Badger,* and *Van der Peet*. Governments must change the way they deal with Aboriginal people, and they must allocate additional resources to ensure that Aboriginal people and their rights are properly considered, and that Aboriginal people are consulted about decisions or activities that may affect their Aboriginal and treaty rights, including Aboriginal title.

For Aboriginal people, a non-negotiated settlement by way of judicial intervention could have the possibility of increasing expanded rights and opportunities on land to which Aboriginal title may vest. However, more than likely, based on the jurisprudence to date from the Supreme Court of Canada, while there may be some degree of rights recognized and granted, as in *Marshall,* these rights will continue to be subject to justifiable regulation by government. Additionally, although compensation is a remedy to be considered, it is not clear the degree to which compensation will factor in adjudication claims of Aboriginal title.

Since the *Delgamuukw* decision, the awareness of Aboriginal title and rights in British Columbia has heightened to the extent that government and industry constantly refer to the uncertainty over the land base as an impediment to economic growth. It is likely that if Aboriginal title were found to exist in the Maritimes, similar charges would be made, and treaty negotiations would clearly help settle this uncertainty. It is also clear, however, that to dispell this unease, governments must be willing and able to put into place management regimes for natural resources, such as fish or timber, that are comprehensive, transparent, and justifiable, and that balance the interests of both Aboriginal and non-Aboriginal users.

Section 35(3) of the *Constitution Act, 1982* and Modern Treaties

Treaties are not only those documents negotiated a hundred years ago or more, they also include modern agreements between Aboriginal people and the Crown. Section 35(3) of the *Constitution Act, 1982* reads:

> (3) For greater certainty, in subsection (1) "treaty rights" includes rights that now exist by way of land claims agreements or may be so acquired.

To date, the Supreme Court of Canada has not made any distinction between historical treaties and modern treaties. Although the precise degree to which all the interpretive principles surrounding treaties apply to land claims agreements is uncertain, it seems safe to assume that the rights contained in land claims agreements and modern treaties are constitutionally protected. These agreements will, therefore, play a significant role in the governance of major portions of Canada's land mass, yet no one knows just how they will affect decisions related to land management and governance. For the Maritimes, an understanding of section 35(3) will become increasingly important as negotiated settlements are reached. This is true because section 35(3) is the mechanism by which the rights contained in modern treaties become "treaty rights" for the purposes of protection under section 35 generally.

The first modern treaty to be signed was the 1975 James Bay and Northern Quebec Agreement regarding lands in northern Quebec. It was signed by the Governments of Canada and Quebec and by the Cree and Inuit of the area concerned. It was followed, in 1978, by the Northeastern Quebec Agreement signed by the Governments of Canada and Quebec and by the Naskapi. Since then, a number of other modern treaties or land claims agreements have been signed.[101] The most recent modern treaty to be signed is the Nisga'a Final Agreement (1999)[102] in British Columbia. The agreement is both a "land claims agreement" and a "treaty" within the meaning of section 35(3), and it provides that the *Canadian Charter of Rights and Freedoms*[103] will apply to the Nisga'a government.

The Nisga'a Nation has a population of approximately 5,500. As a result of the agreement, the former Nisga'a Indian reserves (fifty-six in total, including four villages) will no longer be governed by the *Indian Act,* but rather by the agreement. The Nisga'a Nation now holds a total of 1,992 square kilometers of land in the lower Nass River area, of which approximately 62 square kilometers consists of former Nisga'a Indian reserve land. The Final Agreement provides for the Nisga'a Nation to own the forest resources and allows it to develop its own regulations and standards to govern forest practices on its lands, while at a minimum meeting provincial standards. The Nisga'a Nation holds its land in fee simple and must allow public access to these lands for non-commercial and recreational purposes, including hunting, fishing, and public transportation corridors. With respect to fishing, the Nisga'a are guaranteed an allocation of salmon returning to Canadian waters. In making the

---

101 Inuvialuit Final Agreement (1978), en. by the *Western Arctic (Inuvialuit) Claims Settlement Act,* S.C. 1984, c. 24; Gwich'in Final Agreement (1992), en. by the *Gwich'in Land Claim Settlement Act,* S.C. 1992, c. 53; Sahtu Dene and Metis Land Claim Agreement (1993), en. by the *Sahtu Dene and Metis Land Claim Settlement Act,* S.C. 1994, c. 27; Nunavut Land Claims Agreement (1993), en. by the *Nunavut Land Claim Agreement Act,* S.C. 1993, c. 29; Yukon Final Agreement (1993), en. by the *Yukon First Nations Land Claims Settlement Act,* S.C. 1994, c. 34. Other agreements flow from the Yukon agreements regarding both individual claims and self-government agreements for fourteen Yukon First Nations.

102 Enacted by the *Nisga'a Final Agreement Act,* S.C. 2000, c. 7.

103 *Canadian Charter of Rights and Freedoms, supra* note 32.

allocation, the Crown must consider conservation and equitable distribution among all those affected. Canada and British Columbia continue to manage the fisheries as they relate to the Nisga'a. In return for their undefined Aboriginal rights to hunt, the Nisga'a receive a portion of the total allowable harvest for wildlife such as moose and grizzly bear in the Nass Wildlife Area, which provides a mechanism for an increased Nisga'a role in the management of the area. The Nisga'a Nation remains subject to provincial laws governing conservation, public health, and safety.

The Final Agreement affirms that the Nisga'a Nation has the right to self-government and the authority to make laws as provided for in the agreement. There is a central Nisga'a Lisims government, along with four Nisga'a village governments. The Nisga'a also have a constitution that will set out the necessary rules and procedures for a functioning democratic government. Non-Nisga'a residents on Nisga'a lands are provided with the right to participate in Nisga'a public institutions that directly affect them, such as school boards or health boards, and with the right to be consulted regarding decisions that directly affect them. In general, the Nisga'a Nation governance model is a combination of municipal-style governmental authorities, authorities currently provided for in the *Indian Act,* and new powers not normally held by the former two, such as environmental assessment, wills and estates, and post-secondary education.

The Final Agreement also allows the Nisga'a to provide full policing services on Nisga'a lands, with provincial standards continuing to apply for police training, conduct, and qualifications. A Nisga'a court can also be established pursuant to the agreement to deal with Nisga'a laws on Nisga'a lands. The cash component of the agreement stipulates that the Nisga'a will receive $190 million to be paid out over fifteen years. In addition, the Nisga'a will receive $11.5 million to purchase commercial fishing vessels and licences. The agreement calls for five-year fiscal financing agreements to be negotiated between Canada, British Columbia, and the Nisga'a regarding the funding of public services and programs on Nisga'a lands. A central principle for these agreements is that the level of public programs and services provided on Nisga'a lands will be generally comparable to the level of programs delivered by other local and regional governments in northwestern British Columbia. It is noteworthy that the *Indian Act*'s section 87 income-tax exemption for reserve-based income will be phased out over a twelve-year period.

An outstanding national issue that may have finally been settled by the Nisga'a Final Agreement is the issue of the "cede, release and surrender" language found in most older treaties. The purpose of this language was to ensure that a treaty replaced any outstanding Aboriginal rights and that the First Nations involved ceded, released, and surrendered any interests in the land to the Crown. First Nations have found this language particularly distasteful and have sought flexible, more sensitive language. At the same time, public governments at the treaty table have been concerned that without such strong language, the certainty and finality they seek as a result of treaties cannot be achieved. The Nisga'a agreement appears to have solved this problem by reaching a negotiated outcome. Sections 23 to 27 of chapter 2 of the agreement seek to describe the nature of the rights in such a manner that it is clear that all the Aboriginal and treaty rights of the Nisga'a are contained therein. Section 22 reads: "This Agreement constitutes the full and final settlement in respect of the aboriginal rights, including aboriginal title, in Canada of the Nisga'a Nation." Section 26 reads:

> If, despite this Agreement and the settlement legislation, the Nisga'a Nation has an aboriginal right, including aboriginal title, in Canada, that is other than, or different in attributes or geographical extent from, the Nisga'a section 35 rights as set out in this Agreement, the Nisga'a Nations releases that aboriginal right to Canada to the extent that the aboriginal right is other than, or different in attributes or geographical extent from, the Nisga'a section 35 rights as set out in this Agreement.

The Nisga'a Final Agreement is a significant agreement for the Nisga'a and for the people of British Columbia. It is to be hoped that it is the start of a segment of British Columbia's history that will see many more agreements reached between the Aboriginal people of British Columbia and the Governments of British Columbia and Canada.

While on its face, section 35(3) ensures that rights contained in modern treaties are covered by the application of section 35(1), the precise meaning of this constitutional protection remains unclear. For example, does the liberal and generous interpretive scheme required by section 35(1) and applied to historical treaties apply to modern treaties? Just what is deemed to be a "right" within a land claims agreement? Are all sections of an agreement constitutionally protected, such as those creating advisory boards? If so, what is the impact on the existing division of powers between different levels of government and on the constitutional authority of federal and provincial governments?

There are many outstanding questions relating to the impact and meaning of section 35(3), and there is little by way of judicial or academic commentary to consult.[104] The term "right" probably does not need to be present in every provision of a land claims agreement in order for it to be considered

---

104 T. Isaac, "The *Constitution Act, 1982* and the Constitutionalization of Aboriginal Self-Government in Canada: *Cree-Naskapi of (Quebec) Act*", [1991] 1 C.N.L.R. 1; see also *Eastmain Band* v. *Gilpin,* [1987] 3 C.N.L.R. 54 (Que. Prov. Ct.), and *Waskaganish Band* v. *Blackned,* [1986] 3 C.N.L.R. 168 (Que. Prov. Ct.).

a "right" for the purposes of section 35(1). Elsewhere, I have argued that section 35(3) implicitly recognizes and constitutionally protects the contingent form of self-government, to the extent that self-governing provisions are contained in land claims agreements. In particular, self-government legislation flowing from constitutionally protected land claims agreements, such as the *Cree-Naskapi Act* (from the 1975 James Bay and Northern Quebec Agreement) may have some quasi-constitutional status.[105] In *Cree School Board* v. *Canada* (1998),[106] Supreme Court Justice Croteau held that the Cree school board created under the James Bay and Northern Quebec Agreement enjoys constitutional status, even though the creation of the school board was not phrased as a "right" *per se*. The point to be taken from the above is that although we have section 35(3) in the Constitution, we do not really understand what it means in practical terms.

In *Campbell et al.* v. *British Columbia* (2000),[107] the British Columbia Supreme Court considered an application seeking an order that the Nisga'a Final Agreement is in part inconsistent with the Constitution of Canada and therefore in part of no force or effect. The applicant argued that the treaty was inconsistent because it purports to bestow upon the governing body of the Nisga'a Nation legislative authority inconsistent with the division of powers granted to Parliament and the legislative assemblies of the provinces by sections 91 and 92 of the *Constitution Act, 1867*.[108]

In this case, the court held that the assertion of sovereignty by the British Crown did not necessarily extinguish the right of Aboriginal people to govern themselves. Any Aboriginal right to self-government could be extinguished after Confederation and before 1982 by federal legislation or it could be replaced or modified by the negotiation of a treaty. Post-1982, such rights could not be extinguished, but could be defined and given meaning by way of a treaty. The Nisga'a Final Agreement defines the content of Aboriginal self-government expressly. The court stated that the *Constitution Act, 1867* did not distribute all legislative power to Parliament and the provincial legislatures. It did not purport to, and indeed did not, end the royal prerogative or the Aboriginal and treaty rights, which remained with the Nisga'a in 1982. As of 1982, section 35 constitutionally guarantees the limited form of self-government that remained with the Nisga'a after the assertion of sovereignty, and the Nisga'a Final Agreement gave that limited right definition. The Nisga'a government is subject both to the limitations set out in the treaty itself and to the limited guarantee of section 35 rights.

---

105 Isaac, *ibid.*

106 *Cree School Board* v. *Canada,* [1998] 3 C.N.L.R. 24 (Que. Sup. Ct.).

107 *Campbell et al.* v. *British Columbia,* [2000] 4 C.N.L.R. 1 (B.C.S.C.).

108 *Constitution Act, 1867* (U.K.), 30 & 31 Vict., c. 3 (R.S.C. 1985, App. II, No. 5).

The *Campbell* application may not have posed the more important question: namely, what affect will the Nisga'a Final Agreement have on federal and provincial authority? One of the outstanding issues that affects the power of government is the extent to which the courts will interpret provisions of modern treaties that do not contain the language of "rights" that are affirmed and recognized under section 35(3). Take the example of a right to fish, as opposed to a reference to a "truckhouse" as in *Marshall,* that is interpreted by the Supreme Court as affirming a right to fish. In modern treaties that do not use the term "right" extensively throughout their respective texts, the question must be posed as to what it is that is constitutionally protected. Some argue that only "substantive" provisions of an agreement receive constitutional protection. But, as seen in decisions such as *Nunavut Tunngavik Inc.* v. *Canada* (1997 and 2000), in which the federal court considered the impact of the Nunavut Land Claims Agreement on the minister of Fisheries and Oceans discretionary authority to set turbot quotas.[109] Provisions that may simply be "advisory" or "administrative" in nature can still hold a government to a substantive degree of accountability, all within the ambit of having constitutional protection. Also, as "rights," do the provisions in modern treaties still require the requisite "consultation," the same degree of fiduciary responsibility by the Crown, and do they still invoke, to the same extent, the honour of the Crown when interpreted? The interpretation of self-government provisions may also affect federal and provincial government authority. Self-government provisions may, on their face, appear to delegate power to the First Nations, but the extent to which the powers they delegate may supercede federal and provincial laws remains uncertain.

It is not yet clear how modern treaties are to be interpreted. Should they be interpreted in the same way as historical treaties or should they be interpreted differently? The Federal Court of Appeal in *Eastmain Band* v. *Canada* (1993)[110] held that although the principle of interpreting treaties "liberally" applies to modern treaties, the principle of doubtful expressions being construed in favour of the Indians does not apply. Justice Decar wrote:

> We must be careful, in construing a document as modern as the 1975 [James Bay] Agreement, that we do not blindly follow the principles laid down by the Supreme Court in analyzing treaties entered into in an earlier era. The principle that ambiguities must be construed in favour of the Aboriginals rests, in the case of historic treaties, on the unique vulnerability of the Aboriginal

---

109 In *Nunavut Tunngavik Inc.* v. *Canada (Min. of Fisheries and Oceans),* [1997] 4 C.N.L.R. 193 (F.C.T.D.), and *Nunavut Tunngavik Inc.* v. *Canada (Min. of Fisheries and Oceans),* [2000] 3 C.N.L.R. 136 (F.C.T.D.). See chapter 6 for discussion.
110 *Eastmain Band* v. *Canada,* [1993] 3 C.N.L.R. 55 (F.C.A.).

parties, most of whom were not able to read the documents that they were signing and were compelled to negotiate with parties who had a superior bargaining position. When it is modern treaties that are at stake, the Aboriginal party must now, too, be bound by the informed commitment that it is now in a position to make. No serious and lasting political compromise can be entered into in an atmosphere of distrust and uncertainty.[111]

If the interpretive principles applied to historical treaties are applied to modern treaties, which contain many more administrative and substantive provisions, these treaties will radically affect the traditional understanding of the federal and provincial division of powers. It is not clear what the long-term impact on the Canadian legal and political systems will be of constitutionally protecting the hundreds of pages of dense legal text contained in the modern treaties. Although the answer to this question may be unclear and arguable, its importance is incontestable.

Aboriginal title also poses questions for federal and provincial authority. *Delgamuukw* holds that if Aboriginal title is found to exist, then activities such as forestry can continue and justify an infringement of Aboriginal title.[112] However, the Supreme Court also states that governments must accommodate Aboriginal title, and this can be accomplished in areas such as forestry by ensuring that Aboriginal people participate in resource development by way of leases and licences.[113] What this will mean in practical terms is uncertain, but it surely calls for a balancing of Aboriginal and non-Aboriginal interests and probably in a manner that is "proportional." With the importance of forestry on the East Coast, this area will surely continue to receive increased scrutiny.

These arguments are not to suggest that modern treaties are not productive, or that they are not achieving certainty over the issue of outstanding Aboriginal rights and title in Canada. Rather, the issue is that section 35(3) is an extremely powerful instrument that directly affects the Constitution of Canada and the existing authority of federal and provincial governments. It should be used measurably and only after careful consideration. Both Aboriginal and non-Aboriginal people have a vested interest in understanding the full impact of section 35(3). The Maritimes, like British Columbia, may have to become attuned to the language of negotiating modern treaties.

There continues to be uncertainty for, and continuing duties relating to, the Crown with respect to Aboriginal and treaty rights. Whether the issue is one of outstanding Aboriginal title or of a historical treaty or of a modern

---

111 *Ibid.* at 61 and 64.
112 *Delgamuukw, supra* note 2 at para. 165.
113 *Ibid.* at para. 167.

negotiated settlement, governments will continue to bear the burden of justifying their regulations and authority regarding decisions and actions that affect Aboriginal and treaty rights. Governments must also be prepared to consult properly with Aboriginal peoples in the appropriate circumstances. Thus, the constitutional requirement to consult does not rest with the private sector, it rests with government.

Conclusion

This chapter briefly outlined the nature and extent of Aboriginal title as a subset of Aboriginal rights protected by section 35 of the *Constitution Act, 1982*. In doing so, it made it clear that there are many outstanding issues to be resolved. However, one thing is certain: regardless of what legal perspective one might hold on this issue, Aboriginal title remains an outstanding issue to be determined, either in the courts or by way of negotiation. Either way, the goal must be to settle all the issues in a fair and reasonable manner so that the people of the Maritimes, both Aboriginal and non-Aboriginal, can get on with life. Although *Marshall* represents a significant turning point in the recognition and affirmation of treaty rights in the Maritimes, the underlying issue of Aboriginal title will overshadow *Marshall* and place First Nations' issues at the forefront, providing the impetus for a negotiated solution. In the meantime, governments must balance their obligation to Aboriginal people with their obligation to the rest of society, particularly as it relates to continued economic growth and prosperity.

This situation imposes many burdens on the private sector as well as on government. The economic uncertainty that has been seen in British Columbia as a result of *Delgamuukw* could also affect the Maritimes. This underscores the need for governments to take proactive steps to settle these outstanding matters and, in the meantime, to put in place regulatory regimes that attempt to balance all interests. In the end, most will recognize that no regulatory scheme will be perfectly balanced in all circumstances, particularly considering the complex nature of these issues. Regardless, the onus rests with governments to make their best efforts at being reasonable and fair, and to be prepared to justify their actions so that these issues, whether they concern treaty rights or Aboriginal title, do not impair the social and economic life of the Maritimes and other parts of Canada.

Chapter 5

•••••

The *Marshall* Decisions

Introduction

On September 17 (*Marshall No. 1*)[1] and November 17, 1999 (*Marshall No. 2*),[2] the Supreme Court of Canada delivered the two *Marshall* decisions that acknowledge, and at the same time place limits upon, Mi'kmaq treaty rights to hunt, fish, gather, and trade for necessaries. The first decision dealt with the substantive issue: namely, the charges against Donald Marshall, Jr., under the federal *Fisheries Act*.[3] The second decision provided the reasons the court was rejecting an application for a rehearing brought forward by an intervener. In providing these reasons, the court elaborated on and reiterated its earlier decision. This chapter provides summaries of both *Marshall* decisions and discusses their legal significance. It also discusses the decisions from the perspectives of historical evidence and the role of this evidence in Aboriginal and treaty rights decisions; the authority of the Crown to regulate Aboriginal and treaty rights; the honour of the Crown; and the larger implications of *Marshall* on Aboriginal and treaty rights in the Maritimes.

Nova Scotia Provincial Court

Mr. Marshall is a registered Mi'kmaq Indian under the federal *Indian Act*[4] and a member of the Membertou Indian Band located near Sydney, Nova Scotia. On August 24, 1993, Mr. Marshall went fishing for, and caught, eels

---

1   *R. v. Marshall (Marshall No. 1)*, [1999] 3 S.C.R. 456. Portions of this chapter were originally written for the *Marshall* symposium published in the *Saskatchewan Law Review* in my commentary entitled "The Courts, Government, and Public Policy: The Significance of *R. v. Marshall*" (2000) 63(2) Sask. L. Rev. 701.

2   *R. v. Marshall (Marshall No. 2)*, [1999] 3 S.C.R. 533 (reconsideration refused).

3   R.S.C. 1985, c. F-14.

4   R.S.C. 1985, c. I-5.

in Pomquet Harbour in the County of Antigonish, Nova Scotia. After fishing, Mr. Marshall proceeded to sell the eels he had caught earlier in the day. He sold approximately 463 pounds of eels at $1.70 per pound. He was subsequently charged with a number of offences under the *Fisheries Act.*

Judge Embree of the Nova Scotia Provincial Court[5] found Mr. Marshall guilty on the following charges: fishing for eels without authorization under a licence issued pursuant to the *Maritime Provinces Fishery Regulations* (section 4(1)(a)), the *Fishery (General) Regulations,* and the *Aboriginal Communal Fishing Licences Regulations;* fishing for eels with eel nets during the closed season contrary to section 20 of the *Maritime Provinces Fishery Regulations;* and selling or offering to sell eels not having been caught pursuant to a commercial fishing licence issued under section 35(2) of the *Fishery (General) Regulations.* Each of these charges constituted an offence pursuant to section 78(a) of the *Fisheries Act.*

Judge Embree held that the Treaties of 1760–61 between the governor of the British Colony of Nova Scotia and the Mi'kmaq were valid treaties and that these treaties currently apply to all Mi'kmaq in Nova Scotia. Counsel for Mr. Marshall argued that the defendant's actions were based on the proposition that the Treaties of 1760–61 guaranteed a right to the Mi'kmaq to fish and to sell the fish they caught. The Crown argued that the treaties did not confer any such right and that, even if they did, they were still subject to regulation. That is, a treaty right to fish would still be subject to regulation by the *Fisheries Act.* The crux of Mr. Marshall's defence lay in a restrictive covenant (the "truckhouse clause") contained within the 1760 treaty, which reads in part:

> [W]e will not traffick, barter or exchange any commodities in any manner but with such persons or the managers of such Truck houses as shall be appointed or Established by His Majesty's Governor at Lunenbourg or elsewhere in Nova Scotia or Accadia.[6]

Judge Embree concluded that Mr. Marshall did not meet the burden of establishing that the treaties provided him with the right to fish and sell the fish. The British did not, and did not intend, to convey the rights claimed by Mr. Marshall. Judge Embree wrote:

> Mi'kmaq concerns in 1760 were very focused and immediate. Conveying the right which the defendant here claims from this trade clause is not even

---

5 *R. v. Marshall,* [1996] N.S.J. No. 246 (QL) (N.S. Prov. Ct.).
6 Treaty of 1760. See *Marshall No. 1, supra* note 1 at para. 5.

among the "various possible interpretations of the common intention" of the
Mi'kmaq and the British.[7]

Judge Embree was very thorough in his examination of the trial evidence
placed before him. He examined carefully the historical evidence and the
context within which the Treaties of 1760–61 were drafted. He wrote:

> In interpreting the Treaties of 1760-61 (i.e. determining their contents and
> meaning), I have examined everything that could be considered as providing
> the "context" within which the treaties were created.[8]

Notwithstanding this, the majority of the Supreme Court of Canada had a
different interpretation of the trial evidence.

Nova Scotia Court of Appeal

On March 26, 1997, a unanimous Nova Scotia Court of Appeal dismissed the
appeal by Mr. Marshall to the lower court convictions. Counsel for Mr.
Marshall argued that the lower court had misconstrued a number of items.[9]
First, the court had misconstrued the requirement that treaties contain express provisions guaranteeing rights, rather than implicit terms—such as those
inferred in the truckhouse clause—that reflected the "essence" of the treaty
relationship between the British and the Mi'kmaq. Thus, the defence argued
that the truckhouse clause was of crucial importance to the Mi'kmaq and was
not simply a secondary provision. Second, the court had overlooked the requirement of the honour of the Crown and its fiduciary relationship to the
Mi'kmaq. Third, the court had erroneously placed on Mr. Marshall the burden of proof for whether the Crown's decision to abandon the truckhouse
system terminated, suspended, or limited the rights claimed by Mr. Marshall.
Fourth, the court had neglected to consider that although the Mi'kmaq Treaties of 1760–61 were on the same terms as the Maliseet Treaty of February
23, 1760, the Mi'kmaq treaties did not incorporate by reference earlier treaties, while the Maliseet Treaty did. Fifth, the court had not considered whether
the Crown was estopped or precluded from tendering evidence demonstrating that the Treaty of 1752 was terminated as a result of hostilities and other
events after 1753, as per *R. v. Simon* (1985).[10] The Crown reiterated its argument presented at trial.

---

7   *Ibid.* at para. 129.
8   *Ibid.* at para. 87.
9   *R. v. Marshall*, [1997] 3 C.N.L.R. 209 at 212 (N.S.C.A.).
10 *R. v. Simon*, [1985] 2 S.C.R. 387.

The Court of Appeal held that the Treaties of 1760–61 contained all the terms of the agreement between the Mi'kmaq and the British and that the earlier treaties were not incorporated into them. The relevant clauses in the treaties simply showed a British recognition that the Mi'kmaq traded as opposed to conferring a right to trade. The truckhouse clause simply gave the Mi'kmaq a right to bring goods to a truckhouse to trade. The court wrote:

> The fact that under the Treaties of 1760-61 the Mi'kmaq were authorized and required to trade goods only at truckhouses does not constitute the grant of a right to do so. The truckhouse clause was not a condition of peace with the Mi'kmaq. It was, rather, a mechanism imposed upon them to help ensure that the peace was a lasting one, by obviating their need to trade with enemies of the British. The trial judge was correct when he concluded that the only implication from the demise of the truckhouses and licensed traders was that the Mi'kmaq were free to trade in the same manner as all other residents of the territory. The truckhouse clause simply cannot bear the interpretation placed upon it by the appellant, nor do the judge's words, interpreted in context, support the submission that he found that the Treaties of 1760-61 granted a treaty right to trade at truckhouses.[11]

Truckhouses were basically trading posts. They existed only briefly in Nova Scotia. They were originally promised in the Treaty of 1752 "wherever the Indians desired." It was only after the 1760 treaty that the British established six truckhouses, but due to the lack of trade volume, these were dismantled by 1764.

Marshall No. 1 (September 17, 1999)

The Supreme Court of Canada[12] allowed Mr. Marshall's appeal of the convictions under the *Fisheries Act.* Mr. Marshall admitted that he had illegally caught and sold eels without a licence during a closed season. It was up to the court to decide whether such acts could be justified based on Mr. Marshall's claim of a treaty right to catch and sell fish under the Treaties of 1760–61. A majority of the Supreme Court concluded that although the truckhouse clause appears to restrict the Mi'kmaq to trade at "truckhouses," it is actually a reflection, based on the historical evidence, of the Mi'kmaq demand for trade. In essence, the written terms of the 1760 treaty did not contain the entire agreement reached between the British and the Mi'kmaq. This interpretation is in direct contrast to the Court of Appeal's assertion that the written text

---

11 *Marshall, supra* note 9 at 233.
12 *Marshall No. 1, supra* note 1.

contained the entire treaty. Justice Binnie, on behalf of the majority of the Supreme Court, noted that although the text of the March 10, 1760, treaty does not, by itself, support Marshall's position, the extrinsic evidence surrounding the negotiations supports the parties' general intention at the time the treaty was signed.

In the opening paragraphs of *Marshall,* Justice Binnie acknowledged the unique or *sui generis* nature of treaties and their interpretation in Canada law. He wrote:

> I recognize that if the present dispute had arisen out of a modern commercial transaction between two parties of relatively equal bargaining power, or if, as held by the courts below, the . . . [1760 document] was to be taken as being the "entire agreement" between the parties, it would have to be concluded that the Mi'kmaq had inadequately protected their interests. However, the courts have not applied strict rules of interpretation to treaty relationships.[13]

The court first focussed on the use of extrinsic evidence and affirmed its use in appropriate circumstances. The court noted that (1) even in the commercial context, extrinsic evidence may be used to demonstrate that a written document does not contain all the terms of an agreement,[14] (2) even in a document that is purported to contain all the terms of an agreement, extrinsic evidence, of a cultural or historical significance, may be considered if it assists in understanding the context of the treaty, even if there is no apparent ambiguity,[15] and (3) in the case where the Crown's representatives put into written form only a portion of the verbal agreement with Indians, it would be unconscionable for the Crown to ignore the verbal terms and rely only on that which is written.[16]

Based on this approach to extrinsic evidence, the court rejected the trial judge's assertion that the 1760 document contained the entire agreement. The majority held that the British-drafted treaty did not accurately reflect the British-drafted minutes of the negotiating sessions and other documents and evidence.[17] The court also found that the Court of Appeal had erred by

---

13 *Ibid.* at para. 4.
14 *Ibid.* at para. 10.
15 *Ibid.* at para. 11. See *R.* v. *Taylor and Williams,* [1981] 3 C.N.L.R. 114 at 123 (Ont. C.A.); leave to appeal refused [1981] 2 S.C.R. xi. Cited with approval in *Delgamuukw* v. *British Columbia,* [1997] 3 S.C.R. 1010 at para. 87, and *R.* v. *Sioui,* [1990] 1 S.C.R. 1025 at 1045.
16 *Marshall No. 1, supra* note 1 at para. 12; see *R.* v. *Guerin,* [1984] 2 S.C.R. 335.
17 *Marshall No. 1, ibid.* at paras. 19–20.

distinguishing between land-cession treaties and treaties of peace and friendship, such as the 1760 treaty. Since the Mi'kmaq were largely dispossessed of their lands by 1760, the purpose of a land-cession treaty would have been moot. The court also affirmed that the same rules of interpretation must apply both to peace and friendship treaties and to land-cession treaties.

Justice Binnie stated that the lower courts had erred in concluding that the only enforceable treaty obligations were those set out in the 1760 document, whether it was interpreted in a flexible manner (as by the trial judge) or in a more restrictive manner (as by the Court of Appeal). The common intention of the 1760 document, not simply its written terms, had to be considered.[18] The content of treaty rights need not be special, but their protection, regardless of their content, is special in Canadian law.[19]

Justice Binnie discussed the honour of the Crown and noted that the "honour of the Crown is always at stake in its dealings with Aboriginal people."[20] He summarized the court's interpretation of the events leading up to the 1760 treaty by stating that an interpretation "that turns a positive Mi'kmaq trade demand into a negative Mi'kmaq covenant . . . is [not] consistent with the honour and integrity of the Crown."[21] The lower courts' interpretation of the truckhouse clause left the Mi'kmaq with "an empty shell of a treaty promise."[22] The written promise of a truckhouse is not the entire treaty right, but rather it is the right to continue to obtain necessaries by hunting, fishing, and trading products at these truckhouses (for example), subject to justifiable restrictions as affirmed in the Supreme Court's decision of *R. v. Badger* (1996).[23]

In his conclusion, Justice Binnie affirmed that the test for infringement under section 35(1) of the *Constitution Act, 1982*[24] is the same for both Aboriginal and treaty rights. Also, the court focussed on the fact that the minister of Fisheries' discretionary authority, as set out in the *Maritime Provinces Fishery Regulations,* the *Aboriginal Communal Fishing Licenses Regulations,* and the *Fisheries Act,* imposes no obligation or direction on the minister to explain how he or she should exercise his or her discretionary authority in a way that respects treaty rights.[25]

---

18 *Ibid.* at para. 40.
19 *Ibid.* at para. 48.
20 *Ibid.* at para. 49.
21 *Ibid.* at para. 52.
22 *Ibid.*
23 *Ibid.* at para. 56; *R. v. Badger,* [1996] 1 S.C.R. 771.
24 *Constitution Act, 1982,* Sched. B to the *Canada Act* 1982 (U.K.) 1982, c. 11 as am. by the *Constitution Amendment Proclamation 1983*, R.S.C. 1985, App. II, No. 46 [add. ss. 35(3) and 35(4)].
25 *Marshall No. 1, supra* note 1 at paras. 62–64.

In this case, the court found that fishing without a licence and selling eels without a licence constituted *prima facie* infringements of Mr. Marshall's treaty rights and that such infringements were not justified according to the *Badger* test. Thus, Mr. Marshall was acquitted of selling fish during the closed season because there "can be no limitation on the method, timing and extent of Indian hunting under a treaty . . . apart . . . from a treaty limitation to that effect."[26]

Justice McLachlin's and Justice Gonthier's dissent focussed on the trial judge's conclusion that the historical evidence strongly suggested that there was no guarantee of a general treaty right to trade (and no treaty right to hunt or fish), but simply a "right to bring goods" to truckhouses. This right terminated when the exclusive trading and truckhouse regime ended. Justice McLachlin concluded that the trial judge had made no error of law and, as such, there was no basis upon which the Supreme Court could interfere with the trial court's judgement. She placed emphasis on her reading that the trial judge took a great deal of care to review the historical and other evidence presented. Justice McLachlin found that the actions of the parties, the British and the Mi'kmaq, both before and after the signing of the 1760 treaty, confirmed that the parties did not intend to create a right to hunt, fish, gather, and trade but simply a right to bring goods to a truckhouse to trade.

Marshall No. 2 (November 17, 1999)[27]

Following the release of the September 17, 1999, decision, there was much reaction from both Aboriginal and non-Aboriginal people and, in particular, from representatives of non-Aboriginal fishers. Additionally, there was a notable "non-reaction" from the federal government, especially with respect to any substantive measures it would take to justify its regulation of the Aboriginal fishery.

The West Nova Fishermen's Coalition, an intervener[28] in the September 17, 1999, decision, applied for a rehearing of the decision with respect to the federal government's regulatory authority regarding fisheries. If the rehearing was granted, the intervener would call for a stay in the judgement until the rehearing was complete. The coalition also sought a new trial to determine whether licensing and closed seasons could be justified by the Crown on the basis of conservation or some other ground. The coalition made its

---

26 *Ibid.* at para. 65; see also *Badger, supra* note 23 at para. 90.

27 *Marshall No. 2, supra* note 2.

28 An intervener is an interested party who voluntarily joins an action with the leave of the court.

application in response to a vocal reaction by non-Aboriginal fishers to the decision and in response to members of some First Nations who set lobster traps during the closed season.

The Supreme Court may consider a rehearing of an appeal based on an intervener's submission in "exceptional circumstances."[29] In its estimation, the *Marshall* decision did not constitute such circumstances. Furthermore, the Crown, Mr. Marshall, and other interveners were opposed to a new trial.[30] At the heart of the request for a rehearing was, as the court put it, "a basic misunderstanding of the scope of the Court's majority reasons."[31] In an unusual move, the court decided to give detailed reasoning regarding its rejection of the application for a rehearing. In so doing, the court provided a useful clarification and reiteration of the law relating to treaty rights and their regulation and justifiable infringement by the Crown.

Marshall No. 2 was viewed by some as the Supreme Court caving in to pressure. For instance, commenting on the decision, the national chief of the Assembly of First Nations stated:

[T]he Supreme Court's partial reversal in Marshall #2 must be stated to be what it was: a cowardly retreat from impartial interpretation of the law. It is obvious that the Supreme Court was intimidated by the intense violent reaction from non-Native Canadians on the east coast, and possibly from the officers of the Crown. This was a textbook case of recognition of rights being made subject to mob rule. If non-Native mobs object and make their objections violently known, instead of the Court strengthening and reinforcing its ruling, the Supreme Court heard an additional appeal and beat a retreat.[32]

I disagree. The Supreme court simply reiterated, albeit extensively, earlier pronouncements regarding government's ability to justifiably infringe treaty rights. *Marshall No. 2* is wholly consistent with *Marshall No. 1*.

---

29 Other notable Aboriginal law decisions where reconsideration by the Supreme Court of Canada was refused are *R. v. Van der Peet,* [1996] 2 S.C.R. 507; reconsideration refused January 16, 1997, Doc. 23803 (S.C.C.), and *Ontario (A.G.) v. Bear Island Foundation,* [1991] 2 S.C.R. 570; reconsideration refused (1995), 46 R.P.R. (2d) 91n (S.C.C.).

30 *Marshall No. 2, supra* note 2 at para. 9.

31 *Ibid.* at para. 11.

32 National Chief Matthew Coon Come, "Netukulimk: A Way To Make A Living" (Halifax: National Fisheries Strategy Conference, January 29–31, 2001).

Evidentiary Rules and Historical Evidence

When comparing the majority decision in *Marshall* with the dissent, it is
apparent that two different approaches (liberal and conservative) were taken
in the examination of the relevant historical evidence. On its face, a liberal
interpretation of the historical evidence is not surprising considering the interpretative principles that the Supreme Court has provided regarding treaty
interpretation in this and other decisions. In *R. v. Sioui* (1990), for example,
Justice Lamer noted with approval that in

> *Simon v. The Queen,* . . . [1985] 2 S.C.R. 387 . . . this court adopted the
> comment of Norris J.A. in *R. v. White and Bob,* . . . 50 D.L.R. (2d) 613
> (B.C.C.A.) (affirmed in the Supreme Court (1965), 52 D.L.R. (2d) 481), that
> the courts should show flexibility in determining the legal nature of a docu-
> ment recording a transaction with the Indians. . . . [T]hey must take into
> account the historical context and perception each party might have as to the
> nature of the undertaking contained in the document under consideration.
> . . . As the Chief Justice said in *Simon, supra,* treaties and statutes relating to
> Indians should be liberally construed and uncertainties resolved in favour of
> the Indians (at p. 410) . . . therefore, we should adopt a broad and generous
> interpretation of what constitutes a treaty.[33]

However, the extent to which the majority in *Marshall* were willing to find an
explicit treaty right was surprising to many.

No other Supreme Court of Canada decision involving treaty rights has
interpreted a treaty to guarantee a treaty right when no evidence, either in the
text of the treaty itself or extrinsic, explicitly provided for such a right or a
promise. Although a number of decisions (discussed below) have held that
ancillary or implied rights exist, they have, with the exception of *Marshall,*
always been based in some manner on the evidentiary record. The majority in
Marshall seem to have taken a very broad approach to utilizing the interpretive principles of past decisions in attempting to understand the "intentions"
of the parties, even though no evidence was produced to support the affirmation of specific rights. In her dissent, Justice McLachlin outlined a number of
these principles, including the following:

1. Aboriginal treaties constitute a unique type of agreement and attract special principles of interpretation. . . .
2. Treaties should be liberally construed and ambiguities or doubtful expressions should be resolved in favour of the Aboriginal signatories. . . .

---

33 *R. v. Sioui,* [1990] 1 S.C.R. 1025 at 1035; see also *Badger, supra* note 23 at para. 41.

3. The goal of treaty interpretation is to choose from among the various possible interpretations of common intention the one which best reconciles the interests of both parties at the time the treaty was signed. . . .

4. . . . [I]ntegrity and honour of the Crown is presumed. . . .

5. In determining the signatories' respective understanding and intentions, the court must be sensitive to the unique cultural and linguistic differences between the parties. . . .

6. The words of the treaty must be given the sense which they would naturally have held for the parties at the time. . . .

7. A technical or contractual interpretation of treaty wording should be avoided. . . .

8. While construing the language generously, courts cannot alter the terms of the treaty by exceeding what is "possible on the language" or realistic. . . .

9. Treaty rights of Aboriginal peoples must not be interpreted in a static or rigid way.[34]

Additionally, the Supreme Court went to great lengths in the *Delgamuukw* (1997)[35] decision to outline clearly the importance and usefulness of extrinsic evidence when examining the existence of Aboriginal rights. Chief Justice Lamer, for the majority, wrote:

> Both the principles laid down in *Van der Peet*—first, that trial courts must approach the rules of evidence in light of the evidentiary difficulties inherent in adjudicating Aboriginal claims, and second, that trial courts must interpret that evidence in the same spirit—must be understood against this background. . . . [T]his requires the courts to come to terms with the oral histories of Aboriginal societies, . . . the laws of evidence must be adopted in order that this type of evidence can be accommodated and placed on an equal footing with the types of historical evidence that courts are familiar with, . . . historical documents.[36]

With these principles in mind, the fact that Canadian courts examining an Aboriginal or treaty right claim would take a broad or liberal approach in interpreting Aboriginal or treaty rights is not surprising. What is surprising about the *Marshall* decision is the extent to which the court was prepared to find a treaty right. The issue is not whether the Supreme Court's interpretation or the trial court judge's interpretation is correct, but rather the process the courts

---

34 *Marshall No. 1, supra* note 1 at para. 78.

35 *Delgamuukw v. British Columbia,* [1997] 3 S.C.R. 1010.

36 *Ibid.* at paras. 82, 84, 87; see also *R. v. Van der Peet,* [1996] 2 S.C.R. 507 at para. 68.

used to interpret the evidence given at trial. It is generally held that the trial judge is best placed to comprehend and consider the evidence and the testimony provided at trial. As Justice McLachlin noted, the trial lasted forty days and the judge heard the testimony of three expert witnesses and was presented with four hundred documents.[37] Notwithstanding this, the majority felt comfortable in overturning the trial judge's conclusion and providing their own interpretation of the true intentions of the British and Mi'kmaq at the time the treaty was negotiated.

There is some question as to the ability of higher courts to accurately interpret evidence given at trial. The Crown's expert, Dr. Stephen Patterson, claimed that the Supreme Court distorted his testimony and used selective evidence in the majority decision.[38] Justice Binnie referred extensively to Dr. Patterson's testimony in the majority judgement.[39] Dr. Patterson was quoted as saying:

> Without the rest of the evidence, you don't have the proper context for understanding the meaning in which my remarks were made. . . . I said these treaties made native people subjects of the British Crown, they have rights . . . but it is the same rights as anyone else's rights. They would be subject to the very same regulations that the subjects of the British Crown would have been subject to in 1760 and 1761.[40]

Interestingly, the court released a correction to the text of the majority decision[41] on September 30, 1999. The corrections appeared in paragraph 37 dealing with Dr. Patterson's evidence and attempted to put Dr. Patterson's comments into a more accurate focus. This, along with the court's lengthy reconsideration decision (*Marshall No. 2*), raises questions regarding the process by which this decision was drafted.

Lower courts must continue to examine and consider carefully *Marshall, Delgamuukw,* and other decisions with respect to their treatment of extrinsic evidence. The trial judge is best placed to judge the evidence presented and place it within the proper context. The Supreme Court has affirmed many times that the trial judge's findings should be treated with deference. Appel-

---

37 *Marshall No. 1, supra* note 1 at para. 84.

38 "High Court Accused of 'Distorting' History" *National Post* (28 October 1999) A1; see also "High Court's Rulings Add to Confusion, Experts Say" *National Post* (8 April 2000) A9.

39 *Marshall, No. 1, supra* note 1 at paras. 37–39.

40 "High Court Accused," *supra* note 38.

41 These changes to the majority decision in *Marshall* have been incorporated into the extracts of the decision provided in the appendix to this book.

lant courts should not interfere "unless it can be established that the trial judge made some palpable and overriding error which affected his assessment of the facts."[42] This standard has been applied in Aboriginal rights cases such as *R.* v. *N.T.C. Smokehouse Ltd.,*[43] where Chief Justice Lamer stated: "[T]he findings of fact made by the trial judge should not, absent a palpable and overriding error, be overturned on appeal." In *R.* v. *Adams,*[44] Chief Justice Lamer stated that the trial judge's finding should be held in deference unless they were "made as a result of a clear and palpable error." In *R.* v. *Côté,* the court held:

> [T]he role of this Court is to rely on the findings of fact made by the trial judge and to assess whether those findings of fact are both reasonable and support the claim that an activity is an aspect of a practice, custom or tradition integral to the distinctive culture of the aboriginal community or group in question.[45]

If the trial judge does not place the evidence in its proper context, the trial judgement is vulnerable at appeal. Yet, as seen with *Marshall,* even after a thorough analysis at trial, a superior court may interpret the intentions of the parties in a very different manner. Careful consideration of extrinsic evidence will be an increasingly important task, especially with respect to the development of Aboriginal legal jurisprudence in the Maritimes, where it will more than likely rely heavily upon evidence that is hundreds of years old, in great volume and in different forms. Additionally, because these Maritime treaties are, by their very nature, vague and brief, the potential for courts to be "imaginative" exists and, therefore, an extra degree of caution and consideration should be exercised by all in dealing with this type of evidence.

In *Marshall No. 1,* the Supreme Court rejected a strict approach to using extrinsic evidence when interpreting historical treaties. The court provided three reasons for rejecting this approach: (1) even in the modern commercial context extrinsic evidence is used to illustrate that a written document does not include all the terms of a contract, (2) the court made it clear in recent cases that extrinsic evidence regarding the historical and cultural context of a treaty may be helpful in the absence of any ambiguity on the face of the treaty, and (3) if a treaty was concluded verbally and put into written form

---

42 See *Stein* v. *Kathy K (The)*, [1976] 2 S.C.R. 802 at 808.
43 *R.* v. *N.T.C. Smokehouse Ltd.,* [1996] 2 S.C.R. 672 at 689.
44 *R.* v. *Adams,* [1996] 3 S.C.R. 101 at para. 38.
45 *R.* v. *Côté,* [1996] 3 S.C.R. 139 at 178; see also *R.* v. *Van der Peet,* [1996] 2 S.C.R. 507 at 564–66.
46 *Marshall No. 1, supra* note 1 at paras. 10–12.

later by Crown representatives it would be unconscionable for the Crown to ignore the oral terms but continue to rely on the written terms of the treaty.[46] The court did caution, however, that generous rules of interpretation ought not to be confused with "a vague sense of after-the-fact largesse."[47] Presumably, the court's reference to "after-the-fact largesse" would preclude an overly generous or unrealistic interpretation of treaty rights. This nevertheless remains a subjective element.

In *Mitchell* v. *Canada (Min. of National Revenue),*[48] the Supreme Court of Canada considered whether the Mohawks of Akwesasne possessed a right to bring goods across the St. Lawrence River (the Canada–United States border) for the purposes of trade. Although the trial judge, affirmed by the Federal Court of Appeal, found that there was sufficient evidence to establish an ancestral Mohawk practice of transferring goods across the St. Lawrence River for trading purposes, Chief Justice McLachlin held that the findings of fact at trial represented a "clear and palpable error."[49] In *Mitchell,* Chief Justice McLachlin undertook an intensive review of the evidence and concluded that it was sparse, doubtful, and hardly compelling.[50]

Marshall and *Mitchell* have different results with respect to the Supreme Court's treatment of the evidence. In *Marshall,* the court held that a treaty right existed even though there was no direct evidence supporting the existence of such a right. The court inferred that it would be reasonable to presume that such a right could be contained within the terms of the 1760 treaty. In *Mitchell,* the result was the opposite. There, the court carefully scrutinized all the evidence placed before the trial judge and the Court of Appeal, and held that there was a "clear and palpable" error with respect to the interpretation of the evidence. The conclusion in *Mitchell* was that no such Aboriginal right to bring goods across the border existed. Although both decisions treated the evidence in different ways, they both represent a significant trend in the adjudication of Aboriginal rights in Canada. Specifically, Aboriginal and treaty rights will be held to a high, but reasonable, evidentiary standard, as was the case in *Mitchell,* and—putting aside the issue of evidence—Aboriginal and treaty rights face an ever-increasing number of federal and provincial justificatory factors.

Marshall and *Mitchell,* while similar in their result of affirming federal and provincial jurisdiction, when justified, are fundamentally the opposite of each other with respect to how they each dealt with evidence. *Marshall* cre-

---

47 *Ibid.* at para. 14.
48 *Mitchell* v. *Canada (Min. of National Revenue)* (2001), 199 D.L.R. (4th) 385 (S.C.C.).
49 *Ibid.* at para. 51.
50 *Ibid.* at paras. 47 and 51.

ated a right where one did not appear to exist and overturned the trial courts' interpretation of the evidence. Likewise, *Mitchell* overturned the trial judge's interpretation of the evidence and concluded that no Aboriginal right existed. Although the analytical framework may be in place, its practical application needs to be refined and better understood, particularly for lower courts as they attempt to apply the law in this complex and quickly changing area of adjudication. The evidence used to support the existence of an Aboriginal or treaty right may come under a high degree of scrutiny. Although *Mitchell* supports this suggestion, *Marshall* appears to contradict it. Thus, even as the principles are becoming clearer, their application is far from being consistent or predictable.

In *Marshall,* the court made it clear that it was prepared to examine the broader context within which the negotiations surrounding the 1760 treaty occurred. The court said the question to be answered was "whether the underlying negotiations produced a broader agreement between the British and the Mi'kmaq, memorialized only in part by the Treaty of Peace and Friendship."[51] The court underscored the difficulties that Aboriginal people have proving rights from a historical perspective.[52] After the court concluded that the written terms of the treaty did not include the entire terms of the treaty, it was then necessary to ascertain what other elements of the treaty existed but were not outlined in the 1760 document. The court engaged in a discussion of what it called "implied or incidental" rights. These rights support the meaningful exercise of express rights based on the *sui generis* nature of the Crown's relationship to Aboriginal people. The honour of the Crown, the court stated, required a broad examination and interpretation of the negotiations leading up to the 1760 document.[53] In previous decisions, the Supreme Court had always based its affirmation of an implied or incidental right either on an express promise or right in the text of a treaty or document, or on an examination of the historical record for evidence of such a promise or right being made or granted. No such circumstances existed in *Marshall*.

The court noted that the content of hunting, fishing, and gathering rights may not be any greater than those enjoyed by other Canadians. What is important, however, is that there is a distinction between a liberty enjoyed by all citizens (for example, freedom of expression) and a right that exists by way

---

51 *Marshall No. 1, supra* note 1 at para. 7.

52 *Ibid.* at para. 20. The Supreme Court cited *R. v. Simon,* [1985] 2 S.C.R. 387 at 408; *Badger, supra* note 23 at para. 7, for treaty rights; and *Van der Peet, supra* note 29 at para. 68, and *Delgamuukw, supra* note 35 at paras. 80–82, for Aboriginal rights.

53 *Marshall No. 1, ibid.* at para. 44. In decisions such as *R. v. Sundown,* [1999] 1 S.C.R. 393; *Simon, ibid.;* and *R. v. Sioui,* [1990] 1 S.C.R. 1025.

of specific legal authority, in this case, a treaty (for example, a treaty right to fish).[54] The court pointed out that the rights enjoyed by the Mi'kmaq need not be preferential, but only protected by way of a constitutionally protected treaty. Thus the treaty protection is special in that it protects against interference with its exercise. The court stated that this is similar to the trading arrangement outlined in the 1760 document. The court noted:

> [T]he fact the *content* of Mi'kmaq rights under the treaty to hunt, fish and trade was no greater than those enjoyed by other inhabitants does not, unless those rights were extinguished prior to April 17, 1982, detract from the higher *protection* they presently offer to the Mi'kmaq people. [Emphasis in original][55]

Of course, as noted above, a great deal of analysis and consideration is required before coming to the conclusion that a "right" exists, especially in a case such as *Marshall,* where there is no explicit evidence of a right or a promise ever being granted or made.

The extent to which First Nations may use extrinsic evidence to bolster their claims for existing treaty rights has been strengthened significantly by the majority decision in *Marshall.* Yet, as much of a benefit as that decision may appear to be, it also presents a practical problem. *Marshall* stands for the proposition that one cannot simply look at the written terms of a treaty and deduce what rights may flow therefrom, either directly or incidentally. Rather, *Marshall* moves courts in the direction of leaving this issue open to a wide and broad interpretation. This appears to run counter to the desire by the courts to have the parties negotiate a settlement. It may prove difficult to negotiate when neither party has any understanding of what it may be gaining or relinquishing. It is important to recognize that *Marshall* is a departure from earlier Supreme Court of Canada decisions regarding the existence of implied or incidental rights and the analysis of the "context" within which treaties are negotiated.

Although Justice Binnie went to great lengths to demonstrate that the majority were simply applying a well-referenced set of principles to interpret the 1760 treaty, what the Supreme Court did in reality was to acknowledge the existence of a substantive treaty right in the absence of any direct evidence confirming this view, either written or otherwise. The court seemed to rely on its understanding of what it determined the intentions of the parties to be. For example, the Supreme Court cited the Ontario Court of Appeal decision of *R. v. Taylor and Williams* (1981)[56] as evidence that the historical and

---

54 *Marshall No. 1, supra* note 1 at para. 45.
55 *Ibid.* at para. 48.
56 *R. v. Taylor and Williams,* [1981] 3 C.N.L.R. 114 (Ont. C.A.).

cultural context of a treaty may be considered even when ambiguity on the face of the treaty is absent.[57] However, in *Taylor and Williams*, there was substantial evidence to suggest that substantive promises were made to the Indians to hunt and fish. No such evidence was put before the court in *Marshall*.

Justice Binnie also noted that the approach taken in *Taylor and Williams* was cited with approval in *Delgamuukw* v. *British Columbia* (1997)[58] and in *R.* v. *Sioui* (1990).[59] In *Delgamuukw*, the reference was a general one regarding a flexible approach to the laws of evidence, keeping in mind that in *Delgamuukw* there was an abundance of extrinsic evidence supporting Aboriginal title. In *Sioui*, there was little debate that there existed substantive treaty rights, namely those concerning the practice of customs and traditions. The issue was where these rights could be exercised. Thus, although the court applied *Taylor and Williams*, *Delgamuukw*, and *Sioui* to support its finding of a positive treaty right to hunt, fish, gather, and trade for necessaries, all three of these decisions are distinguishable in that none of them purported to create rights but rather each interpreted evidence that demonstrated the existence of such rights. In *Marshall*, there was no evidence supporting the explicit promise of a right, and this was confirmed by the trial judge and by the Court of Appeal.

Justice Binnie cited *R.* v. *Sundown* (1999)[60] and *R.* v. *Simon* (1985)[61] as authorities for the proposition that one must choose from various possible interpretations of common intention and choose that which best reconciles the interests of the Mi'kmaq and the British. In *Sundown*, the court found an incidental right to shelter when Treaty No. 6 Indians hunt. This was based on an explicit right to hunt being outlined in Treaty No. 6 and on evidence being presented that Treaty No. 6 Indians, namely the Cree, used shelters extensively when they hunted. Similarly, in *Simon*, the court held that hunting and fishing rights were confirmed by the Treaty of 1752, based upon an explicit reference to hunting and fishing in the text of the treaty and supported by extrinsic evidence. No such clause exists with respect to the Treaties of 1760–61, nor did the evidence make any suggestion of a right to hunt, fish, or gather, or trade for necessaries: the majority inferred that such a right was meant to be protected.[62]

57 *Marshall No. 1, supra* note 1 at para. 11.
58 *Delgamuukw* v. *British Columbia*, [1997] 3 S.C.R. 1010 at para. 87, as cited in *Marshall No. 1, supra* note 1 at para. 11.
59 *Sioui, supra* note 53 at 1045, as cited in *Marshall No. 1, supra* note 1 at para. 11.
60 *Sundown, supra* note 53.
61 *Simon, supra* note 52.
62 *Marshall No. 1, supra* note 1 at para. 42.

Conclusion

From the evidentiary perspective, the most startling element of the *Marshall* decision was the Supreme Court's implication of a right, even though no such right was discussed during the negotiations and no evidence was presented to suggest that such a right was promised, in any form. One commentator summarized this notable consequence of the *Marshall* decision as follows:

> [T]he majority has interpreted treaties that the Crown *ought* to have entered into rather than the 1760–1761 treaties that the Crown *did* enter into, and has been led to the conclusion that the Crown *ought* unilaterally to have included a fishing-right term in the treaties by the fact that aboriginal treaty rights were given constitutional protection in 1982. [Emphasis in original][63]

It remains to be seen whether the Supreme Court will continue to follow this liberal and intuitive approach to interpreting treaties. With such an expansive interpretive approach, it becomes increasingly important for governments to understand what their obligations and rights are and to act accordingly.

---

63 W.H. Hurlburt, "Case Comment on *R.* v. *Marshall*" (2000) 38(2) Alta. L. Rev. 563 at 577.

Chapter 6

. . . . . .

Government Responsibilities
Highlighted by *Marshall*

Introduction

Marshall represents the most articulate enunciation of the Supreme Court's views regarding Canadian governments' continued regulatory and legislative authority—and, I suggest, responsibility—in the face of constitutionally protected Aboriginal and treaty rights. One of the most striking characteristics of the *Marshall* decisions is the extent to which the Supreme Court outlined the parameters of governments' legislative authority and responsibility as it relates to treaty rights. This chapter analyzes this aspect of the decisions and maintains that the real onus with respect to these matters rests with government and not with the resource sector or First Nations. Governments must put in place comprehensive regulatory regimes that are sensitive not only to First Nation rights, but also to the economic and social well-being of society in general.

Government's Authority to Regulate

In *Marshall,* the Supreme Court of Canada held that the Mi'kmaq people possess hunting, fishing, and gathering rights and trading rights for "necessaries" as contained in the Treaties of 1760–61, but it also held that these rights are "always subject to regulation."[1] In *Marshall No. 2,* the court wrote:

> The Court was thus most explicit in confirming the regulatory authority of the federal and provincial governments within their respective legislative fields to regulate the exercise of the treaty right subject to the constitutional requirement that restraints on the exercise of the treaty right have to be jus-

---

1   *R.* v. *Marshall (Marshall No. 1),* [1999] 3 S.C.R. 456 at para. 4.

tified on the basis of conservation or other compelling and substantial public interests.[2]

The court also made it clear that the rights protected by the Treaties of 1760–61 are limited to securing "necessaries," which the court defined in a modern context as "equivalent to a moderate livelihood." The court suggested that a moderate livelihood included acquiring food, clothing, and housing, supplemented by a few amenities. A moderate livelihood must address day-to-day needs and does not include the open-ended accumulation of wealth.[3] The problem, of course, for this decision and others like it, is the precise definition of "a moderate livelihood." This ambiguity underscores the necessity for the courts to define "moderate livelihood" on a case-by-case basis, taking into account geographical area, economic realities, and the nature of the available resources at stake.[4]

In *Marshall,* the court noted that the catch limits that could produce a moderate livelihood for individual Mi'kmaq families at present-day standards can be established by regulations that can be enforced without violating any treaty rights. In this way, the regulations would accommodate treaty rights rather than infringe them, and would, therefore, not have to be justified under the *Badger* test.[5] However, the real issue is that the court did not define what a reasonable catch limit would be for an individual Mi'kmaq family. It is most likely that the present fishery resource is insufficient to allow for such broad catch limits to be applied to all Mi'kmaq families and still meet conservation needs and balance the demands of the non-Aboriginal fishery.

Although this is a brief reference by the court, the notion that a government could enact regulations that limit the exercise of a treaty fishing right and that would not have to be justified is significant. This goes back to earlier references that treaty rights are not absolute rights. Thus, the court appears to be saying that treaty rights, by themselves, may have a limited scope imposed upon them by government, so long as government has been sensitive to what it believes are the rights possessed. Therefore, it is only those actions or decisions that are not respectful of Aboriginal or treaty rights that must be justified. The Supreme Court seemed to suggest a similar line of reasoning in

2   *R. v. Marshall (Marshall No. 2),* [1999] 3 S.C.R. 533 at para. 24.

3   *Marshall No. 1, supra* note 1 at para. 59, citing with approval *R. v. Van der Peet* (1993), 80 B.C.L.R. (2d) 75 at 126 (B.C.C.A.), and *R. v. Gladstone,* [1996] 2 S.C.R. 723 at para. 165.

4   *Marshall No. 1, ibid.* at para. 7.

5   See *R. v. Badger,* [1996] 1 S.C.R. 771 at paras. 96 and 97, wherein Cory J. affirmed the application of the *Sparrow* justificatory analysis (see *R. v. Sparrow,* [1990] 1 S.C.R. 1075 at 1113–21).

Sparrow, where the court noted the following with respect to the effect of section 35(1):

> The constitutional entitlement embodied in s. 35(1) requires the Crown to ensure that its regulations are in keeping with that allocation of priority. The objective of this requirement is *not to undermine Parliament's ability and responsibility with respect to creating and administering overall conservation and management plans* regarding the salmon fishery. The objective is rather to guarantee that those plans *treat* aboriginal peoples in a way ensuring that their rights are taken seriously. [Emphasis added][6]

The *Sparrow* analysis, however, also suggests a contrary view. That is, if there is an impairment of a right, then there is an infringement. Only when an infringement exists can the government justify its actions. *Marshall* seems to suggest that within the right itself some impairment can occur before government is required to justify any *excess* impairment. This will be a key element to look for in future decisions because as governments become more sophisticated in how to regulate Aboriginal and treaty rights, this potential new limitation on Aboriginal and treaty rights could have significant consequences.

The court also stated that the treaties and their benefits are local in nature and unless a new agreement with the Crown is reached, the exercise of these treaty rights is limited to the area traditionally used by the local community. The treaty rights do not belong to individuals, but are exercised with the authority of the local community to which the individual belongs.[7]

The court also noted, in *Marshall No. 2,* that certain unjustified assumptions were made by the Native Council of Nova Scotia regarding its interpretation of *Marshall* and so-called economic treaty rights on forestry, minerals, and natural-gas deposits offshore. Also, the Union of New Brunswick Indians suggested that any "gathering" contemplated in *Marshall No. 1* included harvesting of resources from the sea, the forest, and the land. The court made it clear that this interpretation of "gathering" was not considered by the court in its September 17, 1999, decision, and that negotiations with respect to resources such as lumber, minerals, or offshore natural-gas deposits would extend beyond the subject matter of the *Marshall* decision. The court underscored that treaty rights are capable of an evolution in their development, but that this evolution is limited and not absolute. Justice Binnie wrote: "While treaty rights are capable of evolution within limits, . . . their subject matter

---

6   *Sparrow, ibid.* at 1119.
7   *Marshall No. 2, supra* note 2 at para. 17.

(absent a new agreement) cannot be wholly transformed."[8] Thus the treaty right to gather does not include "anything and everything physically capable of being gathered."[9]

The court emphasized throughout both judgements the limit of the right adjudicated. Many non-Aboriginal fishers feared that the treaty right could be expanded, whereas many Aboriginal fishers hoped that *Marshall* could be used as the basis for a more expansive commercial fishery. The court dealt with this issue directly. Justice Binnie noted: "[T]his fear (or hope) is based on a misunderstanding of the narrow ambit and extent of the treaty right."[10] The treaty right recognized by the court is "a regulated right and can be contained by regulation within its proper limits."[11] To date, though, the federal Department of Fisheries and Oceans seems reluctant to regulate and appears to be placing its attention on expanding the Aboriginal commercial fishery without creating a regulatory regime that is sensitive to Aboriginal and treaty rights and balanced with the rights and interests of other Canadians.

In *Marshall No. 2,* the court confirmed that licensing schemes, such as fishery or wildlife licences, are not automatically an unjustified limitation on the exercise of treaty rights. The justification of a licensing requirement depends upon the facts.[12] The court cited with approval an excerpt from its decision in *R. v. Nikal* (1996)[13] as follows:

> It is said that a licence by its very existence is an infringement of the aboriginal right since it infers that government permission is needed to exercise the right and the appellant is not free to follow his own or his band's discretion in exercising that right. This position cannot be correct. . . . The ability to exercise personal or group rights is necessarily limited by the rights of others. The government must ultimately be able to determine and direct the way in which these rights should interact. Absolute freedom in the exercise of even a *Charter* or constitutionally guaranteed aboriginal right has never been accepted, nor was it intended. . . . Absolute freedom without any restriction necessarily infers a freedom to live without any laws. Such a concept is not acceptable in our society.

This is a clear statement affirming government's authority to regulate and,

8   *Ibid.* at para. 19. See also *Marshall No. 1, supra* note 1 at para. 58.
9   *Marshall No. 2, ibid.* at para. 20.
10 *Marshall No. 1, supra* note 1 at para. 57.
11 *Ibid.* at para. 58.
12 *Marshall No. 2, supra* note 2 at para. 28.
13 *R. v. Nikal,* [1996] 1 S.C.R. 1013 at paras. 91 and 92; see *Marshall No. 2, ibid.* at para. 27.

perhaps, its duty to regulate. *Nikal, Marshall, Adams* (1996),[14] and others all support this same theme.

The court also made clear that its September 17, 1999, judgement did not question the validity of the *Fisheries Act* or any of its provisions. It did say, however, that in the absence of any justification of the regulatory prohibitions contained in the *Fisheries Act,* the appellant would be entitled to an acquittal because these regulatory prohibitions interfered with the appellant's treaty right to fish. The court also attempted to define what it meant by the treaty right being a limited right in its nature. For example, the court stated that catch limits that would produce a moderate livelihood for an individual Mi'kmaq at present-day standards could be established by regulation and enforced without violating any treaty rights.[15] Regulations could accommodate the treaty right, and these regulations would not constitute an infringement that would have to be justified under the *Badger* test.[16] The court found that only those regulatory limits that would place the Mi'kmaq harvest below that reasonably expected to produce a moderate livelihood would need to be justified.[17]

The essential theme that runs through all these limitations and much of what the court said is that there is a high onus on government to put its house in order with respect to the regulation and enforcement of fisheries and other areas so that governments can accommodate and consider Aboriginal and treaty rights. In *Marshall No. 2,* the court stated: "It is up to the Crown to initiate enforcement action in the lobster and other fisheries if and when it chooses to do so."[18] Indeed, the court outlined a number of specific authorities held by the federal government in the *Aboriginal Communal Fishing Licences Regulations,*[19] which impose conditions on the Aboriginal fishery, where justified. The court did not appear to state that these regulations are flawed on their face. Rather, the court appeared to suggest that these regulations may need to be amended to accommodate a limited commercial fishery.[20]

Ministerial Discretionary Authority

Nothing in the fishery regulations gives the minister direction on how he or she should exercise his or her discretionary authority respecting decisions that

---

14 *R. v. Adams,* [1996] 3 S.C.R. 101.
15 *Marshall No. 1, supra* note 1 at para. 61.
16 *Marshall No. 2, supra* note 2 at para. 36
17 *Ibid.* at para. 39.
18 *Ibid.* at para. 15.
19 *Aboriginal Communal Fishing Licences Regulations,* SOR/93-332.
20 *Marshall No. 2, supra* note 2 at para. 34.

may affect treaty rights. The court suggested that the minister's discretionary authority should be expressed in a manner that provides the minister with clear directions on how to exercise his or her authority in a way that respects treaty rights. In *R. v. Adams* (1996), Chief Justice Lamer noted:

> In this instance, the regulatory scheme subjects the exercise of the appellant's Aboriginal rights to a pure act of Ministerial discretion, and sets out no criteria regarding how that discretion is to be exercised. . . . Parliament may not simply adopt an unstructured discretionary administrative regime which risks infringing Aboriginal rights in a substantial number of applications in the absence of some explicit guidance. If a statute confers an administrative discretion which may carry significant consequences for the exercise of an Aboriginal right, the statute or its delegate regulations must outline specific criteria for the granting or refusal of that discretion which seek to accommodate the existence of Aboriginal rights.[21]

In *Marshall No. 2*, the court stated that "specific criteria must be established" so that the minister can exercise his or her discretionary authority in a proper manner.[22] *Marshall* is significant in that it recognizes a further limitation to a legislative grant of absolute discretion beyond that contained in the purposes of the enabling legislation.

The issue of the exercise of ministerial discretionary authority was considered in *Nunavut Tunngavik Inc. v. Canada (Min. of Fisheries and Oceans)* (1997)[23] and *Nunavik Inuit v. Canada (Min. of Canadian Heritage)* (1998).[24] In *Nunavut Tunngavik Inc.* (N.T.I.), the issue concerned the minister of Fisheries and Oceans' decision on turbot quotas in an area within the Nunavut Land Claims Agreement (Nunavut Agreement). N.T.I. argued that the minister had failed to consider the advice of the Nunavut Wildlife Management Board (NWMB), which was constituted under the Nunavut Agreement. After a review of the Nunavut Agreement, Judge Campbell held that the reference to consultation in that agreement must mean "*meaningful inclusion* of the NWMB in the Governmental decision-making process before *any* decisions are made"

---

21 *Ibid.* at para. 64. In *R. v. Adams, supra* note 14 at paras. 52 and 54. See also *Marshall No. 2, supra* note 2 at para. 33, where *Adams* is cited with approval regarding the need for guidelines to assist the exercise of ministerial discretionary authority.

22 *Ibid., Marshall No. 2,* at para. 33.

23 *Nunavut Tunngavik Inc. v. Canada (Min. of Fisheries and Oceans),* [1997] 4 C.N.L.R. 193 (F.C.T.D.).

24 *Nunavik Inuit v. Canada (Min. of Canadian Heritage),* [1998] 4 C.N.L.R. 68 (F.C.T.D.).

[emphasis in original].[25] Judge Campbell held that the minister cannot simply receive and examine the advice and recommendations given by the NWMB. He concluded that the relationship between the minister and the NWMB was intended to be "*mandatory, close, cooperative and highly respectful*" [emphasis in original].[26] The message from the court was that government must take a proactive stance when "considering" Aboriginal interests and advice with respect to decisions and actions that may adversely affect Aboriginal people.

The Federal Court of Appeal, while agreeing with the trial court's conclusion to set aside the minister's decision, referred the matter back to the minister for reconsideration. The Appeal Court focussed on whether the minister had given special consideration to the adjacency and economic dependence principles required by the Nunavut Agreement, or whether the minister had misconstrued these principles in their application. The court also rejected a number of the trial judge's conclusions regarding the interpretation given to the relevant provisions of the Nunavut Agreement. The court stressed that it would not "second guess" the minister.[27] The court balanced this by noting that "the Minister's discretion in section 7 of the *Fisheries Act* is no longer absolute when the exercise of that discretion affects the wildlife and the marine areas of the [Nunavut Settlement Area] and the wildlife management."[28]

N.T.I. again challenged the authority of the minister of the Department of Fisheries and Oceans in the decision of *Nunavut Tunngavik Inc.* v. *Canada (Min. of Fisheries and Oceans)* (2000).[29] In that decision, Judge Blais dismissed an application similar to the one noted above made by N.T.I. and stated that the minister had erred in failing to apply the principles set out in the Nunavut Agreement. In dismissing the application, Judge Blais noted:

> [T]he authority of the NWMB was in the nature of advice and recommendations and the minister did look into it. It was within the minister's discretion and within the limits of the Agreement to take into consideration a number of factors including growth and decline in stock. . . . Finally, in view of the situation that prevails in the Atlantic affecting every eastern province and territory with respect to Atlantic fishery, the end result provided by the minister's decision on quota allocation can not be seen as unfair in view of the important decline in stock.[30]

---

25 *Nunavut Tunngavik, supra* note 23 at 211.

26 *Ibid.* at 210.

27 *Nunavut Tunngavik Inc.* v. *Canada (Min. of Fisheries and Oceans)* (1998), 162 D.L.R. (4th) 625 at 634 (F.C.A.).

28 *Ibid.* at 633.

29 *Nunavut Tunngavik Inc.* v. *Canada (Min. of Fisheries and Oceans),* [2000] 3 C.N.L.R. 136 (F.C.T.D.); affirmed [2001] 1 C.N.L.R. iv (F.C.A.).

30 *Ibid.* at paras. 91, 92, and 94 (F.C.T.D.).

The difference in this decision was that there was substantial evidence that the minister took into account all the relevant considerations and disseminated clearly that such consideration occurred. Additionally, there was a clear paper trail that showed the minister receiving and considering the applicable advice. The Federal Court of Appeal affirmed the trial court's decision and stated:

> [B]ecause of the classically polycentric nature of the allocation of a fixed quota among competing groups of fishers, the proper standard of review of the exercise of the Minister's discretion is patent unreasonableness. The Minister's decision easily withstands that test. The decision has a rational basis, because it was open to the Minister to determine the quota by reference to quotas historically allocated for turbot fishing in Davis Strait, rather than to the allocation of quotas in other zones in the Atlantic fishery.[31]

In *Kadlak* v. *Nunavut (Min. of Sustainable Development),*[32] an Inuit applicant sought judicial review of the minister of Sustainable Development's decision to disallow the NWMB's decision related to hunting polar bears. The minister's decision was quashed and the matter was referred back to the minister. Justice Kilpatrick stated:

> Section 35(1) . . . does not promise that the rights under the Nunavut Land Claims Agreement will be immune from all forms of government regulation. It does require the territorial and federal Crown to justify any decision that impacts adversely upon the promises made and rights conferred in the Land Claims Settlement.[33]

As in the *N.T.I.* and *Nunavik* decisions, the court clearly placed the onus on government to be prepared to justify its regulations. For governments in the Maritimes, like other governments in Canada, effort must be made to modify and improve decision-making processes to allow for court scrutiny and to be able to meet the test of justification.

These decisions show the minister initially making a decision that is unclear and not able to be demonstrably justified. The decisions then illustrate a ministerial decision on the same matter being upheld. The difference is in the process of arriving at the decision and is in keeping with the comments made

---

31 *Ibid.* at para. 4, v (F.C.A.).
32 *Kadlak* v. *Nunavut (Min. of Sustainable Development),* [2001] 1 C.N.L.R. 147 (Nun. Ct. J.).
33 *Ibid.* at para. 22.

by the Supreme Court in *Marshall,* that is, requiring government to be held accountable for its decisions and to be prepared to justify those decisions when they affect the rights of Aboriginal people. These decisions clearly indicate that when governments put *effort* into changing their administrative and decision-making processes to expand transparency and reasonableness, their decisions can withstand judicial scrutiny. Although they do not reference *Marshall,* these decisions in many ways exemplify the principles for which *Marshall* stands.

Another case that illustrates the duty on government to consult properly when negotiating treaties is *Nunavik Inuit* v. *Canada (Min. of Canadian Heritage)* (1998).[34] In this case, Appeal Court Justice Richard dealt with a request for a declaration by the Nunavik Inuit that the minister of Canadian Heritage ought not establish a national park. The proposed boundaries of the park would encompass 80 percent of the territory that was then under treaty negotiations between the Nunavik Inuit and the federal government. The court held that the Government of Canada had a duty to consult with the Nunavik Inuit prior to establishing a national park in northern Labrador, and that such a duty to consult included both a duty to inform and a duty to listen. According to the court, prior to the establishment of a national park in northern Labrador, the government also had a duty to consult and to negotiate in good faith with Nunavik Inuit with respect to the Inuit claims to Aboriginal rights in certain parts of Labrador. Finally, the court concluded that if the Governments of Canada and Newfoundland and Labrador reached an agreement to establish a national park before a final treaty was settled with the Nunavik Inuit, those lands were to be set aside as a national park pending land claims negotiations.[35]

Provincial Jurisdiction

One criticism that has been levelled against the Supreme Court regarding *Marshall* and other decisions is that the court has allowed provincial governments to infringe Aboriginal rights, when these rights are at the heart of federal jurisdiction as provided for in section 91(24) of the *Constitution Act, 1867.*[36] Additionally, the court has also appeared to put non-constitutionally protected interests on an equal footing with Aboriginal and treaty rights protected under section 35, by claiming that Aboriginal and treaty rights may be

---

34 *Nunavik Inuit, supra* note 24.
35 *Ibid.* at 103.
36 *Constitution Act, 1867* (U.K.), 30 & 31 Vict., c. 3 (R.S.C. 1985, App. II, No. 5); see K. McNeil, "Aboriginal Title and the Division of Powers: Rethinking Federal and Provincial Jurisdiction" (2000) 61:2 Sask. L. Rev. 431.

balanced with other competing public interests.[37] On their face, these arguments make sense. How can provincial legislatures legislate in areas of federal jurisdiction and how can non-constitutionally protected interests, such as the interests of non-Aboriginal fishers, be *balanced* with Aboriginal and treaty rights? I suggest the answer lies within section 35(1) itself and in the definition that the Supreme Court attributed to the phrase "recognized and affirmed."

Section 35(1) reads: "The existing aboriginal and treaty rights of the aboriginal peoples of Canada are hereby recognized and affirmed." In *R. v. Sparrow* (1990),[38] the Supreme Court, in a unanimous decision, defined the phrase "recognized and affirmed." It is important to remember that prior to *Sparrow* a major preoccupation of scholars in this area was to understand what section 35 meant and what its effects would be. *Sparrow* was the first decision in which the Supreme Court gave views on its meaning.[39] The court noted that "rights that are recognized and affirmed are not absolute."[40] The court reached this conclusion after considering three factors: the history of the entrenchment of section 35 in 1982, general constitutional interpretative principles, and principles relating to Aboriginal rights.[41] The court noted that the words "recognized and affirmed" place "some restraint on the exercise of sovereign power"[42] and give "a measure of control over government conduct and a strong check on legislative power."[43] The court also concluded that although Aboriginal and treaty rights are protected by section 35(1), they are not subject to section 1 of the *Canadian Charter of Rights and Freedoms,* which reads:

> The *Canadian Charter of Rights and Freedoms* guarantees the rights and freedoms set out in it subject only to such reasonable limits prescribed by law as can be demonstrably justified in a free and democratic society.[44]

This does not mean that any law or regulation affecting Aboriginal rights will "automatically be of no force or effect."[45] Also, the rights in the *Charter* are defined in absolute terms as "rights" (save for section 1) and "guarantees" the

---

37 See, for example, K. McNeil, "How Can Infringements of the Constitutional Rights of Aboriginal Peoples be Justified?" (1997) 8:2 Const. Forum 33.

38 *R. v. Sparrow,* [1990] 1 S.C.R. 1075.

39 *Ibid.* at 1082. The court noted: "This appeal requires this Court to explore for the first time the scope of s. 35(1)."

40 *Ibid.* at 1109.

41 *Ibid.* at 1106.

42 *Ibid.* at 1109.

43 *Ibid.* at 1110.

44 *Canadian Charter of Rights and Freedoms,* Part I of the *Constitution Act, 1982,* Sched. B. to the *Canada Act 1982* (U.K.), 1982, c. 11.

45 *Sparrow, supra* note 38 at 1109.

rights contained therein as opposed to "recognizing and affirming" those rights. Legislation affecting Aboriginal and treaty rights will be valid if it can be justified according to the test laid out in *Sparrow* and enhanced in subsequent decisions.[46]

The issue of provincial jurisdiction to regulate Aboriginal and treaty rights has also arisen within the context of section 88 of the *Indian Act*.[47] A number of commentators have argued that section 88 is of "doubtful constitutional validity."[48] The primary basis for this argument appears to rest on section 88's lack of reference to Aboriginal rights and title, thereby suggesting that provincial laws of general application cannot affect matters central or incidental to the exercise of these rights or to the nature of Aboriginal title.[49] These positions also appear to rely on Chief Justice Lamer's comments in *Delgamuukw* on the provincial authority to extinguish Aboriginal rights. Indeed, it is true that there is no reference to either Aboriginal rights or title in section 88. However, I maintain that this reference does not need to be included. One must keep in mind that before 1982, it was necessary to reference treaty rights explicitly, otherwise they could be overridden by ordinary laws. After 1982, any reference to treaty rights, Aboriginal rights, or Aboriginal title is redundant to the extent that these rights are constitutionally recognized and affirmed within section 35. Their constitutional status has changed absolutely since 1982. Provincial, and federal, legislation is subject to the Constitution, including section 35. However, nothing in section 91(24) or section 35 takes away or erodes provincial legislative authority. Section 88 is a valid incorporation by reference of provincial laws into the federal realm. It does not affect the constitutional entrenchment of Aboriginal and treaty rights, but it does mean that provinces, within the parameters of their constitutional authority, can infringe these rights, when justified. Provincial legislative authority continues to exist and is subject to federal jurisdiction, to the *Charter,* and to section 35.

The particular passages from *Delgamuukw* that are most relevant to this

---

46 See chapter 3.

47 See chapter 2.

48 See B. Slattery, "First Nations and the Constitution: A Question of Trust" (1992) 71 Can. Bar Rev. 261 at 285; K. McNeil, "Aboriginal Title and Section 88 of the *Indian Act*" (2000) 34:1 U.B.C. Law Rev. 159; and K. Wilkins, "'Still Crazy After All These Years': Section 88 of the *Indian Act* at Fifty" (2000) 38(2) Alta. L. Rev. 458 at 503.

49 In *Delgamuukw v. British Columbia,* [1997] 3 S.C.R. 1010 at para. 183, Lamer C.J. wrote: "I see nothing in the language of the provision [s. 88] which even suggests the intention to extinguish aboriginal rights. Indeed, the explicit reference to treaty rights in s. 88 suggests that the provision was clearly not intended to undermine aboriginal rights."

discussion are those relating to whether the Province of British Columbia had the power to extinguish Aboriginal rights after 1871, either under its own jurisdiction or by operation of section 88 of the *Indian Act*.[50] In particular, the following excerpt from *Delgamuukw* is helpful. Chief Justice Lamer wrote:

> I conclude with two remarks. First, even if the point were not settled, I would have come to the same conclusion. The judges in the court below noted that separating federal jurisdiction over Indians from jurisdiction over their lands would have a most unfortunate result—the government vested with primary constitutional responsibility for securing the welfare of Canada's aboriginal peoples would find itself unable to safeguard one of the most central of native interests—their interest in their lands. Second, although the submissions of the parties and my analysis have focused on the question of jurisdiction over aboriginal title, in my opinion the same reasoning applies to jurisdiction over any aboriginal right which relates to land. . . . Those relationships with the land, however, may be equally fundamental to aboriginal peoples and, for the same reason that jurisdiction over aboriginal title must vest with the federal government, so too must the power to legislate in relation to other aboriginal rights in relation to land. . . . [T]he Court has held that section 91(24) protects a "core" of Indianness from provincial intrusion, through the doctrine of interjurisdictional immunity. It follows, at the very least, that this core falls within the scope of federal jurisdiction over Indians. That core, for reasons I will develop, encompasses aboriginal rights, including the rights that are recognized and affirmed by section 35(1). Laws which purport to extinguish those rights therefore touch the core of Indianness which lies at the heart of section 91(24), and are beyond the legislative competence of the provinces to enact. The core of Indianness encompasses the whole range of aboriginal rights that are protected by section 35(1). Those rights include rights in relation to land; that part of the core derives from section 91(24)'s reference to "Lands reserved for the Indians". But those rights also encompass practices, customs and traditions which are not tied to land as well; that part of the core can be traced to federal jurisdiction over "Indians". Provincial governments are prevented from legislating in relation to both types of aboriginal rights.[51]

What is interesting about Chief Justice Lamer's comments is that they (1) focus on the power of the province to extinguish aboriginal rights and title, (2) focus on the ability of provinces to *legislate* with respect to Aboriginal rights, including Aboriginal title, and (3) in no manner contradict earlier Su-

---

50 *Ibid.* at paras. 172–83.
51 *Ibid.* at paras. 176, 177, and 178.

preme Court of Canada statements with respect to provincial governments' ability to justifiably interfere with and infringe existing Aboriginal and treaty rights.

Provincial and federal legislation is subject to the Constitution, including section 35. Nothing in section 91(24) or section 35 takes away or erodes provincial legislative authority,[52] *except* to confirm that provinces cannot legislate in areas of exclusive federal jurisdiction and that provincial jurisdiction is subject to existing Aboriginal and treaty rights in section 35(1), subject to being justified.[53]

Section 88 is a valid incorporation by reference of provincial laws into the federal realm. Section 88 does not affect the constitutional entrenchment of Aboriginal and treaty rights, but does extend provincial legislative applicability to Indians and their lands. Provincial legislative authority continues to exist and is subject to areas of federal jurisdiction, the *Charter,* and section 35 rights.

Put another way, Aboriginal rights exist in two realms: constitutional and jurisdictional. In the constitutional realm, Aboriginal rights are "recognized and affirmed" and serve as a major check on the exercise of the Crown's legislative authority (federal *and* provincial). Within this context, provincial governments must consider, and may justifiably infringe, Aboriginal rights. In the jurisdictional realm, Aboriginal rights remain part of federal common law, which affirms, as in *Delgamuukw,* that only the federal government possesses the authority to legislate with respect to Aboriginal rights. This jurisdictional realm is particularly important when examining whether Aboriginal rights have been extinguished (prior to 1982), since prior to 1982 only the federal government possessed that authority. Although these two realms—constitutional and jurisdictional—are related, they are nevertheless distinct. It is this dichotomy in the nature of Aboriginal rights, existing within both section 91(24) and section 35(1), that has caused confusion among commentators and lower and appellate courts. These concepts are not contradictory, but are rather simply the *balancing* of provincial legislative authority with existing Aboriginal and treaty rights.

---

52 Aboriginal rights may be infringed by federal (see *R.* v. *Sparrow, supra* note 38) and provincial (see *R.* v. *Côté,* [1996] 3 S.C.R. 139) governments; see *Delgamuukw, supra* note 49 at para 160.

53 In *R.* v. *Côté,* [1996] 3 S.C.R. 139 at para. 74, the court noted: "[I]t is quite clear that the *Sparrow* test applies where a provincial law is alleged to have infringed an aboriginal or treaty right in a manner which cannot be justified. . . . The text and purpose of s. 35(1) do not distinguish between federal and provincial laws which restrict aboriginal or treaty rights, and they should both be subject to the same standard of scrutiny."

As for provincial intrusion into federal jurisdiction, I believe that the Supreme Court has made a distinction in its decisions between legislation that attempts to legislate with respect to Indians and laws of general application that, although affecting Indians, do not single them out. This latter type of provincial legislation is lawful even though it affects Aboriginal and treaty rights because it does not purport to legislate Indians directly. It is important to recognize that in *Sparrow* the court stated that section 35(1) "affords aboriginal peoples constitutional protection against provincial legislative power." I believe that this means that Aboriginal and treaty rights may not be used as a reason to negate the federal legislative jurisdiction outlined in section 91(24) of the *Constitution Act, 1867.*

I also maintain that, based on the Supreme Court's direction to date and its interpretation of section 35, provincial legislatures could enact legislation that attempts to deal with the provincial role of maintaining the honour of the Crown and the duty to consult in matters that may affect Aboriginal and treaty rights. Although the drafting of such provisions would be complex, they are, nevertheless, a realistic and necessary result of the Supreme Court's direction to all governments. The Supreme Court affirmed this, in part, in *Marshall No. 2,* where it stated with respect to the regulatory authority of the Crown:

> The Court was thus most explicit in confirming the regulatory authority of the federal *and provincial governments* within their respective legislative fields to regulate the exercise of the treaty right [subject to justification]. [Emphasis added][54]

Thus, when one examines the Supreme Court's initial understanding and definition of section 35(1) and the operative words "recognized and affirmed," it ought not come as any surprise that the court is willing to allow infringements of Aboriginal and treaty rights that may be justified and also to allow a "balancing" of interests between Aboriginal and treaty rights and the interests of others in Canadian society. In *Badger* (1996), [55] the Supreme Court cited with approval the Ontario Court of Appeal decision of *R.* v. *Agawa* (1988),[56] where Justice Blair stated: "Rights do not exist in a vacuum and the exercise of any right involves a balancing with the interests and values involved in the rights of others."

The court noted in *Sparrow:*

> While it [constitutional protection] does not promise immunity from government regulation in a society that, in the twentieth century, is increasingly

---

54 *Marshall No. 2, supra* note 2 at para. 24.
55 *Badger, supra* note 5 at para. 80.
56 *R.* v. *Agawa,* [1988] 3 C.N.L.R. 73 at 89–90 (Ont. C.A.).

more complex, interdependent and sophisticated, and where exhaustible resources need protection and management, it does hold the Crown to a substantive promise.[57]

Criticism of *Marshall* or the Supreme Court's other decisions since *Sparrow*
regarding the Crown's ability to regulate and justify its actions must begin
with *Sparrow*.

Practical Measures

The Supreme Court, and other courts, has provided some comments on how
governments can improve their regulatory regimes as they relate to the rights
of Aboriginal people. Based upon a review of these decisions, the following
can be ascertained:

1. Discretionary authority conferred by statute must outline specific criteria
    for the granting or refusal of that discretion when Aboriginal or treaty
    rights may be affected.
2. Where discretionary authority is exercised and where Aboriginal or treaty
    rights may be affected, governments must always be prepared to explain
    their decisions in a justifiable and transparent manner.
3. Regulations that, at their core, affect Aboriginal or treaty rights, such as
    hunting or fishing, must be drafted so that they are clear and unambigu-
    ous in their meaning and intent. That is, if the goal is safety, conserva-
    tion, or some other compelling public interest, then this should be stated
    clearly in the regulation.
4. Where it is clear that regulations may affect Aboriginal or treaty rights,
    the regulations should provide for a meaningful consideration of these
    rights and a mechanism to disseminate that such consideration occurred.
5. Regulations that accommodate Aboriginal and treaty rights, such as set-
    ting catch limits that provide a "moderate livelihood" for Mi'kmaq (which
    was the issue in *Marshall*) do not require justification since they would
    not infringe any rights, although how this principle would apply to rights
    other than fishing is unclear.

The above are a few examples of what could be done to meet the standard of justification the Supreme Court has imposed on governments. It is
true that these suggestions would require a wholesale re-examination of thou-
sands of pages of laws and regulations, but this is the onus that the courts
have placed on governments. It is important to note that although these suggestions may appear to impede governmental authority, quite the opposite is

---

57 *Ibid.* at 1110.

true. By re-tooling the existing regulatory regime, governments could significantly reduce their exposure to having their laws and decision-making processes overturned or deemed inapplicable when they affect Aboriginal people.

The Honour of the Crown

The Supreme Court's discussion of the honour of the Crown in *Marshall*
focussed on the interpretation of the events leading up to the 1760 treaty.
When it looked at the trade arrangement that had been made, the court held
that it had to be interpreted in a way that gave it meaning in light of promises
made by the Crown.[58] Both the majority and the dissenting judgements referred to the role of the honour of the Crown when interpreting treaties. Indeed, *Marshall* is one of a number of Supreme Court of Canada decisions
dealing with the honour of the Crown in the context of Aboriginal-Crown
relations. For example, in *R. v. Sparrow,* the Supreme Court stated:

> The way in which a legislative objective is to be attained must uphold the
> honour of the Crown and must be in keeping with the unique contemporary
> relationship, grounded in history and policy, between the Crown and Canada's
> aboriginal peoples.[59]

In *R. v. Badger,* the court noted: "In each case, the honour of the Crown is
engaged through its relationship with the Native people."[60]

As important as the concept of the honour of the Crown has been in the
development of recent Aboriginal jurisprudence, there appears to be a continuing question of what precisely the concept means. This is evidenced clearly
in the *Marshall* decision when one compares the majority decision with the
dissenting opinions. In the majority decision, Justice Binnie referred to the
honour of the Crown a number of times.[61] Early in the decision he wrote that
he would allow the appeal "because nothing less would uphold the honour
and integrity of the Crown in its dealings with the Mi'kmaq people to secure
their peace and friendship."[62] The majority decision noted that the honour of
the Crown may be used to amend deficiencies in the written record and, in the
case of *Marshall,* to attempt to make sense of the 1760 negotiations.[63] To
explain its position, the court cited *Badger:*

---

58 *Marshall No. 1, supra* note 1 at para. 52.
59 *R. v. Sparrow, supra* note 38 at 1110.
60 *Badger, supra* note 5 at para. 78.
61 *Marshall No. 1, supra* note 1 at paras. 4, 40, 43, 44, 49–52.
62 *Ibid.* at para. 4.
63 *Ibid.* at paras. 43 and 44.

[T]he honour of the Crown is always at stake in its dealings with Indian people. Interpretations of treaties and statutory provisions which have an impact upon treaty or aboriginal rights must be approached in a manner which maintains the integrity of the Crown. It is always assumed that the Crown intends to fulfil its promises. No appearance of "sharp dealing" will be sanctioned.[64]

The majority in *Marshall* equated the honour of the Crown with placing what the intention "ought" to have been on the Crown or, for that matter, on the Mi'kmaq as well. Keep in mind that no evidence was produced in *Marshall* to suggest that an explicit promise was made for hunting, fishing, gathering, or trading rights; such rights were inferred. This expansive interpretation of the honour of the Crown is new. Justice McLachlin affirmed that the honour of the Crown is presumed and must be upheld.[65] The dissenting opinion focussed on the fact that a right must first be found to exist before the question of a law derogating from that right can be examined.

There is another aspect to the notion of the "honour of the Crown," and that is that the Crown should be proactively examining its regulations *before* litigation is commenced. This kind of proactive action, I submit, is also part of the Crown's fiduciary duty and honour. The courts to date have been clear about the responsibilities that rest with governments. Governments have the authority to regulate, but they must do so in a manner that is respectful of, and sensitive to, Aboriginal and treaty rights. If governments continue to make decisions that do not take these rights into consideration or, in the alternative, refuse to make decisions that may affect these rights (for example, by not regulating the fishery but by simply issuing fishing licences to Aboriginal fishers, leaving the issue of regulation outstanding and uncertain), this can be interpreted as a breach of the Crown's fiduciary duty towards Aboriginal people and their rights. Some may argue that inaction and not putting regulations into place is respectful of Aboriginal and treaty rights, but this is not the case if the resource at issue is one that must be regulated, sooner or later. The lack of clear rules and a clear understanding of the nature of the regulation to be imposed is as problematic to Aboriginal resource users (in the *Marshall* case, fishers) as it is to non-Aboriginal resource users.

Thus, the honour of the Crown can place the onus on the Crown to determine how it is going to manage Aboriginal and treaty rights in Canada. In the *Marshall* case, the Crown argued that there were no treaty rights and even if there had been, they would have been "subject *ab initio* to regulations." No alternative argument was made in case a treaty right was held to exist. The

---

64   *Ibid.* at para. 49; *Badger, supra* note 5 at para. 41.
65   *Ibid.* at para. 110.

Crown should always be prepared to justify any and all of its statutes, regulations, and actions that may interfere with existing Aboriginal and treaty rights. In the eleven years since the *Sparrow* decision was released, governments have been slow in developing sophisticated and comprehensive schemes to ensure that their laws take into account existing Aboriginal and treaty rights. This may seem a high onus, but the courts have been clear that a failure to do so will usually result in a regulation, statute, or action not being justifiable. As has been noted by the Supreme Court, it was "always open to the Minister . . . to seek to justify the limitation on the treaty right because of the need to conserve the resource in question or for other compelling and substantial public objectives."[66]

In *Marshall,* the Crown also argued that no *Badger* justification was required. Although this is an interesting argument, one cannot help but question why the Crown would try to distinguish such a seminal decision as *Badger* on the interpretation of Maritime treaties. *Badger* made it clear that a *Sparrow*-type justification test is required when interpreting treaty rights, and to argue that these treaty rights would be subject to regulations rather than attempt to justify them simply does not consider the existing case law from the Supreme Court. It must become standard practice for governments in Canada to justify laws and regulations that may adversely affect Aboriginal people. If they are not in a position to justify those laws, then those laws need to be revisited. Given the *Marshall, Delgamuukw, Badger, Sparrow,* and other decisions, governments must address how they will justify infringements of Aboriginal and treaty rights. To address these matters comprehensively and proactively is simply a matter of good public policy.

Marshall has reaffirmed how important it is for governments to be proactive in justifying regulations that may affect Aboriginal and treaty rights. I submit that the honour and integrity of the Crown, as defined by the Supreme Court, demands this kind of proactive action. The Supreme Court has clearly outlined the types of governmental objectives that can justify the infringement of Aboriginal rights and title. These objectives include conservation and resource management and "other objectives"[67] and must be for a "compelling and substantial" purpose.[68] In *Gladstone,* the Supreme Court affirmed that there is a broad range of objectives that can justify the infringement of Aboriginal rights:

---

66 *Marshall No. 2, supra* note 2 at para. 19. Also, in *Badger,* for example, the Crown chose not to put arguments forward justifying their regulations. See *Badger, supra* note 5 at para. 98.

67 See *Sparrow, supra* note 38 at 1113.

68 *Ibid.* and *R. v. N.T.C. Smokehouse Ltd.,* [1996] 2 S.C.R. 672 at para. 97.

Because, however, distinctive Aboriginal societies exist within, and are a part of, a broader social, political and economic community, over which the Crown is sovereign, there are circumstances in which, in order to pursue objectives of compelling and substantial importance to that community as a whole (. . . Aboriginal societies are a part of that community), some limitation of those rights will be justifiable. . . . [L]imits placed on those rights are, where the objectives . . . are of sufficient importance to the broader community . . . *equally* a necessary part of that reconciliation. [Emphasis in original][69]

The court also noted that objectives such as economic and regional fairness and the historical reliance of non-Aboriginal people on the fishery, for example, satisfy the *Sparrow* justificatory standard.[70] In *Delgamuukw* (1997), the Supreme Court held that the justification standard outlined in *Sparrow* (1990) and *Gladstone* (1996) also applies to Aboriginal title cases.[71] As noted earlier, under *Delgamuukw,* the justification standard was further expanded and articulated by including such justifiable activities as agriculture, mining, forestry, hydroelectric power, general economic development, environmental protection, protection of endangered species, infrastructure development, and settlement. It is worth noting that the application of the justification standard requires a case-by-case analysis.[72]

Additionally, the Supreme Court, in *Gladstone,* noted that the priority of the Aboriginal fishery cannot be at the expense of other participants in the fishery. Rather a much more fluid and subjective approach was enunciated by the court:

Where the Aboriginal right is one that has no internal limitation then the doctrine of priority does not require that, after conservation goals have been met, the government allocate the fishery so that those holding an Aboriginal right to exploit that fishery on a commercial basis are given an exclusive right to do so. Instead, the doctrine of priority requires that the government demonstrate that, in allocating the resource, it has taken account of the existence of Aboriginal rights and allocated the resource in a manner respectful of the fact that those rights have priority over the exploitation of the fishery by other users. . . . The content of this priority—something less than exclusivity but which nonetheless gives priority to the Aboriginal right—must

---

69 *R. v. Gladstone,* [1996] 2 S.C.R. 723 at para. 73.
70 *Ibid.* at para. 75.
71 *Delgamuukw, supra* note 49 at para. 165.
72 *Ibid.*

remain somewhat vague pending consideration of the government's actions in specific cases.[73]

This approach to the doctrine of priority was reaffirmed in both *Marshall No. 1*[74] and *Marshall No. 2*.[75]

Unlike the other historical treaties in Canada, the Maritime treaties of peace and friendship did not require the First Nations to cede, release, or surrender their rights in return for enumerated rights. Therefore, although the *Marshall* decision affirms certain treaty rights for the Mi'kmaq, there may very well be, and most likely are, other rights in the Maritimes that are protected as Aboriginal rights within the meaning of section 35(1). This creates the unique and interesting situation of Aboriginal rights co-existing with treaty rights. This possibility may be made even more dynamic and complex by the continued existence of Aboriginal title in the Maritimes.[76]

Conclusion

The *Marshall* decisions are interesting examples of the development and evolution of Aboriginal and treaty rights law in Canada. Justice Binnie, on behalf of the majority, noted that there is a distinction to be made between a liberty or freedom enjoyed by all citizens and a right conferred by a specific legal authority, such as a treaty. When interpreting a liberty or freedom, one does so with the intent of understanding how the liberty or freedom may be limited in its application. For a right, the interpretation is affirmative: that is, the interpretation stresses what a right *is* as opposed to what it *is not*.

In Canada, most of the substantive case law surrounding Aboriginal and treaty rights has developed over the past decade or so. Of course, there was much case law prior to the 1990 *Sparrow* decision, but not within the ambit of constitutionally protected rights and freedoms as set out in the *Constitution Act, 1982*.[77] If one examines *Sparrow* (1990),[78] *Van der Peet* (1996),[79]

---

73 *Gladstone, supra* note 69 at paras. 62–63.
74 *Marshall No. 1, supra* note 1 at para. 57.
75 *Marshall No. 2, supra* note 2 at paras. 41–42.
76 See chapter 4.
77 Important pre-1990 decisions include *St. Catherine's Milling and Lumber Co.* v. *R.* (1889), 14 App. Cas. 46 (J.C.P.C.); *Hamlet of Baker Lake* v. *Min. of Indian Affairs and Northern Development*, [1979] 3 C.N.L.R. 17 (F.C.T.D.); *R.* v. *Guerin*, [1984] 2 S.C.R. 335; and *Calder* v. *British Columbia (A.G.)*, [1973] S.C.R. 313.
78 *Sparrow, supra* note 38.
79 *R.* v. *Van der Peet*, [1996] 2 S.C.R. 507.

Badger (1996),[80] and *Delgamuukw* (1997)[81] closely, one notices an expansive and liberal approach to this developing area of Canadian jurisprudence. It is as though Aboriginal and treaty rights were being treated or interpreted as freedoms or liberties. Given the number of basic and broad principles of law stated by the Supreme Court in these decisions, it is inevitable that the court will soon reach a stage where, in its application of these principles, it begins to apply these principles in a manner that places restrictions or limitations on Aboriginal and treaty rights. In so doing, the process of interpreting freedoms or liberties will become—and has indeed become—the process of interpreting rights conferred by a specific legal authority. So, although the court may have taken an expansive and liberal approach with respect to the historical evidence and in the development of broad interpretative principles, the application of the principles to date leads to a different conclusion. That is to say, the court has gone to great lengths in both *Marshall* decisions to put inherent limitations upon the treaty rights to fish, hunt, gather, and trade for necessaries.

The Supreme Court of Canada decisions over the past decade have, at times, caused confusion in this rapidly developing area of the law. Nevertheless, the court has made clear the standard expected of government and the importance of negotiated settlements. Governments in Canada must ensure that they have the mechanisms in place for consultation and for regulation of resources in a way that respects any Aboriginal and treaty rights that may exist. The purpose of including the term "may" is to state that governments need to be proactive in drafting and delivering legislation and regulations. This is the standard to which public governments ought to be held. It is a standard that not only Aboriginal peoples but also the general public should expect. Litigation is expensive and time consuming, and it does not resolve the matters that affect people, either Aboriginal or non-Aboriginal, on a daily basis. Governments, therefore, have an obligation to be clear and precise about how laws will apply to Aboriginal people in Canada.

The courts have given many suggestions to government on how to exercise their legislative authority in a manner that is consistent with Aboriginal and treaty rights. Examples include amending any legislated discretionary authority that may affect Aboriginal and treaty rights; being prepared to justify governmental actions based on factors such as conservation and other substantive and compelling public purposes; showing how Aboriginal and treaty rights have been carefully considered in decision-making that may adversely affect these rights; and establishing full and proper consultation regimes throughout governments' administrative structures. Governments have

---

80 *Badger, supra* note 5.
81 *Delgamuukw, supra* note 49.

been slow to respond to these suggestions. Until governments respond in a full and comprehensive way to these issues, decisions such as *Marshall* will continue.

Although there is an onus being placed on governments, it is one that ought to become standard. It is simply a cost of doing business in a post-1982 Canada. The problem for many public governments has been to identify Aboriginal issues as being pan-government in scope and not relegated to one distinct agency. Although there are numerous Aboriginal affairs departments and agencies in the federal, provincial, and territorial government structures, what is needed is a recognition that these agencies need real authority to begin what will be a massive change in how governments deal with Aboriginal and treaty rights. This is not to say that these are simply "Aboriginal affairs" type matters. Rather, these matters affect all elements of a functioning government, including fiscal considerations, natural resources, environmental management, governance, taxation, education, transportation, fisheries, et cetera. Until this dynamic shift takes place, Aboriginal and treaty rights decisions will continue to catch governments off-guard.

Although many Aboriginal people view *Marshall* as a victory in the broad sense, which to some extent is accurate, there is another side to the *Marshall* decision. This other side is that government has at its disposal a wide array of tools it can use to curtail the absolute expression of Aboriginal and treaty rights. However, the onus is on government to ensure that the mechanisms it uses to curtail or limit the absolute expression of Aboriginal or treaty rights are transparent, are used for purposes that are justifiable, and operate in ways that are respectful of Aboriginal and treaty rights.

To date, much of the focus of Aboriginal rights discourse has been in western Canada. *Marshall* has opened up the debate regarding Aboriginal and treaty rights in the Maritimes. The real challenge will be for governments and First Nations in the Maritimes to arrive at some common understanding on how these rights are going to be accommodated and reconciled within the fabric of the mainstream judicial and legislative structures. This is no easy challenge. For First Nations, it means coming to grips with the reality that their rights are not absolute and that some compromise is expected and required in order for these rights to be fully accommodated. For governments, it means taking a proactive stance in considering the effects of their legislation and actions on the Aboriginal and treaty rights that may exist. All Canada has an interest in what occurs in the Maritimes since it will, very likely, affect other parts of the country. Finally, for the Aboriginal and non-Aboriginal public, the challenge is to exercise patience and exert pressure on both governments and First Nations to work out mutually acceptable understandings of the incorporation of First Nations' interests in the laws and activities governing all people of the Maritimes.

Chapter 7

· · · · · ·

The Impact of *Marshall*

Introduction

The *Marshall* decisions[1] have dramatically increased the attention being paid to, and appreciation for, Aboriginal and treaty rights issues in the Maritimes. Prior to *Marshall,* the only decision of substance by the Supreme Court of Canada regarding treaty rights in the Maritimes was *Simon* (1985).[2] However, with this increased attention has also come increased anxiety. For non-Aboriginal people, their concerns relate to their livelihoods and the preservation of the fishery and other resources. Aboriginal people, on the one hand, have expressed jubilation over the *Marshall* decision but, on the other hand, have expressed concern over governments' willingness and ability to react. This chapter examines the judicial application of *Marshall* to date, events surrounding the Aboriginal and non-Aboriginal reaction to *Marshall*—particularly at Burnt Church, New Brunswick—and the federal response to *Marshall.*

Judicial Application of *Marshall*

The few decisions that have directly applied *Marshall* to date demonstrate that it is far too early to make any concrete analysis of *Marshall*'s long-term impact. Nevertheless, the following decisions illustrate how lower courts have attempted to "*Marshall*-proof" their reasoning, either by demonstrably illuminating the law on a particular subject matter in a manner that is comprehensive (*Shubenacadie*) or by dealing extensively with the historical and other evidence presented to the court (*Bernard*).

In *Shubenacadie Indian Band* v. *Canada (Min. of Fisheries and Oceans)*

---

1   *R.* v. *Marshall (Marshall No. 1),* [1999] 3 S.C.R. 456, and *R.* v. *Marshall (Marshall No. 2),* [1999] 3 S.C.R. 533 (reconsideration refused).
2   *R.* v. *Simon,* [1985] 2 S.C.R. 387.

(2000),[3] Justice Pelletier of the Federal Court, Trial Division considered an application by the Shubenacadie Indian Band (also known as the Indian Brook Band) for an interlocutory injunction enjoining the minister of Fisheries and Oceans from seizing the band's and its members' lobster traps, fishing vessels, equipment used to harvest lobsters, lobsters harvested by them, and from otherwise impeding with their lobster fishing and sales. The band referenced the *Marshall* decision as evidence of the Mi'kmaq right to engage in a livelihood fishery as opposed to a commercial fishery. In dismissing the motion, Justice Pelletier outlined the test for granting interlocutory injunctions, as set out in *Manitoba (A.G.)* v. *Metropolitan Stores Ltd.*[4] and *R.J.R.-MacDonald Inc.* v. *Canada.*[5] The test comprises three questions: (1) Is there a serious issue to be tried? (2) Would there be irreparable harm? and (3) What is the balance of convenience?[6]

The court was concerned with an interlocutory injunction amounting to an interlocutory declaration,[7] as considered in *Gould* v. *Canada (A.G.).*[8] Injunctions that determine rights, and therefore amount to a declaration of rights, should not be made on an interlocutory basis. Justice Pelletier determined that the application in *Shubenacadie* came within the *Gould* principle, in that it would likely be the final disposition of the matter and would affect rights beyond those of the immediate parties and therefore should not be made on an interlocutory basis. The court held that the underlying issue of the validity of the legislation should be tested on a full record in other proceedings and that the damage suffered by the band did not make success at the application hearing illusory. The rights in question stretch a long way into the future, and this case, therefore, did not come within the limited exceptions set out in *R.J.R.-MacDonald.*

Justice Pelletier stated that it was against the public interest to create a vacuum of authority with respect to the fishery resource—by impairing the

---

3   *Shubenacadie Indian Band* v. *Canada (Min. of Fisheries and Oceans)*, [2001] 1 C.N.L.R. 282 (F.C.T.D.).

4   *Manitoba (A.G.)* v. *Metropolitan Stores Ltd.*, [1987] 1 S.C.R. 110.

5   *R.J.R.-MacDonald Inc.* v. *Canada (A.G.)*, [1994] 1 S.C.R. 311.

6   "Balance of convenience" refers to examining and considering the interests of others in arriving at a decision.

7   An injunction is a judicial remedy that is made to require a party to refrain from doing a particular act. Injunctions are normally granted without the benefit of a full trial and complete evidence. Therefore, courts must be careful in granting such extraordinary relief and, as in this case, ensure that the granting of an injunction is not tantamount to a recognition of rights that normally would not exist without a full trial.

8   *Gould* v. *Canada (A.G.)*, [1984] 1 F.C. 1133 (Fed. C.A.).

authority of the Department of Fisheries and Oceans—and with respect to the necessary negotiations and consultations that will occur. He determined that to grant injunctive relief in this case would be to grant the same ability to every other band entitled to claim the benefit of the peace and friendship treaties. According to Justice Pelletier, determination of this matter can be made only after all the issues have been fully canvassed, including the issue of justification. In his opinion, the balance of convenience did not favour the band.

In a similar fact situation as *Shubenacadie*, *Barlow* v. *Canada (A.G.)*[9] dealt with Justice MacKay considering an application for declaratory and injunctive relief by Mr. Barlow, a New Brunswick Mi'kmaq who claimed that *Marshall* affirmed his right to fish under the 1760 treaty. Mr. Barlow sought to have the federal Department of Fisheries and Oceans (DFO) return his seized lobster traps and make a declaration affirming that DFO had breached Mi'kmaq treaty rights by enforcing existing fishery regulations. Justice MacKay held that the DFO actions did not meet the standard for imposing extraordinary relief as set out in *Manitoba (A.G.)* v. *Metropolitan Stores Ltd.*[10] and *R.J.R.-MacDonald Inc.* v. *Canada (A.G.).*[11]

Again in *Barlow*,[12] Justice Teitelbaum considered a motion by the Government of Canada to strike the application by Mr. Barlow and convert the application into an action. Mr. Barlow applied for judicial review, asserting that the minister of DFO had breached his rights under the 1760 treaty. The claim was based on *Marshall*'s affirmation of a treaty right to fish. The order was granted and the application was converted into a trial of an action—that is, a full trial rather than simply a hearing—because "the key test is whether the judge can see that affidavit evidence will be inadequate, not that trial evidence will be superior."[13] On the issue of the *Marshall* decision and the treaties referred to therein, Justice Teitelbaum stated:

> I am satisfied that the applicants [Mr. Barlow] have the obligation to be precise. It is not sufficient for the applicants to say "we are speaking of the treaty or treaties mentioned in *R.* v. *Marshall*," supra without producing the treaty or treaties relied upon or if not, at least by stating, in writing, what are the treaties relied upon.[14]

---

9 *Barlow* v. *Canada (A.G.)*, [1999] F.T.R. Uned. 748 (F.C.T.D.).
10 *Metropolitan Stores Ltd.*, *supra* note 4.
11 *R.J.R.-MacDonald Inc.*, *supra* note 5.
12 *Barlow* v. *Canada* (2000), 186 F.T.R. 194 (F.C.T.D.).
13 *Ibid.* at para. 76.
14 *Ibid.*

In *R. v. Muise (W.T.)* (2000),[15] Justice Glennie considered the conviction of a non-Aboriginal person who had assisted an Aboriginal hunter who claimed they both possessed hunting rights under the 1760 treaty and who relied upon the reasoning in *Marshall* as a defence. The court held that the trial judge correctly applied *Marshall,* in that *Marshall* provides no defence to a non-Aboriginal person assisting an Aboriginal person in exercising treaty rights, and in particular, no defence to a non-Aboriginal person purchasing meat hunted by an Aboriginal person. The rights of Aboriginal people can be exercised only by Aboriginal people and cannot be transferred to a non-Aboriginal person.

In another application of *Marshall,* Judge Lordon of the New Brunswick Provincial Court held that under treaties signed in 1761 and 1779, the Mi'kmaq of the Miramichi do not hold a treaty right to commercially harvest wood. In *R. v. Bernard,*[16] the accused, a Mi'kmaq registered under the *Indian Act,*[17] had been charged and convicted for unlawfully possessing timber contrary to section 67(1)(c) of the New Brunswick *Crown Lands and Forests Act.* Mr. Bernard claimed that he possessed treaty rights to commercially harvest and sell forest products and that these rights were part of his community's Aboriginal title. The Crown argued that no such rights existed, either as part of a treaty or under Aboriginal title. The Court of Queen's Bench affirmed the trial court's decision.

Applying the principles set out in *Marshall,* Judge Lordon held that the commercial harvesting of wood products is not an evolution of traditional Miramichi Mi'kmaq gathering activities and therefore is not protected as a treaty right under section 35 of the *Constitution Act, 1982.*[18] Although there was no evidence that the Miramichi Mi'kmaq ever ratified or signed the treaties made by some Mi'kmaq in 1749 and 1752, there was evidence that they signed a treaty at Belcher's farm in 1761. A subsequent treaty was signed by some Mi'kmaq in 1779, which renewed and ratified the 1761 treaty. The treaties of 1761 and 1779 were signed by the Miramichi Mi'kmaq as a hunting, fishing, and gathering society.

To interpret the right to gather as a right to participate in the wholesale uncontrolled exploitation of natural resources would change the terms of the treaty and completely alter the rights thereby conferred. No evidence was

---

15 *R. v. Muise (W.T.)* (2000), 227 N.B.R. (2d) 95 (N.B.Q.B.).

16 *R. v. Bernard,* [2000] 3 C.N.L.R. 184 (N.B. Prov. Ct.); affirmed by [2001] N.B.J. No. 259 (N.B.Q.B.).

17 *Indian Act,* R.S.C. 1985, c. I-5.

18 *Constitution Act, 1982,* Sched. B. to the *Canada Act 1982* (U.K.), 1982, c. 11, as am. by the *Constitution Amendment Proclamation, 1983,* R.S.C. 1985, App. II, No. 46 [am. ss. 25(b) and add. 35(3), 35(4), 35.1 and 37.1 and 54.1].

presented to suggest that the Mi'kmaq ever harvested or traded logs with either the British or French. Nothing in Belcher's Proclamation of 1762 provides a basis for such a treaty right. Likewise, no evidence was found to suggest that language posed a difficulty in the ability of the Mi'kmaq to understand and appreciate the written documents as well as the oral representations made prior to and after the treaties were signed. Finally, no evidence was presented suggesting that the harvesting of logs was part of the distinctive culture of the Miramichi Mi'kmaq at the time of contact.

Throughout the fifty-page decision, Judge Lordon paid special attention to expert testimony, oral evidence, and the historical evidence provided. He wrote:

> Given the cultural and historical context in which the Treaties of 1761 and 1779 were signed by the Mi'kmaq . . . as a hunting, fishing and gathering society, it is my opinion that to interpret the right to "gather" as a right to participate in the wholesale uncontrolled exploitation of natural resources would "alter the terms of the treaty" and "wholly transform" the rights therein contained.[19]

Using the test set out by the Supreme Court of Canada in *Delgamuukw* v. *British Columbia* (1997),[20] Judge Lordon held that the accused failed to establish that his ancestors occupied the land in question at the time the Crown asserted sovereignty over it. Judge Lordon held that the British had acquired sovereignty from Halifax to Quebec by 1759, although the area was not formally ceded by France until 1763. The *Royal Proclamation of 1763* did not reserve land for Indians in Nova Scotia. He also concluded that the *Proclamation* does not recognize reserved land unless it was reserved prior to the issuance of the *Proclamation*.[21] Judge Lordon stated that occasional uses of the land in question for hunting, fishing, and gathering purposes are not sufficient to establish Aboriginal title to the land. He also stated that the Mi'kmaq were not the only occasional visitors to the area and therefore were not the exclusive users of the area. The court therefore held that the accused failed to meet the standard for proving Aboriginal title. This appears to be contrary to *Delgamuukw*, wherein the Supreme Court held that exclusive possession does not mean other First Nations were not present. Rather, it means that the First Nation had the intent, or capacity, to possess exclusive occupation.[22] What this may mean in practical terms has yet to be determined.

---

19 *Bernard, supra* note 16 at 206 and para. 87.
20 *Delgamuukw* v. *British Columbia,* [1997] 3 S.C.R. 1010.
21 *Bernard, supra* note 16.
22 *Delgamuukw, supra* note 20 at para. 143.

In *Pictou* v. *Canada* (2000),[23] Justice Bowie considered an appeal by a number of Mi'kmaq who were appealing the minister of National Revenue's assessment for not collecting the Goods and Services Tax. The appellants operated a gas bar and convenience store on their reserve. They claimed they possessed treaty rights that excluded them from the operation of the federal *Excise Tax Act*. Justice Bowie, although giving favourable consideration to the Treaties of 1760–61 and the *Marshall* decision, found that neither the trade clause nor the promises of peace and friendship could support a finding that the Treaties of 1760–61 rendered the Mi'kmaq immune from taxation and legislation. Justice Bowie stated that the appellants' type of business did "not correspond, either quantitatively or qualitatively, to the type of trade that the signatories to the treaties could have had in contemplation in 1760."[24]

In *R.* v. *Marshall* (Stephen Marshall) (2001),[25] Provincial Court Judge Curran considered the case of thirty-five Mi'kmaq who had been charged with cutting timber on, and removing timber from, Crown land without authorization contrary to Nova Scotia's *Crown Lands Act*.[26] The Mi'kmaq offered as a defence that they possessed Aboriginal title to all Nova Scotia and that their Treaties of 1760–61 include a right to harvest forest products for sale. In adjudicating this case, Judge Curran extensively reviewed the history of the Mi'kmaq, but he spent little time in analyzing the Aboriginal title claim according to the test outlined in *Delgamuukw*.[27]

Judge Curran concluded that the Treaties of 1760–61 and Belcher's Proclamation of May 4, 1762, do not provide a basis for claiming a right to harvest wood. He referenced *Marshall No. 1* and *Marshall No. 2* in coming to this conclusion.[28] He dismissed using the Treaties of 1760–61 as a defence, stating that there was "no evidence the Mi'kmaq sold or traded timber up to the time of the treaties and no reason to believe they did."[29] In dealing directly with the inferences made by the Supreme Court in *Marshall*, Judge Curran stated:

> Trade in logging is not the modern equivalent or a logical evolution of
> Mi'kmaq use of forest resources in daily life in 1760 even if those resources
> sometimes were traded. Commercial logging does not bear the same relation
> to the traditional limited use of forest products as fishing for eels today bears

23 *Pictou* v. *Canada,* [2001] 1 C.N.L.R. 230 (T.C.C.).
24 *Ibid.* at para. 37.
25 *R.* v. *Marshall,* [2001] 2 C.N.L.R. 256 (N.S. Prov. Ct.); also discussed in chapter 3.
26 *Crown Lands Act,* R.S.N.S. 1989, c. 114, s. 29.
27 *Marshall, supra* note 25, see paras. 136–42.
28 *Ibid.* at paras. 90, 93–95.
29 *Ibid.* at para. 92.

to fishing for eels or any other species in 1760. Fishing is fishing whether or not the boats and equipment used to do it remains the same. Using a few trees to make things for personal use or incidental trade while leaving the surrounding forests standing is not the same as demolishing entire stands of forest for sales to sawmills or pulp-mills. Whatever rights the defendants have to trade in forest products are far narrower than the activities which gave rise to these charges.[30]

This last sentence is interesting in that Judge Curran left the door open to a right to a "moderate livelihood," but on a very limited and more personal basis than modern logging would typically allow.

Judge Curran dismissed using Belcher's Proclamation as the source for a treaty right to log since it did not apply to the cutting sites in question. Finally, it is also noteworthy that Judge Curran agreed with the conclusion noted earlier in this book that the *Royal Proclamation of 1763* applies to Nova Scotia.[31] This decision underscores the immense onus on First Nations to produce evidence to prove Aboriginal title and treaty rights, and the corresponding onus on courts to consider that evidence carefully and to refer to it appropriately when considering the merits of a case.

These decisions are an early indication of the application of *Marshall*. It would be premature to make any substantive comments after such a limited number of decisions. However, these decisions, like *Marshall*, emphasize government regulation and its need to be consistent and comprehensive.[32]

Burnt Church and Indian Brook[33]

After the release of the initial *Marshall* decision on September 17, 1999, there were immediate reactions from representatives for both Aboriginal and non-Aboriginal fishers. For Aboriginal fishers, the reaction was primarily one of jubilation at having their treaty rights acknowledged by Canada's highest court. For non-Aboriginal fishers, the reaction was one of confusion over

---

30 *Ibid.* at para. 95.
31 *Ibid.* at para. 107.
32 *R.* v. *Savard,* [2001] 1 C.N.L.R. 272 (C. Que. (Crim.)).
33 For a good discussion of a chronology of events after the release of the *Marshall* decision, see K. Coates, "The *Marshall* Crisis and East Coast Confrontations," *The Marshall Decision and Native Rights* (Montreal & Kingston: McGill-Queen's University Press, 2000) at 127–68; P. Barss Donham, "Lobster Wars" (February 2000) Canadian Dimension 26–28; P. Barss Donham, "Marshall Decision Book Needs Better Storyteller" (January/February 2001) Canadian Dimension 7; and D. Peacock, "Burnt Church Affair Needs Closer Look" (January/February 2001) Canadian Dimension 3.

what the treaty rights meant in practical terms and frustration over the lack of an immediate and coordinated federal response. A newspaper report quoted an internal federal Department of Justice document as stating that DFO "is concerned about the outcome of this case as it will affect their ability to regulate an already volatile situation surrounding the fishery on the East Coast."[34] Nowhere was the tension between these two groups more evident than at the Burnt Church First Nation in New Brunswick and at the Indian Brook First Nation in Nova Scotia.

In a display of frustration, on October 3, 1999, approximately 150 non-Aboriginal fishing boats made their way into Miramichi Bay—an area known for its lobster fishery—to protest Burnt Church members fishing there out of season for lobster. Although the protest was peaceful to begin with, it soon turned violent and hundreds of Aboriginal lobster traps were destroyed. While the other thirty-two First Nations in Atlantic Canada voted to halt lobster fishing for thirty days so the federal government could figure out how it would regulate the fishery in light of *Marshall,* Burnt Church and Indian Brook rejected this plan. Indian Brook (also known as Shubenacadie Indian Band) applied for an interlocutory injunction preventing DFO from enforcing the fishery regulations as they related to the lobster fishery, with a number of conditions. The application was rejected.[35] Justice Pelletier noted in that decision: "The unfortunate confrontations in St. Mary's Bay and at Burnt Church are a throbbing reminder that despite the Peace and Friendship treaties, we have some way to go to achieve that objective."[36]

The First Nations' moratorium on lobster fishing was withdrawn in October 1999. It was then that DFO decided to impose regulations on Burnt Church and Indian Brook. DFO imposed limits of six hundred lobster traps on Burnt Church and eight hundred lobster traps on Indian Brook. This did not end the tension. The frustration of many non-Aboriginal fishers was expressed in the Maritime Fishermen's Union November presentation to the Parliamentary Standing Committee on Fisheries and Oceans:

> We are left with communities that are torn apart, where tension remains high, where commercial fishermen's attitudes have hardened, where native people feel aggressed, and where no one looks good. We should equally recognize the high pressure position that many Band leaders have been put in as a result of native peoples' desire to exercise their rights.[37]

---

34 R. Mofina, "Ottawa Feared Native Fishing Rights Ruling" *Vancouver Sun* (9 July 2001) A6.
35 See *Shubenacadie Indian Band, supra* note 3.
36 *Ibid.* at para. 70.
37 Maritime Fishermen's Union, Presentation to the Parliamentary Standing Committee on Fisheries and Oceans (November 25, 1999) at 6.

DFO's response to this tension was to appoint James MacKenzie on October 15, 1999, as the chief federal representative to negotiate interim fisheries agreements with all thirty-four First Nations in the Maritimes. At the time of writing, thirty of the thirty-four have signed, or are in the process of finalizing, such agreements.[38] The intent of these agreements is not only to provide access to the food and commercial fishery, but also to provide training, gear, boats, and capacity-building opportunities. The initial round of negotiations had a budget of approximately $160 million. Additionally, some First Nations decided to place the interim fisheries agreements within the framework of their existing Aboriginal Fisheries Strategy Agreement, which gives them access to the food and commercial fishery. An Indian Affairs "Backgrounder" summarized the federal government's view with respect to the success of this initiative:

> To ensure the viability of the fishery, which is fully subscribed, the Department created space for this increased access through voluntary retirement of licences held by non-Aboriginal fishers. As a result of these initiatives, Mi'kmaq and Maliseet communities have increased their participation in the Atlantic fishery. More than 130 fishing vessels have been allocated to Aboriginal communities. There has been a 174% increase in the number of commercial lobster enterprises owned and operated by First Nations. Prior to the *Marshall* decision, First Nations held one tuna licence. They now have 10. In 2000, 5% of the shrimp in Quebec was harvested by First Nations, and 7% of the crab quota for the southern Gulf of St. Lawrence and Scotian Shelf was allocated to First Nation fishers.[39]

Although this demonstrates an effort to increase the Aboriginal involvement in the fishery, it does not deal with the issue that the courts have been raising to governments time and time again. That is, modify and revitalize the regulatory regime so that it is sensitive to and respects the rights of Aboriginal people in a manner that is sensitive to the interests of other Canadians.

Although the interim fisheries agreements substantially reduced the levels of frustration and anxiety that existed in the region, they did not meet the expectations of a number of First Nations, including Indian Brook and Burnt Church. In February 2000, DFO seized two crab-fishing boats from the members of Indian Brook. Between late July and early August 2000, seven more Indian Brook fishing vessels were seized and eighteen people were charged with illegally fishing lobster. By late August 2000, tension had reached an

---

38 Those not signing include the Bear River, Burnt Church, Indian Brook, and Afton First Nations.

39 Indian and Northern Affairs Canada, "Backgrounder: The *Marshall* Judgement and the Federal Government's Response" (B-HQ-01-09(149), February 2001) at 2.

extreme level at Burnt Church. After Burnt Church rejected an interim fishing agreement, the First Nation was raided again; this time over seven hundred traps were seized and four people were arrested.[40]

As of June 14, 2001, five new fishing agreements were signed with the Glooscap First Nation and Pictou Landing First Nation of Nova Scotia, the Redbank First Nation of New Brunswick, and le Nation micmaque de Gespeg and les Malicites de Viger of Quebec. These new agreements—with the exception of Pictou Landing agreement, which is for only one year—have three-year terms and similar terms and conditions as the earlier agreements. Along with these agreements, DFO has established an Industry Advisory Committee (comprising fishing, DFO, and First Nation representatives) to advise DFO on the implementation of its Licence Retirement Program, which was established to make room for First Nations fishers, in response to *Marshall*. As of April 3, 2001, the minister of DFO reported that 248 licence packages had been retired under this program or about 3 percent of the almost eight thousand core enterprises in the Maritimes and Quebec.[41] A separate sub-committee was established to advise on matters relating to Atlantic Canada.[42]

In an attempt to prevent a repeat of the fall 2000 confrontations on Miramichi Bay, the minister of DFO issued a short-term communal licence to Burnt Church, valid from August 20 to August 27, 2001. This licence permits Burnt Church to set up to five hundred lobster traps for food, social, and ceremonial purposes in a restricted zone in the vicinity of Burnt Church.[43] It does not allow commercial fishing (during the spring 2001 lobster season, DFO reported, Burnt Church utilized thirteen of seventeen commercial lobster licences available to the community). The restricted licence was later renewed from August 27 to October 20, 2001.[44] Although this restricted licence may have prevented confrontation for the short term, it raises serious concerns about DFO's long-term strategy to manage the fishery, in light of *Marshall*. That said, it is productive that DFO has reached an agreement with the Mari-

---

40 "Minister Says Bands Can Fish Without Federal Agreements" *[Saint John] Telegraph Journal* (8 April 2000) A3.
41 Canada, DFO, "Speaking Notes for the Hon. Herb Dhaliwal at the Standing Committee on Fisheries and Oceans (SCOFO): *Marshall* Update, House of Commons" (Ottawa: April 3, 2001) at 5.
42 Canada, DFO, "News Release: Dhaliwal Establishes Industry Advisory Committee for the Licence Retirement Program" (Ottawa: May 31, 2001).
43 Canada, DFO, "Statement by Herb Dhaliwal, Minister of Fisheries and Oceans— Update on Fisheries Affected by the Supreme Court's *Marshall* Decision" (Ottawa: August 20, 2001).
44 Canada, DFO, "Statement by Herb Dhaliwal, Minister of Fisheries and Oceans— Update on Fisheries Affected by the Supreme Court's *Marshall* Decision" (Ottawa: August 27, 2001).

time Fishermen's Union to establish the Community and Fisheries Relations Office in Richibucto, New Brunswick.

The events involving the Burnt Church First Nation and DFO exemplify the difficult situation that Aboriginal and treaty rights present in the Maritimes. Although *Marshall* did much to recognize and clarify the Mi'kmaq treaty right to fish, hunt, gather, and trade for necessaries, it also created a considerable amount of ambiguity about how the decision would be implemented. This ambiguity brings with it a considerable financial burden. CBC News reported that DFO expected to spend almost $2 million in relation to the *Marshall* decision for 2000–01.[45] Even before the decision came down, Marshall had proved to be expensive. A federal Department of Justice document is quoted as stating that the Department of Indian Affairs and Northern Development had contributed $30,512 in test-case funding to counsel for Mr. Marshall's Supreme Court appeal. In a similar situation, a Mi'kmaq charged with obstructing a fisheries officer during the Burnt Church stand-off referenced *Marshall* in his application for state-funded counsel. A stay of proceedings was ordered until state-funded counsel could be provided to assist in a constitutional defence based on a treaty right to fish.[46]

At the heart of the Burnt Church situation is whether the imposition of a limited number of lobster traps for Burnt Church is reasonable and justifiable for the purposes of their 1760 treaty right. Between July and September 2000, Burnt Church continued to set lobster traps, to obstruct fisheries officers, and to erect roadblocks. The situation escalated to more serious confrontations on the water, where Burnt Church fishing boats were rammed and sunk by DFO, and Aboriginal leaders involved in the fishery were arrested. At the time, both parties claimed they possessed the right to do what they were doing: Burnt Church claiming that *Marshall* affirmed their right to regulate their fishery, and DFO claiming that it possessed the authority to regulate the fishery, so long as the regulations were justifiable according to the *Marshall* decision.

On September 11, 2000, former Ontario premier Bob Rae agreed to act as mediator between the federal government and Burnt Church. Mediation has been used successfully in many situations where the parties involved have some apparent misunderstandings and differing perspectives; however, in this situation, the issue of mediation raised deeper questions about its appropriateness and potential for a long-term resolution. These issues involve many First Nations, are inherently complex, and deal with a scarce resource. In the end, Mr. Rae's involvement did not result in an agreement.[47] The reasons for

---

45 See "Costs of Enforcing Marshall Decision Revealed" (Toronto: cbc.ca, 14 March 2001).

46 See *R. v. Dedam,* [2001] N.B.J. No. 186 (N.B. Prov. Ct.).

47 T. Isaac, "No End in Sight" *The Globe & Mail* (19 September 2000) A15.

not reaching a mutually acceptable agreement are many. However, it is clear that the nature of these type of disputes go to the core of sovereign authority in Canada, the honour of the Crown in dealing with Aboriginal people, and respecting decisions from the Supreme Court of Canada.[48]

Part of the dilemma in dealing with judicial decisions concerning Aboriginal and treaty rights relates to their interpretation. Burnt Church, along with other First Nations, claims that *Marshall* includes something akin to a right to self-regulate their share of the fishery; DFO argues that the department holds the ultimate authority to regulate the fishery. The Supreme Court was clear in limiting the decision to the facts at hand. It did not deal with the issue of self-government, nor did it indicate that the federal government has the right to regulate the fishery: the authority of the federal government to regulate the Mi'kmaq treaty right to fish is limited to those actions that can be "justified." Although the definition of what is "justified" is unclear in *Marshall,* in a number of other decisions, the court has said that justification requires a compelling and substantive legislative objective, such as the conservation of a natural resource. The tension continues. As Professor Ken Coates has observed:

> Maritimers remain nervous about the *Marshall* decision, and little has been done to assure them that governments have the matter well in hand. Largely private negotiations between the federal government and individual First Nations move the agenda slowly towards a settlement, but the public has little sense of the broader picture that will emerge once agreements are in place. In this situation, with other cases moving through the courts and frustration building again among fishers and First Nations, public anxiety remains high.[49]

As discussed earlier, other Supreme Court of Canada decisions, including *Sparrow* (1990), *Adams* (1996), and *Delgamuukw* (1997), place the onus on government with respect to how it deals with Aboriginal people and their rights. *Marshall* is an additional example where the Supreme Court has squarely put the burden on government to get its house in order. However, the courts have also made it clear that if governments can justify their actions and if their decision-making process is clear and transparent, then Aboriginal and treaty rights may be justifiably infringed.

The Burnt Church situation raises interesting questions regarding the ability of the First Nation to self-regulate its fishery. The Supreme Court has

---

48 T. Isaac, "Where Does Burnt Church Go From Here?" *[Saint John] Telegraph Journal* (2 November 2000) B4.

49 Coates, *supra* note 33 at 128.

not yet dealt with this issue in a broad sense, let alone its specific application to Burnt Church. Although the unauthorized actions by Burnt Church got the attention of many, they did not result in any substantive move towards an affirmation of what the band members believe to be their rights. Despite the lack of a sensitive regulatory regime, DFO was exercising its jurisdiction within the scope of the *Marshall* decision in its response to Burnt Church. To test the limits of Burnt Church's jurisdiction requires either going back to the same court that affirmed their treaty right or negotiating a settlement.

The interim fisheries agreements that have been negotiated so far throughout the Maritimes may be a partial answer for Burnt Church because of the immediate and pragmatic effect of these agreements. However, whether an interim agreement is negotiated or not, the larger issues for Burnt Church and other First Nations remain outstanding: (1) how does self-government relate to treaty rights such as those outlined in the *Marshall* decision? and (2) what rights, if any, does Burnt Church possess with respect to self-regulating its share of the fishery? Interim agreements are expensive, they do not settle outstanding legal uncertainties, and they take energy and resources from ameliorating the regulatory vacuum that currently exists. They are at best a stopgap measure and should not be seen as a solution to the problem.

Negotiating a modern Mi'kmaq treaty is one possible solution to the situation in the Maritimes.[50] On January 10, 2001, representatives of the Governments of Nova Scotia and Canada and the First Nations chiefs of Nova Scotia signed a joint statement of intent and reaffirmation. The agreement calls on all three parties to appoint chief negotiators who will negotiate an umbrella agreement to guide the establishment of a more formal process to negotiate asserted Mi'kmaq Aboriginal and treaty rights and Aboriginal title. Like interim agreements and court decisions, an umbrella agreement can be only a partial solution. A modern treaty will not necessarily resolve all the issues, there will continue to be a need for regulatory reform to meet the terms and conditions of any negotiated settlement, and there needs to be political will from all parties to negotiate such a modern treaty. The problem for many First Nations is that although they want to negotiate modern treaties, they have not yet exhausted all the legal remedies available to them. This leaves many First Nations in the situation where additional litigation through the courts may expand or further interpret the rights they believe they possess. By negotiating too early, many First Nations believe they run the risk of unnecessarily fettering their rights by written agreements that otherwise could be implemented by way of judicial interpretation.

It is important to note that the impact of *Marshall* has not been restricted

---

50 T. Isaac, "Fishing Dispute Has No Simple Solution" *[Saint John] Telegraph Journal* (2 September 2000) C2.

to the East Coast. On the West Coast, fourteen First Nations on Vancouver Island relied on their interpretation of the mid-1800 Douglas Treaties to support their claims to an Aboriginal fishery. DFO offered them fishing licences, gear, and capacity-building in order to avoid litigation.[51] On August 22, 2001, in a demonstration of frustration, a group of non-Aboriginal commercial fishers participated in an illegal fishery. The fishers were protesting the fact that the Aboriginal food fishery was allocated a reported 450,000 sockeye salmon and no allocation was made for the non-Aboriginal commercial fishery.[52] As this book goes to press, Mi'kmaq fishers at Burnt Church continue to place their lobster traps outside the DFO designated zone.

The Federal Perspective

One of the most surprising elements following the release of the *Marshall* decisions was the federal government's lack of a comprehensive and thoughtful strategy to deal with the decision. There was neither a clear and transparent communications strategy nor a substantive regulatory response. It appears that the federal government was, quite simply, caught off-guard. Even if the details of *Marshall* caught some by surprise, it should have been no surprise that a comprehensive regulatory regime on the East and West Coasts of Canada regarding Aboriginal people and the fishery was required. In many ways, DFO has dropped the ball by not being as assertive or as clear as is required. In remarks made to a conference in Halifax, the national chief of the Assembly of First Nations stated the following about the federal response:

> The federal response to the *Marshall* Supreme Court judgement demonstrated that the federal government is incapable of acting as a fiduciary for aboriginal peoples. Canada was unwilling to even consider contingency planning to implement a judgement of the Supreme Court that would have been favourable to the aboriginal peoples.[53]

In early January 2001, a memorandum to the federal Cabinet[54] concerning the federal government's long-term strategy to deal with the effects of the *Marshall* decision was leaked. The twenty-seven-page document outlines in

51 "Dhaliwal Offers Fishing Deals to B.C. Natives to Avoid Litigation" *National Post* (8 April 2000) A7.
52 "Commercial Fishermen Protest on the Fraser" *The [Vancouver] Province* (23 August 2001) A4.
53 National Chief Matthew Coon Come, "Netukulimk: A Way To Make A Living" (Halifax, N.S.: National Fisheries Strategy Conference, January 29–31, 2001).
54 Canada, PCO, Cabinet, "Memorandum to Cabinet: Long Term Response to R. v. Marshall (phase II)" (December 5, 2000).

detail the federal perspective with respect to the decision and the proposals put forward by the Department of Indian Affairs and Northern Development (DIAND) and DFO. The document proposes that the federal government pursue a long-term strategy to build a sustainable treaty relationship with the Mi'kmaq and Maliseet in Nova Scotia, New Brunswick, and Prince Edward Island, and with the four First Nations in Quebec's Gaspé area that the federal Department of Justice believes are covered by the Treaties of 1760–61. The document supports a two-pronged approach. In the short term, a focus on practical measures such as economic development, capacity building, additions to existing reserve lands, and settling outstanding specific claims. In the longer term, a strategy of entering into comprehensive treaty negotiations relating to Aboriginal and treaty rights to lands, resources, and self-government in Nova Scotia and New Brunswick. The document notes that the federal government should be prepared to initiate negotiations with the Nova Scotia and New Brunswick First Nations, with or without, provincial participation.

Interestingly, the document notes that if the comprehensive treaty negotiations option were to be pursued as the sole option, it would address "the long term goal of resolving outstanding claims to Aboriginal rights and title in the Atlantic."[55] Clearly, the document underscores the importance that federal officials are putting on this major outstanding matter, and it recognizes that there may be outstanding Aboriginal rights and title issues that go beyond those dealt with in the *Marshall* decision. To date, the Government of Nova Scotia has agreed to enter into tripartite negotiations, while the Government of New Brunswick wants more time to study the issue. Meanwhile, Prince Edward Island, according to the memorandum, believes that Aboriginal rights and title were extinguished through British land grants prior to Confederation and is therefore not interested in tripartite negotiations. As fee simple title and Aboriginal title can co-exist,[56] Prince Edward Island's perspective on this matter is questionable.

On February 9, 2001, the ministers of DIAND and DFO announced the federal government's strategy to address *Marshall* and build a better relationship with the Mi'kmaq and Maliseet communities. This strategy tracks the language contained in the leaked Cabinet memorandum. There are two parts to the strategy: (1) DIAND will seek to reach long-term agreements with Maritime First Nations regarding their treaty rights, including the possibility of a modern treaty, and (2) DFO will continue to negotiate fishing agreements (supplemented by a budget of approximately $500 million over three years) to provide First Nations with increased access to the fishery. Initially, DIAND will focus on Nova Scotia, where the Mi'kmaq and the Government of Nova

---

55 *Ibid.* at para. 83.
56 See chapter 3.

Scotia have agreed to enter into tripartite negotiations to discuss Aboriginal rights and title and treaty rights to self-government, land, and resources. DIAND has since appointed a chief negotiator and preliminary discussions among the Province of Nova Scotia, Canada, and the First Nations have started. The minister of DFO described the DIAND portion of the federal *Marshall* strategy as a broad negotiation process that

> looks *beyond* fishery access and considers more fundamental questions about Aboriginal and treaty rights. . . . [W]hile this is a parallel and complimen-tary process, it is *distinct* from the process DFO is engaged in. To put it sim-ply, DIAND is looking at long-term solutions to Aboriginal and treaty rights issues, while DFO is implementing immediate fisheries measures over the next three years. [Emphasis in original][57]

A few days before the announcement of this joint strategy to deal with *Marshall,* DFO announced the release of a discussion paper entitled "The Management of Fisheries on Canada's Atlantic Coast." This paper will form the basis for the Atlantic Fisheries Policy Review (AFPR). The AFPR discus-sion paper states that once DFO determines an acceptable level of harvest for a particular species, Aboriginal rights to fish for food and for social and cer-emonial purposes "take precedence over other users of the resource." *Marshall, Gladstone* (1996), and other Supreme Court of Canada decisions stand for the proposition that other resource users and other factors, including "non-Aboriginal regional/community dependence," can provide a legitimate justi-fication for limiting the allocation to the Aboriginal fishery, either for commercial or for "moderate livelihood" purposes. The courts have called for a balancing of interests, which includes giving priority to Aboriginal and treaty rights but also considers the rights of other resource users. The balanc-ing of interests can still mean that priorities can be met. It means, however, that the prioritization must be sensitive and proportional, and that it must consider regional realities.

Since the release of the *Marshall* decision, the public focus on the fishery and the role Aboriginal people play in it has increased substantially. The events at Burnt Church, where there was a confrontation between members of that First Nation and DFO officers on the waters of Miramichi Bay to protect what Burnt Church claimed to be their right to fish lobster, garnered much media attention. On its face, a strategy that attempts to put Aboriginal fishers in a better economic position than they have been in historically is important.

---

57   Canada, DFO, "Speaking Notes for the Hon. Herb Dhaliwal at the Standing Com-mittee on Fisheries and Oceans (SCOFO): *Marshall* Update, House of Commons" (Ottawa: April 3, 2001) at 2–3.

Clearly, the economic and social conditions of Aboriginal people in Canada are not good, and any attempt to enhance their well-being can only benefit all Canadians. The Atlantic fishery requires proactive management and regulation, balanced with sensitivity towards the constitutionally protected rights of Aboriginal people.

The AFPR has been met with resistance by Maritime First Nations. Atlantic Policy Congress of First Nations chiefs responded disapprovingly to the AFPR's discussion paper. Its statement concluded that the AFPR

> has paid token acknowledgment to the DFO's "legal obligations" regarding aboriginal and treaty rights stemming from decisions such as Marshall but it is apparent to us that it intends to only discharge legal obligations based on very narrow interpretations of aboriginal and treaty rights.[58]

To simply put more money into the Aboriginal fishery without resolving the real outstanding issue is a disservice to both Aboriginal and non-Aboriginal fishers. At the heart of the Aboriginal fishery issue on both the East and West Coasts of Canada is the lack of a sensitive regulatory regime that is applicable to all Aboriginal fishers and that balances other substantive public interests, such as conservation and the interests of the non-Aboriginal fishery. Any strategy to lessen the tension surrounding the Aboriginal fishery should include an economic component and a treaty strategy, but must also include a regulatory component.

The lack of a sensitive and balanced regulatory regime with respect to the Aboriginal fishery, which was an issue in *Marshall,* can be traced all the way back to the Supreme Court's decision in *Sparrow* (1990). Since that time, DFO has attempted to put into place *ad hoc* measures to deal with Aboriginal interests and rights in the fishery. For the most part, DFO's measures have resulted in increased expectations on the part of Aboriginal people, coupled with increased frustration by Aboriginal people that their aspirations are not being met and an increasingly large amount of frustration and misunderstanding by non-Aboriginal fishers.

Although recent events in Atlantic Canada have focussed the issue regarding the Aboriginal fishery on the *Marshall* decision, in reality there is a much broader public-policy issue facing not only the federal government but provincial and territorial governments as well. The issue is the extent to which the government is willing to regulate in areas where Aboriginal and treaty rights may be affected in a manner that is respectful not only of those rights

---

58 Atlantic Policy Congress of First Nations Chiefs, "The Management of Fisheries on Canada's Atlantic Coast: A Discussion Document on Policy Direction and Principles" (Halifax, N.S.: March 9, 2001) at 4.

but also of the interests of non-Aboriginal people. Government regulatory regimes have swung from one extreme to the other. At one end of the spectrum, some governments appear to ignore the constitutionally protected rights of Aboriginal people; at the other end of the spectrum, some governments appear to go out of their way to accommodate Aboriginal people at the expense of either the resources or other resource users. Neither extreme fulfils the Crown's fiduciary duty towards Aboriginal people or upholds the honour of the Crown, and neither extreme is sustainable in the long term.

The lack of a consistent and well-thought-out regulatory regime that balances the interests of other resource users with the rights of Aboriginal people will continue to cause unnecessary litigation, confusion, and expense for governments, Aboriginal people, and non-Aboriginal resource users. In *Marshall No. 2,* the court stated: "It is up to the Crown to initiate enforcement action in the lobster and other fisheries if and when it chooses to do so."[59] This raises the question whether government has a duty to pro-actively regulate resources to protect them from undue exploitation in order to preserve reasonable access by Aboriginal people to the resource at issue.

Although the Supreme Court has provided a liberal interpretation of Aboriginal and treaty rights in *Marshall* and in other decisions, the court has also been clear that the ultimate authority to regulate resources rests with government, provided that government can justify any potential impairment of Aboriginal and treaty rights. Although courts have laid out general parameters regarding the rights of Aboriginal people, these judicial decisions are limited in their scope and cannot resolve broader disputes. Moreover, since the 1990 *Sparrow* decision, the Supreme Court has generally established the nature of Aboriginal rights in Canada, but it has left more specific questions about these rights unanswered.

The Supreme Court of Canada has strongly endorsed negotiated settlements. In *Delgamuukw*, the Supreme Court stated:

> [T]he Crown is under a moral, if not a legal, duty to enter into and conduct those negotiations in good faith. Ultimately it is through negotiated settlements, with the good faith and give and take on all sides . . . that we will achieve . . . a basic purpose of s. 35(1).[60]

However, even with negotiated settlements, governments will be required to place these negotiated agreements within their existing legislative frameworks as they apply to resources such as fish and wildlife. Thus, governments sooner or later will have to face the reality that one way or the other they must deal

59 *Marshall No. 2, supra* note 1 at para. 15.
60 *Delgamuukw, supra* note 20 at para. 186.

with the issue of regulating Aboriginal and treaty rights within their legislative realm. To date, DFO has been reluctant to put a regulatory regime in place that is sensitive to Aboriginal and treaty rights. Although this will not be an easy task, it is a task that must nevertheless be undertaken. By not putting such a regime in place, the government is relinquishing a major public-policy obligation and creating a regulatory vacuum.

The AFPR has the potential, albeit unclear right now, to fill the regulatory gap that has existed since the 1990 *Sparrow* decision. Whether they are in the form of economic fishing agreements or modern treaties, there is a need for fishery regulations. The AFPR has not clearly stated whether it will follow *Marshall* and put new regulations in place that not only recognize the rights of Aboriginal people, but also balance those rights with the rights of other resource users.

Helping Aboriginal fishers enhance their commercial presence is an important goal, and it is a strategy that fits within the broader context of encouraging Aboriginal people to become full participants in Canadian society. Even though DFO is under no obligation to provide $500 million to this cause, it does have an obligation, as directed numerous times by the courts, to get its regulatory house in order. Economic incentives or new treaties are only parts of an incomplete picture. Without a comprehensive and sensitive regulatory regime within which to operate, these economic incentives will only be *ad hoc* and short term in nature. A long-term solution requires governmental leadership and sustainable regulation that is balanced, thoughtful, and honourable.

The Burnt Church First Nation was quick to criticize the federal government's actions after *Marshall*. Burnt Church First Nation councillor Brian Bartibogue stated:

> We in our First Nation here designed our own management plan and we feel we have the authority to initiate our own fisheries act. . . . If we do opt into the MacKenzie [DFO] process we have to tell 90 per cent of fishermen that you can't go fishing.[61]

He was also quoted as saying: "We will not allow the federal government to come in here and dangle a few carrots in front of a starving, impoverished people to take away our entire future."[62] His comments show that there appears to be a general unease among most of the Maritime First Nations towards the

---

61 "Burnt Church Cool to New Fishery Plan" *[Saint John] Telegraph Journal* (10 February 2001) A1 and A11.
62 "Burnt Church Turns Down Dhaliwal Proposal" CBC *News Online: New Brunswick* (9 February 2001).

government's interim fisheries agreements.[63]

Where, then, will the solution be found? It seems clear that, one way or the other, negotiated settlements of some nature must be concluded. These agreements must be coupled with a regulatory regime that can be justified. Since negotiated settlements will most likely take a number of years to complete, the regulatory regime should be the first priority. As noted by the Supreme Court in *Delgamuukw*[64] and re-affirmed in *Marshall No. 2*,[65] the process of accommodating treaty rights in Canada may best be resolved by proper and full consultation and by the negotiation of modern agreements that meet the interests of both governments and the Aboriginal people in question.

Marshall has confirmed, as have *Delgamuukw* and *Sparrow,* that modern negotiated agreements are the best solution to the dilemma in which Canada finds itself regarding Aboriginal issues. Litigation has served a useful purpose—namely, to put Aboriginal and treaty rights on the mainstream political and legislative agenda and to delineate some basic legal parameters within which these rights operate—but it cannot resolve the day-to-day issues facing Aboriginal peoples in Canada, such as poverty, high unemployment, health problems, and high suicide rates. Negotiated settlements that are fair and transparent in their meaning serve all Canadians. In *R. v. Sparrow,* the Supreme Court stated that section 35(1) "provides a solid constitutional base upon which subsequent negotiations can take place."[66] In *Delgamuukw,* Chief Justice Lamer noted that

> [u]ltimately, it is through negotiated settlements, with good faith and give and take on all sides, reinforced by the judgments of this court, that we will achieve . . . "the reconciliation of the pre-existence of Aboriginal societies with the sovereignty of the Crown".[67]

Sonia Lawrence and Patrick Macklem have argued that the duty on governments to consult also contains a duty to negotiate in good faith agreements that outline each of the parties' rights when an action is commenced that may adversely affect Aboriginal interests.[68] Finally, as the Supreme Court stated in *R. v. Sparrow:*

---

63 "Natives Wary About Signing Fishing Deals with Federal Negotiator" *[Saint John] Telegraph Journal* (10 March 2001) A2.
64 *Delgamuukw, supra* note 20 at para. 207.
65 *Marshall No. 2, supra* note 1 at para. 22.
66 *R. v. Sparrow,* [1990] 1 S.C.R. 1075 at 1105.
67 *Delgamuukw, supra* note 20 at para. 186.
68 S. Lawrence and P. Macklem, "From Consultation to Reconciliation: Aboriginal Rights and the Crown's Duty to Consult" (2000) 79:1 Can. Bar Rev. 252–79.

The constitutional entitlement embodied in s. 35(1) requires the Crown to ensure that its regulations are in keeping with that allocation of priority. The objective of this requirement is not to undermine Parliament's ability and responsibility with respect to creating and administering overall conservation and management plans regarding the salmon fishery. The objective is rather to guarantee that those plans treat aboriginal peoples in a way ensuring that their rights are taken seriously.[69]

Conclusion

In *Mitchell* v. *Canada (Min. of National Revenue)* (2001),[70] Justice Binnie, commenting on the context for constitutional protection within section 35(1), wrote: "The *Constitution Act, 1982* ushered in a new chapter but it did not start a new book." This comment is indicative of the Supreme Court's approach to interpreting section 35(1) and of its understanding of the constitutional protection afforded to treaty rights as explained in the *Marshall* decisions.

As our understanding of Aboriginal and treaty rights evolves and as the courts continue to apply broad interpretive principles to these rights, there is the potential for misunderstanding and confusion about the meaning of judicial decisions such as *Marshall* and *Delgamuukw*. Because the lexicon on Aboriginal and treaty rights has become much more prevalent in mainstream Canadian political discourse, the attention being paid to these decisions is considerable and their usefulness in political forums has become exemplified.

For example, there are many different interpretations of *Delgamuukw*. Although many claims of Aboriginal title have been made in British Columbia since *Delgamuukw*, *Delgamuukw* did not provide a general blanket recognition of Aboriginal title in British Columbia. Some have claimed that, based on *Delgamuukw*, First Nations have something akin to a "veto" over various resource-based activities regulated by government. Nothing in *Delgamuukw* confers such authority on First Nations.

Despite the conflicting opinions, this much is clear: Aboriginal title exists in British Columbia, but it is up to First Nations to prove that such title exists. The onus is not on the Crown, but rather on the First Nation claiming title. First Nations' interest in the land is not absolute, but must be reconciled with mainstream uses of the land. Activities such as mining, agriculture, economic development, forestry, hydroelectric power, environmental protection, infrastructure building, and settlement are all justifiable legislative objectives

---

69 *Sparrow, supra* note 66 at 1119.
70 *Mitchell* v. *Canada (Min. of National Revenue)*, 2001 S.C.C. 33 at para. 115.

that could lead governments to infringe Aboriginal title.[71] The list of examples of justifiable activities is so broad that it could conceivably justify a wide array of government actions. Although *Delgamuukw* was a step forward in terms of understanding Aboriginal title, it also set parameters on the existence and meaning of such title. It is this other factor, the factor of the limitations imposed by the court, that is sometimes overlooked in the political environment.

The *Marshall* decision contains the same elements of recognition and limitation that are present in *Delgamuukw.* In both *Marshall No. 1* and *Marshall No. 2,* the Supreme Court went to great lengths to explain that its decision was not an absolute recognition of treaty rights, but in fact limited these rights to hunting, fishing, and gathering and trading for necessaries. Notwithstanding the limitations and parameters of *Marshall,* the public perception of this decision, indeed the perception by many First Nations in Atlantic Canada and across Canada, has been that *Marshall* has created an expansive treaty right to hunt, fish, and gather and has impeded the Crown's ability to regulate resource exploitation. Such is not the case. Indeed, *Marshall* illustrates a court going to great lengths to spell out the authority of government to regulate and justifiably infringe constitutionally protected rights.

In a newspaper interview published in January 2001, Justice Bastarache of the Supreme Court of Canada was quoted as making a number of comments regarding *Marshall* that were contrary to the majority decision. He stated:

> The first reaction of the public, especially in the Maritimes, is that the court was very result-oriented and inventing rights that weren't even in the treaties that were brought before the court in that case. . . .The second problem, I think, was also that the court was maybe seen as being unduly favourable to the native position in all cases, and that it sort of has an agenda for extending these [aboriginal] rights and that it has no concern for the rights of others.[72]

Justice Bastarache's comments are interesting given that he did not sit on the court deciding the case. On the one hand, he is probably correct that the court gave a very liberal interpretation of what constitutes a treaty right, in this case relying on the court's understanding of the "intentions" of the treaty-makers. On the other hand, Justice Bastarache's comments about the court not having regard for the rights of others must be questioned. Throughout

---

71 *Delgamuukw, supra* note 20 at para. 165.
72 "scc Wrong Forum For Native Land Claims: Bastarache" (January 19, 2001) 20:34 The Lawyer's Weekly 20.

both *Marshall* decisions, the court went to extremes to underscore that government possesses the authority to regulate Aboriginal and treaty rights and may do so by balancing these rights with the rights of other Canadians.

Justice Bastarache also received criticism from the national chief of the Assembly of First Nations. In remarks made to a conference in Halifax, Nova Scotia, National Chief Matthew Coon Come stated:

> This Justice [Bastarache's] comments demonstrated an ignorance of aboriginal history. They also displayed a prejudice that favours the economic rights of the non-aboriginal population over that of aboriginal peoples.[73]

Following the remarks of Justice Bastarache, the Atlantic Policy Congress of First Nation Chiefs and the Ontario Criminal Lawyers Association filed complaints with the Canadian Judicial Council claiming that Justice Bastarache had an "anti-Aboriginal bias." The Canadian Judicial Council dismissed the complaints.[74]

As these incidents make clear, *Marshall* did not solve all the issues surrounding these treaty rights, or other rights that may exist in the Maritimes for Aboriginal people, including Aboriginal title. Even within the Treaties of 1760–61, it is not clear whether there may be other as-yet-to-be-determined rights. This uncertainty is coupled with the unique possibility of having treaty rights co-existing with other Aboriginal rights and Aboriginal title.

The majority and dissenting decisions in *Marshall* epitomize the difficulty in the analytical approach taken by the Supreme Court to date in Aboriginal and treaty rights decisions. Although both decisions rely on an interpretation of the concept of the "honour of the Crown," two different approaches to the application of this concept made for competing results. For Justice Binnie, the "honour of the Crown" meant that the courts must prevent making "an empty shell of a treaty promise."[75] For Justice McLachlin the "honour of the Crown" included not implying treaty rights where none exist or were not intended to exist. In both cases, the same general rules of interpretation were applied; yet they resulted in fundamentally different conclusions.

It is clear that the courts will continue to play a role in sorting out these matters in the Maritimes and across Canada. Even negotiated settlements will not negate the need for the court to interpret these documents or apply the justification test or determine whether the amount of consultation undertaken

---

73 National Chief Matthew Coon Come, "Netukulimk: A Way To Make A Living" (Halifax, N.S.: National Fisheries Strategy Conference, January 29–31, 2001).

74 R. Mofina, "Complaint Dismissed Against High Court Judge" *The Globe and Mail* (17 March 2001) A4.

meets the applicable requirements. The Supreme Court sees itself continuing to arbitrate these matters and expects that litigation will play an integral role in the development and maintenance of Aboriginal and treaty rights. For example, in *Marshall No. 2*, the court stated with respect to the role that consultation plays in the justification of governmental interference of Aboriginal and treaty rights: "[I]f the consultation does not produce an agreement, the adequacy of the justification of the government's initiative will have to be litigated in the courts."[76] The court also noted: "The various governmental, Aboriginal and other interests are not, of course, obliged to reach an agreement. In the absence of a mutually satisfactory solution, the courts will resolve the points of conflict as they arise case by case."[77]

Even with the reality of continuing litigation, it is clear that a reconciliation of interests between government and Aboriginal people must be achieved, and agreements of some sort must be reached. In recent years, there has been an interest in the idea that Aboriginal jurisprudence may form the foundation for reconciliation between Aboriginal and non-Aboriginal people in Canada. A central theme of the *Report of the Royal Commission on Aboriginal Peoples* is reconciliation.[78] Under a discussion of the treaties, the commissioners wrote: "By reconciliation we mean . . . embracing the spirit and intent of the treaty relationship itself, a relationship of mutual trust and loyalty."[79]

The term "reconciliation" is loaded and has as many meanings as there are commentators; however, in many ways, *Marshall, Delgamuukw,* and *Sparrow* exemplify such an approach.[80] These decisions interpret Aboriginal and treaty rights in a liberal manner, provide substantive rights to the First Nations involved, and place those rights within the context of Canadian society generally. They also recognize the importance of oral evidence and Aboriginal history and stress the need for First Nations and governments in Canada to negotiate rather than litigate. These decisions affirm that the onus rests with governments in Canada to be clear about how their decision-making affects Aboriginal and treaty rights and to be prepared to justify their actions.

---

75 *Marshall No. 1, supra* note 1 at para. 52.
76 *Marshall No. 2, supra* note 1 at para. 43.
77 *Ibid.* at para. 23.
78 *Report of the Royal Commission on Aboriginal Peoples* (Ottawa: Minister of Supply and Services Canada, 1996).
79 *Ibid.* vol. 2 at 38. See also Lawrence and Macklem, *supra* note 68, and J.Y. Henderson *et al., Aboriginal Tenure in the Constitution of Canada* (Toronto: Carswell, 2000) at 87–88, 331–33, and 427–35.
80 For example, *R. v. Gladstone,* [1996] 2 S.C.R. 723 at para. 73, where the court equated "reconciliation" with a balancing of Aboriginal societies as *part of* the broader social, political, and economic community.

The *Marshall* decisions, however, also stress that reconciliation does not mean the absolute expression of rights but rather a compromise against the backdrop of a market-driven society and the demand for scarce resources. This is the realpolitik of judicial interpretation. In both *Marshall* decisions,[81] the Supreme Court cited with approval its statement in *Gladstone* (1996), which reads:

> Although by no means making a definitive statement on this issue, I would suggest that with regards to the distribution of the fisheries resource after conservation goals have been met, objectives such as the pursuit of economic and regional fairness, and the recognition of the historical reliance upon, and participation in, the fishery by non-aboriginal groups, are the type of objectives which can (at least in the right circumstances) satisfy this standard. *In the right circumstances, such objectives are in the interests of all Canadians and, more importantly, the reconciliation of aboriginal societies with the rest of Canadian society may well depend on their successful attainment.* [Emphasis in original][82]

This is clearly a call for government to take a leadership role in reconciling and balancing the interests of Aboriginal and non-Aboriginal people. It requires government to develop a clear and balanced action plan based on science and sound public policy that can be disseminated for all to understand. *Marshall* will continue to have a significant impact on the East Coast fishery in particular, and on Aboriginal and treaty rights jurisprudence generally. *Marshall* underscores the Supreme Court's analytical approach to section 35(1); namely, that there are very few differences between interpreting "Aboriginal" rights and interpreting "treaty" rights. For example, that the *Sparrow* (1990) justificatory analysis is applicable to treaty rights cases was confirmed by *Badger* (1996) and reaffirmed by *Marshall* and the Supreme Court's approach to understanding how ministerial discretionary authority meshed with Aboriginal rights as outlined in *Adams* and was adopted for treaty rights cases in *Marshall No. 2*.[83]

Marshall confirms the courts' liberal approach to interpreting historical evidence and the "intentions" of those who made the treaties. Yet, the court attempts to balance this approach with an increasingly large number of limitations and restrictions on the exercise of treaty rights. In particular, *Marshall No. 2* acts almost as a blueprint for justifiable government regulation of Ab-

---

81 *Marshall No. 1, supra* note 1 at para. 57, and *Marshall No. 2, supra* note 1 at para. 41.
82 *Gladstone, supra* note 80 at para. 75.
83 *Marshall No. 2, supra* note 1 at para. 33.

original and treaty rights. Despite this direction by the courts, as this is written, the federal government has been slow to put any substantive fisheries regulations in place that meet the *Marshall* standard and balance the interests of other Canadians.

Marshall signals an increased interest in Aboriginal issues in the Maritimes, where these issues have been largely ignored or not present. For the Maritimes, the impact of *Marshall* and related lower court decisions has been significant. Federal and provincial governments are paying attention to these issues, as are First Nations and Maritimers generally. Resource companies also have a vital interest in the outcome of these matters when trying to balance their need for economic stability and growth with the new pressures now facing them from Aboriginal people. In many cases, the resource sector, and other sectors of the economy, finds itself between government and Aboriginal groups. Only time and the commitment of all those involved will determine whether Aboriginal people and governments in the Maritimes can come to an understanding on how each will co-exist with the other. It is in the best interests of all Maritimers, indeed all Canadians, for such an understanding to be reached.

Appendix I

••••••

Decisions Relating to Maritime Treaties

Treaty of 1713

R. v. *Isaac* (1975), 13 N.S.R. (2d) 460 (N.S.C.A.). *General reference.*

R. v. *McCoy*, [1993] 1 C.N.L.R. 135 (N.B.Q.B.). *Did not evidence the surrender of Aboriginal rights in New Brunswick.*

R. v. *Paul*, [1998] 1 C.N.L.R. 209 (N.B.Q.B.). *General reference; the Passamaquoddy not identified as a separate tribe at the time of 1713 Treaty.*

Treaty of 1725 (December 15)

R. v. *Simon* (1958), 124 C.C.C. 110 (N.B.S.C. App. Div.). *Treaty not demonstrated to be relevant to parties claiming benefits thereunder.*

R. v. *Francis* (1969), 10 D.L.R. (3d) 189 (N.B.S.C., App. Div.). *Treaty no basis for affirmation of rights.*

R. v. *Isaac* (1975), 13 N.S.R. (2d) 460 (N.S.C.A.). *General reference.*

R. v. *Nicholas*, [1979] 1 C.N.L.R. 69 (N.B. Prov. Ct.). *Treaty limited in geographical application; federal legislation overrides Aboriginal and treaty rights.*

R. v. *Atwin and Sacobie*, [1981] 2 C.N.L.R. 99 (N.B. Prov. Ct.). *Affirms treaty right to hunt.*

R. v. *Paul*, [1981] 2 C.N.L.R. 83 (N.B.C.A.). *Not applicable to New Brunswick Indians.*

R. v. *Sacobie*, [1981] 2 C.N.L.R. 115 (N.B.Q.B.). *General reference; does not provide a defence.*

R. v. *Saulis*, [1981] 2 C.N.L.R. 121 (N.B.Q.B.). *General reference; federal legislation supercedes treaty rights.*

R. v. *Polchies*, [1982] 4 C.N.L.R. 167 (N.B.Q.B.); affirmed by [1983] 3 C.N.L.R. 131 (N.B.C.A.). *General reference.*

R. v. *Perley*, [1982] 2 C.N.L.R. 185 (N.B.Q.B.). *General reference.*

R. v. *Paul; R.* v. *Polchies*, [1988] 4 C.N.L.R. 107 (N.B.Q.B.). *General reference; not established that treaty was abrogated by subsequent hostilities.*

R. v. *Fowler*, [1993] 3 C.N.L.R. 178 (N.B. Prov. Ct.). *Treaty confers rights on Maliseet.*

R. v. *Paul*, [1994] 2 C.N.L.R. 167 (N.B.C.A.). *Treaty confirms Maliseet right to hunt.*

R. v. McCoy, [1994] 2 C.N.L.R. 129 (N.B.C.A.). *Treaty affirms right to hunt by Maliseet; must be exercised in a safe manner.*

Peter Paul v. R., [1998] 3 C.N.L.R. 221 (N.B.C.A.). *Does not create or acknowledge Aboriginal title.*

R. v. Paul, [1998] 1 C.N.L.R. 209 (N.B.Q.B.). *Outlines land rights; Crown lands in New Brunswick are reserved for Indians; guarantees rights of beneficial ownership and possession.*

R. v. Tomah, [1999] 3 C.N.L.R. 311 (N.B.Q.B.). *Does not apply in New Brunswick.*

R. v. Bernard, [2000] 3 C.N.L.R. 184 (N.B. Prov. Ct.). *General reference.*

Pictou v. Canada, [2001] 1 C.N.L.R. 230 (T.C.C.). *General reference.*

Treaty of 1726 (Dummer's at Annapolis Royal)

R. v. Paul; R. v. Polchies, [1988] 4 C.N.L.R. 107 (N.B.Q.B.). *General reference; not established that treaty was abrogated by subsequent hostilities.*

R. v. McCoy, [1994] 2 C.N.L.R. 129 (N.B.C.A.). *Treaty affirms right to hunt by Maliseet; must be exercised in a safe manner.*

R. v. Bernard, [2000] 3 C.N.L.R. 184 (N.B. Prov. Ct.). *General reference.*

Pictou v. Canada, [2001] 1 C.N.L.R. 230 (T.C.C.). *General reference.*

Treaty of 1749

R. v. Paul; R. v. Polchies, [1988] 4 C.N.L.R. 107 (N.B.Q.B.). *General reference; not established that treaty was abrogated by subsequent hostilities.*

R. v. Bernard, [2000] 3 C.N.L.R. 184 (N.B. Prov. Ct.). *No evidence that the Miramichi Mi'kmaq ratified or signed treaty.*

Treaty of 1752 (November 22)

R. v. Syliboy, [1929] 1 D.L.R. 307 (N.S. Co. Ct.). *Not a real treaty; no hunting rights acquired; did not extend to Cape Breton.*

Warman v. Francis (1958), 20 D.L.R. (2d) 627 (N.B.S.C.). *General reference; treaty did not grant title to land.*

R. v. Simon (1958), 124 C.C.C. 110 (N.B.S.C. App. Div.). *Treaty not deemed relevant to parties claiming benefits thereunder.*

R. v. Francis (1969), 10 D.L.R. (3d) 189 (N.B.S.C., App. Div.). *Treaty no basis for affirmation of rights.*

R. v. Isaac (1975), 13 N.S.R. (2d) 460 (N.S.C.A.). *General reference.*

R. v. Nicholas, [1979] 1 C.N.L.R. 69 (N.B. Prov. Ct.). *Treaty is limited in geographical application; federal legislation overrides Aboriginal and treaty rights.*

R. v. Saulis, [1981] 2 C.N.L.R. 121 (N.B.Q.B.). *General reference; federal legislation supercedes treaty rights.*

R. v. Atwin and Sacobie, [1981] 2 C.N.L.R. 99 (N.B. Prov. Ct.). *Affirms treaty right to hunt.*

R. v. Paul, [1981] 2 C.N.L.R. 83 (N.B.C.A.). *Treaty not made with Mi'kmaq Nation as a whole, only with a small group of Mi'kmaq inhabiting what is now known as eastern Nova Scotia.*

R. v. *Secretary of State*, [1981] 4 C.N.L.R. 86 (Eng. C.A.). *General reference.*

R. v. *Cope*, [1982] 1 C.N.L.R. 23 (N.S.C.A.). *Affirmed Mi'kmaq right to hunt and fish; rights can be extinguished by federal legislation.*

R. v. *Simon*, [1985] 2 S.C.R. 387 (S.C.C.). *Validly created treaty affirming Mi'kmaq right to hunt; not terminated by subsequent hostilities.*

R. v. *Johnson*, [1994] 1 C.N.L.R. 129 (N.S.C.A.). *General reference.*

R. v. *Johnson* (1996), 156 N.S.R. (2d) 71 (N.S.C.A.); leave to appeal refused (1997), 162 N.S.R. (2d) 80n (S.C.C.). *General reference; treaty does not support right to possess tobacco from unauthorized dealer.*

Peter Paul v. *R.*, [1998] 3 C.N.L.R. 221 (N.B.C.A.). *Trade provisions do not give rights to Indians other than the Shubenacadie Mi'kmaq.*

R. v. *Marshall*, [1999] 3 S.C.R. 456 (S.C.C.). *General discussion.*

R. v. *Bernard*, [2000] 3 C.N.L.R. 184 (N.B. Prov. Ct.). *No evidence that Miramichi Mi'kmaq ratified or signed treaty.*

Treaty of February 23, 1760

R. v. *Paul; R.* v. *Polchies*, [1988] 4 C.N.L.R. 107 (N.B.Q.B.). *General reference; not established that treaty was abrogated by subsequent hostilities.*

Treaties of 1760–61

R. v. *Marshall*, [1999] 3 S.C.R. 456 (S.C.C.). *Established Mi'kmaq treaty right to hunt, fish, gather, and trade for necessaries; justifiable federal fisheries regulations continue to apply.*

R. v. *Bernard*, [2000] 3 C.N.L.R. 184 (N.B. Prov. Ct.). *General reference.*

Shubenacadie Indian Band v. *Canada (Min. of Fisheries and Oceans)*, [2001] 1 C.N.L.R. 282 (F.C.T.D.). *Application of Marshall decision; interlocutory injunction application denied; fishing regulations required to protect fisheries resource.*

Pictou v. *Canada*, [2001] 1 C.N.L.R. 230 (T.C.C.). *Application of Marshall decision; treaties not a basis for tax exemption.*

R. v. *Marshall*, [2001] 2 C.N.L.R. 256 (N.S. Prov. Ct.). *Application of Marshall No. 1 and No. 2; treaties do not establish timber harvesting rights for sale.*

Belcher's Proclamation of May 4, 1762

Warman v. *Francis* (1958), 20 D.L.R. (2d) 627 (N.B.S.C.). *General reference.*

R. v. *Isaac* (1975), 13 N.S.R. (2d) 460 (N.S.C.A.). *General reference.*

R. v. *Sacobie*, [1981] 2 C.N.L.R. 115 (N.B.Q.B.). *General reference; does not provide a defence.*

R. v. *Saulis*, [1981] 2 C.N.L.R. 121 (N.B.Q.B.). *General reference; federal legislation supercedes treaty rights.*

R. v. *Perley*, [1982] 2 C.N.L.R. 185 (N.B.Q.B.). *General reference.*

R. v. *Bernard*, [2000] 3 C.N.L.R. 184 (N.B. Prov. Ct.) and [2001] N.B.J. No. 259 (N.B.Q.B.). *General reference; Belcher exceeded his authority.*

R. v. *Marshall*, [2001] 2 C.N.L.R. 256 (N.S. Prov. Ct.). *General reference; does not support a claim for logging rights.*

Treaty of 1778

R. v. *Polchies*, [1982] 4 C.N.L.R. 167 (N.B.Q.B.); affirmed by [1983] 3 C.N.L.R. 131 (N.B.C.A.). *Treaty did not preserve right to hunt off-reserve; a treaty within the meaning of s. 88 of the* Indian Act.

R. v. *Paul; R.* v. *Polchies*, [1988] 4 C.N.L.R. 107 (N.B.Q.B.). *General reference.*

R. v. *Nicholas and Bear*, [1985] 4 C.N.L.R. 153 (N.B. Prov. Ct.). *General reference.*

R. v. *Bernard*, [2000] 3 C.N.L.R. 184 (N.B. Prov. Ct.). *General reference.*

Treaty of 1779

R. v. *Francis* (1969), 10 D.L.R. (3d) 189 (N.B.S.C., App. Div.). *Treaty right cannot prevent application of provincial regulation.*

R. v. *Isaac* (1975), 13 N.S.R. (2d) 460 (N.S.C.A.). *General reference.*

R. v. *Paul*, [1981] 2 C.N.L.R. 83 (N.B.C.A.). *Applies to Mi'kmaq reserves between Cape Tormentine and the Bay DeChaleurs, including Red Bank.*

R. v. *Dedam, Sommerville and Ward*, [1984] 4 C.N.L.R. 83 (N.B. Prov. Ct.). *Valid Mi'kmaq treaty protecting fishing and hunting rights.*

Augustine and Augustine v. *R.; Barlow* v. *R.*, [1987] 1 C.N.L.R. 20 (N.B.C.A.). *Extensive discussion of treaty.*

R. v. *Bernard*, [2000] 3 C.N.L.R. 184 (N.B. Prov. Ct.). *Signed by Miramichi Mi'kmaq; renewed 1761 treaty.*

Treaty of 1794

R. v. *Secretary of State*, [1981] 4 C.N.L.R. 86 (Eng. C.A.). *General reference.*

Appendix II

• • • • • •

Marshall No. I (Edited)

R v. *Marshall*, (*Marshall No. 1*) [1999] 3 S.C.R. 456, Lamer C.J. and L'Heureux-Dubé, Gonthier, Cory, McLachlin, Iacobucci, and Binnie JJ., September 17, 1999.

1   BINNIE J. (Lamer C.J., L'Heureux-Dubé, Cory, and Iacobucci, JJ. concurring)— . . . the appellant and a companion, both Mi'kmaq Indians, slipped their small outboard motorboat into the coastal waters of Pomquet Harbour, Antigonish County, Nova Scotia to fish for eels. They landed 463 pounds, which they sold for $787.10, and for which the appellant was arrested and prosecuted. . . .

4   I would allow this appeal because nothing less would uphold the honour and integrity of the Crown in its dealings with the Mi'kmaq people to secure their peace and friendship, as best the content of those treaty promises can now be ascertained. In reaching this conclusion, I recognize that if the present dispute had arisen out of a modern commercial transaction between two parties of relatively equal bargaining power, or if, as held by the courts below, the short document prepared at Halifax under the direction of Governor Charles Lawrence on March 10, 1760 was to be taken as being the "entire agreement" between the parties, it would have to be concluded that the Mi'kmaq had inadequately protected their interests. However, the courts have not applied strict rules of interpretation to treaty relationships. In *R. v. Denny* (1990), 55 C.C.C. (3d) 322, and earlier decisions cited therein, the Nova Scotia Court of Appeal has affirmed the Mi'kmaq aboriginal right to fish for food. The appellant says the treaty allows him to fish for trade. In my view, the 1760 treaty does affirm the right of the Mi'kmaq people to continue to provide for their own sustenance by taking the products of their hunting, fishing and other gathering activities, and trading for what in 1760 was termed "necessaries". This right was always subject to regulation. The Crown does not suggest that the regulations in question accommodate the treaty right. The Crown's case is that no such treaty right exists. Further, no argument was made that the treaty right was extinguished prior to 1982, and no justification was offered by the Crown for the several prohibitions at issue in this case. Accordingly, in my view, the appellant is entitled to an acquittal.

Analysis

5   The starting point for the analysis of the alleged treaty right must be an examination of the specific words used in any written memorandum of its terms. In this case,

the task is complicated by the fact the British signed a series of agreements with individual Mi'kmaq communities in 1760 and 1761 intending to have them consolidated into a comprehensive Mi'kmaq treaty that was never in fact brought into existence. . . . Despite some variations among some of the documents, Embree Prov. Ct. J. was satisfied that the written terms applicable to this dispute were contained in a Treaty of Peace and Friendship entered into by Governor Charles Lawrence on March 10, 1760, which in its entirety provides as follows:

> Treaty of Peace and Friendship concluded by [His Excellency Charles Lawrence] Esq. Govr and Comr. in Chief in and over his Majesty's Province of Nova Scotia or Accadia with Paul Laurent chief of the LaHave tribe of Indians at Halifax in the Province of N.S. or Acadia.

> I, Paul Laurent do for myself and the tribe of LaHave Indians of which I am Chief do acknowledge the jurisdiction and Dominion of His Majesty George the Second over the Territories of Nova Scotia or Accadia and we do make submission to His Majesty in the most perfect, ample and solemn manner.

> And I do promise for myself and my tribe that I nor they shall not molest any of His Majesty's subjects or their dependents, in their settlements already made or to be hereafter made or in carrying on their Commerce or in any thing whatever within the Province of His said Majesty or elsewhere and if any insult, robbery or outrage shall happen to be committed by any of my tribe satisfaction and restitution shall be made to the person or persons injured.

> That neither I nor any of my tribe shall in any manner entice any of his said Majesty's troops or soldiers to desert, nor in any manner assist in conveying them away but on the contrary will do our utmost endeavours to bring them back to the Company, Regiment, Fort or Garrison to which they shall belong.

> That if any Quarrel or Misunderstanding shall happen between myself and the English or between them and any of my tribe, neither I, nor they shall take any private satisfaction or Revenge, but we will apply for redress according to the Laws established in His said Majesty's Dominions.

> That all English prisoners made by myself or my tribe shall be sett at Liberty and that we will use our utmost endeavours to prevail on the other tribes to do the same, if any prisoners shall happen to be in their hands

> And I do further promise for myself and my tribe that we will not either directly nor indirectly assist any of the enemies of His most sacred Majesty King George the Second, his heirs or Successors, nor hold any manner of Commerce traffick nor intercourse with them, but on the contrary will as much as may be in our power discover and make known to His Majesty's

Governor, any ill designs which may be formed or contrived against His Majesty's subjects. And I do further engage that we will not traffick, barter or Exchange any Commodities in any manner but with such persons or the managers of such Truck houses as shall be appointed or Established by His Majesty's Governor at Lunenbourg or Elsewhere in Nova Scotia or Accadia.

And for the more effectual security of the due performance of this Treaty and every part thereof I do promise and Engage that a certain number of persons of my tribe which shall not be less in number than two prisoners shall on or before September next reside as Hostages at Lunenburg or at such other place or places in this Province of Nova Scotia or Accadia as shall be appointed for that purpose by His Majesty's Governor of said Province which Hostages shall be exchanged for a like number of my tribe when requested.

And all these foregoing articles and every one of them made with His Excellency C. L., His Majesty's Governor I do promise for myself and on of sd part—behalf of my tribe that we will most strictly keep and observe in the most solemn manner.

In witness whereof I have hereunto putt my mark and seal at Halifax in Nova Scotia this day of March one thousand

Paul Laurent

I do accept and agree to all the articles of the forgoing treaty in Faith and Testimony whereof I have signed these present I have caused my seal to be hereunto affixed this day of march in the 33 year of His Majesty's Reign and in the year of Our lord - 1760

Chas Lawrence [Emphasis added.]

6   The underlined portion of the document, the so-called "trade clause", is framed in negative terms as a restraint on the ability of the Mi'kmaq to trade with non-government individuals. A "truckhouse" was a type of trading post. The evidence showed that the promised government truckhouses disappeared from Nova Scotia within a few years and by 1780 a replacement regime of government licensed traders had also fallen into disuse while the British Crown was attending to the American Revolution. The trial judge, Embree Prov. Ct. J., rejected the Crown's argument that the trade clause amounted to nothing more than a negative covenant. He found, at para. 116, that it reflected a grant to the Mi'kmaq of the positive right to "bring the products of their hunting, fishing and gathering to a truckhouse to trade". The Court of Appeal ((1997), 159 N.S.R. (2d) 186) found that the trial judge misspoke when he used the word "right". It held that the trade clause does not grant the Mi'kmaq any rights. Instead, the trade clause represented a "mechanism imposed upon them to help ensure that the peace was a lasting one, by obviating their need to trade with enemies of the

British" (p. 208). When the truckhouses disappeared, said the court, so did any vestiges of the restriction or entitlement, and that was the end of it.

7   The appellant's position is that the truckhouse provision not only incorporated the alleged right to trade, but also the right to pursue traditional hunting, fishing and gathering activities in support of that trade. It seems clear that the words of the March 10, 1760 document, standing in isolation, do not support the appellant's argument. The question is whether the underlying negotiations produced a broader agreement between the British and the Mi'kmaq, memorialized only in part by the Treaty of Peace and Friendship, that would protect the appellant's activities that are the subject of the prosecution. I should say at the outset that the appellant overstates his case. In my view, the treaty rights are limited to securing "necessaries" (which I construe in the modern context, as equivalent to a moderate livelihood), and do not extend to the open-ended accumulation of wealth. The rights thus construed, however, are, in my opinion, treaty rights within the meaning of s. 35 of the *Constitution Act, 1982,* and are subject to regulations that can be justified under the *Badger* test (*R. v. Badger,* [1996] 1 S.C.R 771). . . .

Evidentiary Sources
9   The Court of Appeal took a strict approach to the use of extrinsic evidence when interpreting the Treaties of 1760-61. . . . I think this approach should be rejected for at least three reasons.

10   Firstly, even in a modern commercial context, extrinsic evidence is available to show that a written document does not include all of the terms of an agreement. Rules of interpretation in contract law are in general more strict than those applicable to treaties, yet Professor Waddams states in *The Law of Contracts* (3rd ed. 1993), at para. 316:

> The parol evidence rule does not purport to exclude evidence designed to show whether or not the agreement has been "reduced to writing", or whether it was, or was not, the intention of the parties that it should be the exclusive record of their agreement. Proof of this question is a pre-condition to the operation of the rule, and all relevant evidence is admissible on it. This is the view taken by Corbin and other writers, and followed in the Second Restatement. . . .

11   Secondly, even in the context of a treaty document that purports to contain all of the terms, this Court has made clear in recent cases that extrinsic evidence of the historical and cultural context of a treaty may be received even absent any ambiguity on the face of the treaty. MacKinnon A.C.J.O. laid down the principle in *Taylor and Williams, supra,* at p. 236:

> . . . if there is evidence by conduct or otherwise as to how the parties understood the terms of the treaty, then such understanding and practice is of assistance in giving content to the term or terms.

The proposition is cited with approval in *Delgamuukw v. British Columbia,* [1997] 3 S.C.R. 1010, at para. 87, and *R. v. Sioui,* [1990] 1 S.C.R. 1025, at p.1045.

12   Thirdly, where a treaty was concluded verbally and afterwards written up by representatives of the Crown, it would be unconscionable for the Crown to ignore the oral terms while relying on the written terms, *per* Dickson J. (as he then was) in *Guerin v. The Queen,* [1984] 2 S.C.R. 335. Dickson J. stated for the majority, at p. 388:

> Nonetheless, the Crown, in my view, was not empowered by the surrender document to ignore the oral terms which the Band understood would be embodied in the lease. The oral representations form the backdrop against which the Crown's conduct in discharging its fiduciary obligation must be measured. They inform and confine the field of discretion within which the Crown was free to act. After the Crown's agents had induced the Band to surrender its land on the understanding that the land would be leased on certain terms, it would be unconscionable to permit the Crown simply to ignore those terms.

The *Guerin* case is a strong authority in this respect because the surrender there could only be accepted by the Governor in Council, who was not made aware of any oral terms. The surrender could *not* have been accepted by the departmental officials who were present when the Musqueam made known their conditions. Nevertheless, the Governor in Council was held bound by the oral terms which "the Band understood would be embodied in the lease" (p. 388). In this case, unlike *Guerin,* the Governor did have authority to bind the Crown and was present when the aboriginal leaders made known their terms.

13   The narrow approach applied by the Court of Appeal to the use of extrinsic evidence apparently derives from the comments of Estey J. in *R. v. Horse,* [1988] 1 S.C.R. 187, where, at p. 201, he expressed some reservations about the use of extrinsic materials, such as the transcript of negotiations surrounding the signing of Treaty No. 6, except in the case of ambiguity. (Estey J. went on to consider the extrinsic evidence anyway, at p. 203.) Lamer J., as he then was, mentioned this aspect of *Horse* in *Sioui, supra,* at p. 1049, but advocated a more flexible approach when determining the existence of treaties. Lamer J. stated, at p. 1068, that "[t]he historical context, which has been used to demonstrate the existence of the treaty, may equally assist us in interpreting the extent of the rights contained in it".

14   Subsequent cases have distanced themselves from a "strict" rule of treaty interpretation, as more recently discussed by Cory J., in *Badger, supra,* at para. 52:

> . . . <u>when considering a treaty, a court must take into account the context in</u> <u>which the treaties were negotiated, concluded and committed to writing.</u> <u>The treaties, as written documents, recorded an agreement that had already</u> <u>been reached orally and they did not always record the full extent of the oral</u> <u>agreement</u>: see Alexander Morris, *The Treaties of Canada with the Indians*

of Manitoba and the North-West Territories (1880), at pp. 338-42; *Sioui, supra,* at p. 1068; *Report of the Aboriginal Justice Inquiry of Manitoba* (1991); Jean Friesen, *Grant me Wherewith to Make my Living* (1985). The treaties were drafted in English by representatives of the Canadian government who, it should be assumed, were familiar with common law doctrines. Yet, the treaties were not translated in written form into the languages (here Cree and Dene) of the various Indian nations who were signatories. Even if they had been, it is unlikely that the Indians, who had a history of communicating only orally, would have understood them any differently. As a result, it is well settled that the words in the treaty must not be interpreted in their strict technical sense nor subjected to rigid modern rules of construction. [Emphasis added.]

"Generous" rules of interpretation should not be confused with a vague sense of after-the-fact largesse. The special rules are dictated by the special difficulties of ascertaining what in fact was agreed to. The Indian parties did not, for all practical purposes, have the opportunity to create their own written record of the negotiations. Certain assumptions are therefore made about the Crown's approach to treaty making (honourable) which the Court acts upon in its approach to treaty interpretation (flexible) as to the existence of a treaty (*Sioui, supra,* at p. 1049), the completeness of any written record (the use, e.g., of context and implied terms to make honourable sense of the treaty arrangement: *Simon v. The Queen,* [1985] 2 S.C.R. 387, and *R. v. Sundown,* [1999] 1 S.C.R. 393), and the interpretation of treaty terms once found to exist (*Badger*). The bottom line is the Court's obligation is to "choose from among the various possible interpretations of the <u>common</u> intention [at the time the treaty was made] the one which best reconciles" the Mi'kmaq interests and those of the British Crown (*Sioui, per* Lamer J., at p. 1069 (emphasis added)). In *Taylor and Williams, supra,* the Crown conceded that points of oral agreement recorded in contemporaneous minutes were included in the treaty (p. 230) and the court concluded that their effect was to "preserve the historic right of these Indians to hunt and fish on Crown lands" (p. 236). The historical record in the present case is admittedly less clear-cut, and there is no parallel concession by the Crown. . . .

Findings of Fact by the Trial Judge

18   The appellant admitted that he did what he was alleged to have done on August 24, 1993. The only contentious issues arose on the historical record and with respect to the conclusions and inferences drawn by Embree Prov. Ct. J. from the documents, as explained by the expert witnesses. The permissible scope of appellate review in these circumstances was outlined by Lamer C.J. in *R. v. Van der Peet,* [1996] 2 S.C.R. 507, at para. 82:

In the case at bar, Scarlett Prov. Ct. J., the trial judge, made findings of fact based on the testimony and evidence before him, and then proceeded to make a determination as to whether those findings of fact supported the appellant's claim to the existence of an aboriginal right. The second stage of Scarlett Prov. Ct. J.'s analysis—his determination of the scope of the appellant's aboriginal rights on the basis of the facts as he found them—is a determination of a question of law which, as such, mandates no deference from this Court. The first stage of Scarlett Prov. Ct. J.'s analysis, however—the findings of fact from which that legal inference was drawn—do mandate such deference and should not be overturned unless made on the basis of a "palpable and overriding error".

19   In the present case, the trial judge, after a careful and detailed review of the evidence, concluded at para. 116:

> I accept as inherent in these treaties that the British recognized and accepted the existing Mi'kmaq way of life. Moreover, it's my conclusion that the British would have wanted the Mi'kmaq to continue their hunting, fishing and gathering lifestyle. The British did not want the Mi'kmaq to become a long-term burden on the public treasury although they did seem prepared to tolerate certain losses in their trade with the Mi'kmaq for the purpose of securing and maintaining their friendship and discouraging their future trade with the French. <u>I am satisfied that this trade clause in the 1760-61 Treaties gave the Mi'kmaq the right to bring the products of their hunting, fishing and gathering to a truckhouse to trade.</u> [Emphasis added.]

The treaty document of March 10, 1760 sets out a restrictive covenant and does not say anything about a positive Mi'kmaq right to trade. In fact, the written document does not set out any Mi'kmaq rights at all, merely Mi'kmaq "promises" and the Governor's acceptance. I cannot reconcile the trial judge's conclusion, at para. 116, that the treaties "gave the Mi'kmaq the right to bring the products of their hunting, fishing and gathering to a truckhouse to trade", with his conclusion at para. 112 that:

> The written treaties with the Mi'kmaq in 1760 and 1761 which are before me contain, and fairly represent, all the promises made and all the terms and conditions mutually agreed to.

It was, after all, the aboriginal leaders who asked for truckhouses "for the furnishing them with necessaries, in Exchange for their Peltry" in response to the Governor's inquiry "Whether they were directed by their Tribes, to propose any other particulars to be Treated upon at this Time". It cannot be supposed that the Mi'kmaq raised the subject of trade concessions merely for the purpose of subjecting themselves to a trade restriction. As the Crown acknowledges in its factum, "The restrictive nature of the truckhouse clause was British in origin". The trial judge's view that the treaty obligations are all found within the four corners of the March 10, 1760 document, albeit generously interpreted, erred in law by failing to give adequate weight to the concerns and perspective of the Mi'kmaq people, despite the recorded history of the negotiations, and by giving excessive weight to the concerns and perspective of the British, who held the pen. (See *Badger,* at para. 41, and *Sioui,* at p. 1036.) The need to give balanced weight to the aboriginal perspective is equally applied in aboriginal rights cases: *Van der Peet,* at paras. 49-50; *Delgamuukw,* at para. 81.

20   While the trial judge drew positive implications from the negative trade clause (reversed on this point by the Court of Appeal), such limited relief is inadequate where the British-drafted treaty document does not accord with the British-drafted minutes of the negotiating sessions and more favourable terms are evident from the other documents and evidence the trial judge regarded as reliable. Such an overly deferential attitude to the March 10, 1760 document was inconsistent with a proper recognition of the difficulties of proof confronted by aboriginal people, a principle emphasized in the treaty context by *Simon,* at p. 408, and *Badger,* at para. 4, and in the aboriginal rights context in *Van der Peet,* at para. 68, and *Delgamuukw,* at paras. 80-82. The trial judge interrogated himself on the scope of the March 10, 1760 text. He thus asked himself the wrong question. His narrow view of what constituted "the treaty" led to the equally narrow legal conclusion that the Mi'kmaq trading entitlement, such as it was, terminated in the 1780s. Had the trial judge not given undue weight to the March 10, 1760 document, his conclusions might have been very different. . . .

23   I take the following points from the matters particularly emphasized by the trial judge at para. 90 following his thorough review of the historical background:

1   The 1760-61 treaties were the culmination of more than a decade of intermittent hostilities between the British and the Mi'kmaq. Hostilities with the French were also prevalent in Nova Scotia throughout the 1750's, and the Mi'kmaq were constantly allied with the French against the British.

2   The use of firearms for hunting had an important impact on Mi'kmaq society. The Mi'kmaq remained dependant on others for gun powder and the primary sources of that were the French, Acadians and the British.

3   The French frequently supplied the Mi'kmaq with food and European trade goods. By the mid-18th century, the Mi'kmaq were accustomed to, and in some cases relied on, receiving various European trade goods [including shot, gun powder, metal tools, clothing cloth, blankets and many other things].
. . .
6   The British wanted peace and a safe environment for their current and future settlers. Despite their recent victories, they did not feel completely secure in Nova Scotia. . . .

25   . . . It is apparent that the British saw the Mi'kmaq trade issue in terms of peace, as the Crown expert Dr. Stephen Patterson testified, "people who trade together do not fight, that was the theory". Peace was bound up with the ability of the Mi'kmaq people to sustain themselves economically. Starvation breeds discontent. The British certainly did not want the Mi'kmaq to become an unnecessary drain on the public purse of the colony of Nova Scotia or of the Imperial purse in London, as the trial judge found. To avoid such a result, it became necessary to protect the traditional Mi'kmaq economy, including hunting, gathering and fishing. A comparable policy was pursued at a later date on the west coast where, as Dickson J. commented in *Jack v. The Queen,* [1980] 1 S.C.R. 294, at p. 311:

What is plain from the pre-Confederation period is that the Indian fishermen were encouraged to engage in their occupation and to do so for both food and barter purposes.

The same strategy of economic aboriginal self-sufficiency was pursued across the prairies in terms of hunting: see *R. v. Horseman*, [1990] 1 S.C.R. 901, *per* Wilson J., at p. 919, and Cory J., at p. 928.

26   The trial judge concluded that in 1760 the British Crown entered into a series of negotiations with communities of first nations spread across what is now Nova Scotia and New Brunswick. These treaties were essentially "adhesions" by different Mi'kmaq communities to identical terms because, as stated, it was contemplated that they would be consolidated in a more comprehensive and all-inclusive document at a later date, which never happened. The trial judge considered that the key negotiations took place not with the Mi'kmaq people directly, but with the St. John River Indians, part of the Maliseet First Nation, and the Passamaquody First Nation, who lived in present-day New Brunswick.

27   The trial judge found as a fact, at para. 108, that the relevant Mi'kmaq treaty did "make peace upon the <u>same</u> conditions" (emphasis added) as the Maliseet and Passamaquody. Meetings took place between the Crown and the Maliseet and the Passamaquody on February 11, 1760, twelve days before these bands signed their treaty with the British and eighteen days prior to the meeting between the Governor and the Mi'kmaq representatives, Paul Laurent of LaHave and Michel Augustine of the Richibucto region, where the terms of the Maliseet and Passamaquody treaties were "communicated" and accepted.

. . .

29   The genesis of the Mi'kmaq trade clause is therefore found in the Governor's earlier negotiations with the Maliseet and Passamaquody First Nations. . . .

30   It is true, as my colleague points out at para. 97, that the British made it clear from the outset that the Mi'kmaq were not to have any commerce with "any of His Majesty's Enemies". A Treaty of Peace and Friendship could not be otherwise. The subject of trading with the British government as distinguished from British settlers, however, did not arise until after the Indians had first requested truckhouses. The limitation to government trade came as a response to the request for truckhouses, not the other way around.

31   At a meeting of the Governor's Council on February 16, 1760 (less than a week later), the Council and the representatives of the Indians proceeded to settle the prices of various articles of merchandise. . . . Prices of "necessaries" for purchase at the truckhouse were also agreed, . . . The British took a liberal view of "necessaries". . . . At trial the Crown expert and the defence experts agreed that fish could be among the items that the Mi'kmaq would trade.

32   In furtherance of this trade arrangement, the British established six truckhouses

following the signing of the treaties in 1760 and 1761, including Chignecto, Lunenburg, St. John, Windsor, Annapolis and "the Eastern Battery" along the coast from Halifax. The existence of advantageous terms at the truckhouses was part of an imperial peace strategy. As Governor Lawrence wrote to the Board of Trade on May 11, 1760, "the greatest advantage from this [trade] Article . . . is the friendship of these Indians". The British were concerned that matters might again become "troublesome" if the Mi'kmaq were subjected to the "pernicious practices" of "unscrupulous traders". The cost to the public purse of Nova Scotia of supporting Mi'kmaq trade was an investment in peace and the promotion of ongoing colonial settlement. The strategy would be effective only if the Mi'kmaq had access *both* to trade *and* to the fish and wildlife resources necessary to provide them with something to trade.

33   Accordingly, on March 21, 1760, the Nova Scotia House of Assembly passed *An Act to prevent any private Trade or Commerce with the Indians,* 34 Geo. II, c. 11. In July 1761, however, the "Lords of Trade and Plantation" (the Board of Trade) in London objected and the King disallowed the Act as a restraint on trade that disadvantaged British merchants. This coincided with exposure of venality by the local truckhouse merchants. . . .

34   By 1762, Garrish was removed and the number of truckhouses was reduced to three. By 1764, the system itself was replaced by the impartial licensing of private traders approved by the London Board of Trade's "Plan for the Future Management of Indian Affairs", but that eventually died out as well, as mentioned earlier.

35   In my view, all of this evidence, reflected in the trial judgment, demonstrates the inadequacy and incompleteness of the written memorial of the treaty terms by selectively isolating the restrictive trade covenant. Indeed, the truckhouse system offered such advantageous terms that it hardly seems likely that Mi'kmaq traders had to be compelled to buy at lower prices and sell at higher prices. At a later date, they objected when truckhouses were abandoned. The trade clause would not have advanced British objectives (peaceful relations with a self-sufficient Mi'kmaq people) or Mi'kmaq objectives (access to the European "necessaries" on which they had come to rely) unless the Mi'kmaq were assured at the same time of continuing access, implicitly or explicitly, to wildlife to trade. This was confirmed by the expert historian called by the Crown, as set out below.

(ii) *The Expert Evidence*
36   The courts have attracted a certain amount of criticism from professional historians for what these historians see as an occasional tendency on the part of judges to assemble a "cut and paste" version of history: . . .

37   While the tone of some of this criticism strikes the non-professional historian as intemperate, the basic objection, as I understand it, is that the judicial selection of facts and quotations is not always up to the standard demanded of the professional historian, which is said to be more nuanced. Experts, it is argued, are trained to read the various historical records together with the benefit of a protracted study of the

period, and an appreciation of the frailties of the various sources. The law sees a finality of interpretation of historical events where finality, according to the professional historian, is not possible. The reality, of course, is that the courts are handed disputes that require for their resolution the finding of certain historical facts. The litigating parties cannot await the possibility of a stable academic consensus. The judicial process must do as best it can. In this particular case, however, there was an unusual level of agreement amongst all of the professional historians who testified about the underlying expectations of the participants regarding the treaty obligations entered into by the Crown with the Mi'kmaq. I set out, in particular, the evidence of the Crown's expert, Dr. Stephen Patterson, who spent many days of testimony reviewing the minutiae of the historical record. While he generally supported the Crown's narrow approach to the interpretation of the Treaty, which I have rejected on points of law, he did make a number of important concessions to the defence in a relatively lengthy and reflective statement which should be set out in full:

Q. I guess it's fair to say that the British would have understood that the Micmac lived and survived by hunting and fishing and gathering activities.

A. Yes, of course.

Q. And that in this time period, 1760 and '61, fish would be amongst the items they would have to trade. And they would have the right under this treaty to bring fish and feathers and furs into a truckhouse in exchange for commodities that were available.

A. Well, it's not mentioned but it's not excluded. So I think it's fair to assume that it was permissible.

Q. Okay. It's fair to say that it's an assumption on which the trade truckhouse clause is based.

A. That the truckhouse clause is based on the assumption that natives will have a variety of things to trade, some of which are mentioned and some not. Yes, I think that's fair.

Q. Yes. And wouldn't be out of line to call that a right to fish and a right to bring the fish or furs or feathers or fowl or venison or whatever they might have, into the truckhouses to trade.

A. Ah, a right. I think the implication here is that there is a right to trade under a certain form of regulation—

Q. Yes.

A. —that's laid down. And if you're saying right to fish, I've assumed that in recognizing the Micmac by treaty, the British were recognizing them as the people they were. They understood how they lived and that that meant that those people had a *right* to live in Nova Scotia in their traditional ways. And, to me, that *implies* that the British were accepting that the Micmac would continue to be a hunting and gathering people, that they would fish, that they would hunt to support themselves. I don't see any problem with that.

It seems to me that that's implicit in the thing. Even though it doesn't say it, and I know that there seems to, in the 20th century, be some reluctance to see the value of the 1760 and 1761 treaties because they're not so explicit on these matters, but I personally don't see the hang-up. Because it strikes me that there is a recognition that the Micmac are a people and they have the right to exist. And that has—carries certain implications with it.

More than this, the very fact that there is a truckhouse and that the truckhouse does list some of the things that natives are expected to trade, implies that the British are condoning or recognizing that this is the way that natives live. They do live by hunting and, therefore, this is the produce of their hunting. They have the *right* to trade it.

Q. And you have, in fact, said that in your May 17th, 1994 draft article.

A. That's correct.

Q. Yeah. And you testified to that effect in the *Pelletier* case, as well.

A. Well, my understanding of this issue, Mr. Wildsmith, has developed and grown with my close reading of the material. It's the position that I come to accept as being a reasonable interpretation of what is here in these documents. [Emphasis added.]

38   The trial judge gave effect to this evidence in finding a *right* to bring fish to the truckhouse to trade, but he declined to find a treaty right to fish and hunt to obtain the wherewithal to trade, and concluded that the right to trade expired along with the truckhouses and subsequent special arrangements. The Court of Appeal concluded, at p. 207, that Dr. Patterson used the word "right" interchangeably with the word "permissible", and that the trade clause gave rise to no "rights" at all. I think the view taken by the courts below rather underestimates Dr. Patterson. No reason is given for doubting that Dr. Patterson meant what he said about the common understanding of the parties that he considered at least implicit in this particular treaty arrangement. He initially uses the words "permissible" and "assumption", but when asked specifically by counsel about a "right" to fish and to trade fish, he says, "Ah, a *right*" (emphasis added), then, weighing his words carefully, he addresses a "right to fish" and concludes that "by treaty" the British did recognize that the Mi'kmaq "had a right to live in Nova Scotia in their traditional ways" (emphasis added) which included hunting and fishing and trading their catch for necessaries. (Trading was traditional. The trial judge found, at para. 93, that the Mi'kmaq had already been trading with Europeans,

including French and Portuguese fishermen, for about 250 years prior to the making of this treaty.) Dr. Patterson said his opinion was based on the historic documents produced in evidence. He said that this was "the position that I come to accept as being a reasonable interpretation of what is here in these documents" (emphasis added). Dr. Patterson went on to emphasize that the understanding of the Mi'kmaq would have been that these treaty rights were subject to regulation, which I accept.

39   Dr. Patterson's evidence regarding the assumptions underlying and "implicit" in the treaty were generally agreed with by the defence experts, Dr. John Reid and Dr. William Wicken. . . .

40   In my view, the Nova Scotia judgments erred in concluding that the only enforceable treaty obligations were those set out in the written document of March 10, 1760, whether construed flexibly (as did the trial judge) or narrowly (as did the Nova Scotia Court of Appeal). The findings of fact made by the trial judge taken as a whole demonstrate that the concept of a disappearing treaty right does justice neither to the honour of the Crown nor to the reasonable expectations of the Mi'kmaq people. It is their common intention in 1760—not just the terms of the March 10, 1760 document—to which effect must be given.

Ascertaining the Terms of the Treaty
41   Having concluded that the written text is incomplete, it is necessary to ascertain the treaty terms not only by reference to the fragmentary historical record, as interpreted by the expert historians, but also in light of the stated objectives of the British and Mi'kmaq in 1760 and the political and economic context in which those objectives were reconciled.

42   I mentioned earlier that the Nova Scotia Court of Appeal has held on several occasions that the "peace and friendship" treaties with the Mi'kmaq did not extinguish aboriginal hunting and fishing rights in Nova Scotia: *R. v. Isaac* (1975), 13 N.S.R. (2d) 460, *R. v. Cope* (1981), 132 D.L.R. (3d) 36, *Denny, supra*. We are not here concerned with the exercise of such a right. . . .

43   The law has long recognized that parties make assumptions when they enter into agreements about certain things that give their arrangements efficacy. Courts will imply a contractual term on the basis of presumed intentions of the parties where it is necessary to assure the efficacy of the contract, e.g., where it meets the "officious bystander test": . . . Here, if the ubiquitous officious bystander had said, "This talk about truckhouses is all very well, but if the Mi'kmaq are to make these promises, will they have the right to hunt and fish to catch something to trade at the truckhouses?", the answer would have to be, having regard to the honour of the Crown, "of course". If the law is prepared to supply the deficiencies of written contracts prepared by sophisticated parties and their legal advisors in order to produce a sensible result that accords with the intent of both parties, though unexpressed, the law cannot ask less of the honour and dignity of the Crown in its dealings with First Nations. The honour of the Crown was, in fact, specifically invoked by courts in the early 17th century to

ensure that a Crown grant was effective to accomplish its intended purpose: . . .

44   An example of the Court's recognition of the necessity of supplying the deficiencies of aboriginal treaties is *Sioui, supra,* where Lamer J. considered a treaty document that stated simply (at p. 1031) that the Huron tribe "are received upon the same terms with the Canadians, being allowed the free Exercise of their Religion, their Customs, and Liberty of trading with the English". Lamer J. found that, in order to give real value and meaning to these words, it was necessary that a territorial component be supplied, as follows, at p. 1067:

> The treaty gives the Hurons the freedom to carry on their customs and their religion. No mention is made in the treaty itself of the territory over which these rights may be exercised. There is also no indication that the territory of what is now Jacques-Cartier park was contemplated. However, <u>for a freedom to have real value and meaning</u>, it must be possible to exercise it somewhere. [Emphasis added.]

Similarly, in *Sundown, supra,* the Court found that the express right to hunt included the implied right to build shelters required to carry out the hunt. See also *Simon, supra,* where the Court recognized an implied right to carry a gun and ammunition on the way to exercise the right to hunt. These cases employed the concept of implied rights to support the meaningful exercise of express rights granted to the first nations in circumstances where no such implication might necessarily have been made absent the *sui generis* nature of the Crown's relationship to aboriginal people. While I do not believe that in ordinary commercial situations a right to trade implies any right of access to things to trade, I think the honour of the Crown requires nothing less in attempting to make sense of the result of these 1760 negotiations.

Rights of the Other Inhabitants
45   My colleague, McLachlin J., takes the view that, subject to the negative restriction in the treaty, the Mi'kmaq possessed only the liberty to hunt, fish, gather and trade "enjoyed by other British subjects in the region" (para. 103). The Mi'kmaq were, in effect, "citizens minus" with no greater liberties but with greater restrictions. I accept that in terms of the *content* of the hunting, fishing and gathering activities, this may be true. There is of course a distinction to be made between a liberty enjoyed by all citizens and a right conferred by a specific legal authority, such as a treaty, to participate in the same activity. Even if this distinction is ignored, it is still true that a general right enjoyed by all citizens can nevertheless be made the subject of an enforceable treaty promise. In *Taylor and Williams, supra,* at p. 235, the treaty was found to include a term that "[t]he Rivers are open to all & you have an equal right to fish & hunt on them", and yet, despite the reference to equal rather than preferential rights, "the historic right of these Indians to hunt and fish" was found to be incorporated in the treaty, *per* MacKinnon A.C.J.O., at p. 236. . . .

47   The Crown objects strongly to any suggestion that the treaty conferred "*preferential* trading rights". I do not think the appellant needs to show *preferential* trading

rights. He only has to show *treaty* trading rights. The settlers and the military undoubtedly hunted and fished for sport or necessaries as well, and traded goods with each other. The issue here is not so much the content of the rights or liberties as the level of legal protection thrown around them. A treaty could, to take a fanciful example, provide for a right of the Mi'kmaq to promenade down Barrington Street, Halifax, on each anniversary of the treaty. Barrington Street is a common thoroughfare enjoyed by all. There would be nothing "special" about the Mi'kmaq use of a common right of way. The point is that the treaty rights-holder not only has the *right* or liberty "enjoyed by other British subjects" but may enjoy special treaty *protection* against interference with its exercise. So it is with the trading arrangement. . . .

48   Until enactment of the *Constitution Act, 1982,* the treaty rights of aboriginal peoples could be overridden by competent legislation as easily as could the rights and liberties of other inhabitants. The hedge offered no special protection, as the aboriginal people learned in earlier hunting cases such as *Sikyea v. The Queen,* [1964] S.C.R. 642, and *R. v. George,* [1966] S.C.R. 267. On April 17, 1982, however, this particular type of "hedge" was converted by s. 35(1) into sterner stuff that could only be broken down when justified according to the test laid down in *R. v. Sparrow,* [1990] 1 S.C.R. 1075, at pp. 1112 et seq., as adapted to apply to treaties in *Badger, supra, per* Cory J., at paras. 75 *et seq.* See also *R. v. Bombay,* [1993] 1 C.N.L.R. 92 (Ont. C.A.). The fact the *content* of Mi'kmaq rights under the treaty to hunt and fish and trade was no greater than those enjoyed by other inhabitants does not, unless those rights were extinguished prior to April 17, 1982, detract from the higher *protection* they presently offer to the Mi'kmaq people.

The Honour of the Crown
49   This appeal puts to the test the principle, emphasized by this Court on several occasions, that the honour of the Crown is always at stake in its dealings with aboriginal people. . . .

50   This principle that the Crown's honour is at stake when the Crown enters into treaties with first nations dates back at least to this Court's decision in 1895, *Province of Ontario v. Dominion of Canada and Province of Quebec; In re Indian Claims* (1895), 25 S.C.R. 434. In that decision, Gwynne J. (dissenting) stated, at pp. 511-12:

> . . . what is contended for and must not be lost sight of, is that the British sovereigns, ever since the acquisition of Canada, have been pleased to adopt the rule or practice of entering into agreements with the Indian nations or tribes in their province of Canada, for the cession or surrender by them of what such sovereigns have been pleased to designate the Indian title, by instruments similar to these now under consideration to which they have been pleased to give the designation of "treaties" with the Indians in possession of and claiming title to the lands expressed to be surrendered by the instruments, and further that the terms and conditions expressed in those instruments as to be performed by or on behalf of the Crown, have always been regarded as involving a trust graciously assumed by the Crown to the

fulfilment of which with the Indians the faith and honour of the Crown is pledged, and which trust has always been most faithfully fulfilled as a treaty obligation of the Crown. [Emphasis added.]

See also *Ontario Mining Co. v. Seybold* (1901), 32 S.C.R. 1, at p. 2.
. . .

52   I do not think an interpretation of events that turns a positive Mi'kmaq trade demand into a negative Mi'kmaq covenant is consistent with the honour and integrity of the Crown. Nor is it consistent to conclude that the Lieutenant Governor, seeking in good faith to address the trade demands of the Mi'kmaq, accepted the Mi'kmaq suggestion of a trading facility while denying any treaty protection to Mi'kmaq access to the things that were to be traded, even though these things were identified and priced in the treaty negotiations. This was not a commercial contract. The trade arrangement must be interpreted in a manner which gives meaning and substance to the promises made by the Crown. In my view, with respect, the interpretation adopted by the courts below left the Mi'kmaq with an empty shell of a treaty promise.

Contradictory Interpretations of the Truckhouse Clause

53   The appellant argues that the Crown has been in breach of the treaty since 1762, when the truckhouses were terminated, or at least since the 1780s when the replacement system of licensed traders was abandoned. This argument suffers from the same quality of unreasonableness as does the Crown's argument that the treaty left the Mi'kmaq with nothing more than a negative covenant. It was established in *Simon, supra,* at p. 402, that treaty provisions should be interpreted "in a flexible way that is sensitive to the evolution of changes in normal" practice, and *Sundown, supra,* at para. 32, confirms that courts should not use a "frozen-in-time" approach to treaty rights. The appellant cannot, with any show of logic, claim to exercise his treaty rights using an outboard motor while at the same time insist on restoration of the peculiar 18th century institution known as truckhouses.

54   The Crown, on the other hand, argues that the truckhouse was a time-limited response to a temporary problem. As my colleague McLachlin J. sets out at para. 96, the "core" of the treaty was said to be that "[t]he Mi'kmaq agreed to forgo their trading autonomy and the general trading rights they possessed as British subjects, and to abide by the treaty trade regime. The British, in exchange, undertook to provide the Mi'kmaq with stable trading outlets where European goods were provided at favourable terms while the exclusive trade regime existed". My disagreement with that view, with respect, is that the aboriginal people, as found by the trial judge, relied on European powder, shot and other goods and pushed a trade agenda with the British because their alternative sources of supply had dried up; the real inhibition on trade with the French was not the treaty but the absence of the French, whose military had retreated up the St. Lawrence and whose settlers had been expelled; there is no suggestion in the negotiating records that the truckhouse system was a sort of transitional arrangement expected to be temporary, it only became temporary because the King unexpectedly disallowed the enabling legislation passed by the Nova Scotia House of Assembly; and the notion that the truckhouse was merely a response to a trade restriction over-

looks the fact the truckhouse system offered very considerable financial benefits to the Mi'kmaq which they would have wanted to exploit, restriction or no restriction. The promise of access to "necessaries" through trade in wildlife was the key point, and where a right has been granted, there must be more than a mere disappearance of the mechanism created to facilitate the exercise of the right to warrant the conclusion that the right itself is spent or extinguished.

55   The Crown further argues that the treaty rights, if they exist at all, were "subject to regulation, *ab initio*". The effect, it is argued, is that no *Badger* justification would be required. The Crown's attempt to distinguish *Badger* is not persuasive. *Badger* dealt with treaty rights which were specifically expressed in the treaty (at para. 31) to be "subject to such regulations as may from time to time be made by the Government of the country". Yet the Court concluded that a *Sparrow*-type justification was required.

56   My view is that the surviving substance of the treaty is not the literal promise of a truckhouse, but a treaty right to continue to obtain necessaries through hunting and fishing by trading the products of those traditional activities subject to restrictions that can be justified under the *Badger* test.

The Limited Scope of the Treaty Right
57   The Crown expresses the concern that recognition of the existence of a constitutionally entrenched right with, as here, a trading aspect, would open the floodgates to uncontrollable and excessive exploitation of the natural resources. Whereas hunting and fishing for food naturally restricts quantities to the needs and appetites of those entitled to share in the harvest, it is argued that there is no comparable, built-in restriction associated with a trading right, short of the paramount need to conserve the resource. The Court has already addressed this issue in *R. v. Gladstone*, [1996] 2 S.C.R. 723, *per* Lamer C.J., at paras. 57-63, L'Heureux-Dubé J., at para. 137, and McLachlin J., at para. 164; *Van der Peet, supra, per* L'Heureux-Dubé J., at para. 192, and *per* McLachlin J., at para. 279; *R. v. N.T.C. Smokehouse Ltd.*, [1996] 2 S.C.R. 672, *per* L'Heureux-Dubé J., at para. 47; and *Horseman, supra, per* Wilson J., at p. 908, and Cory J., at pp. 928-29. The ultimate fear is that the appellant . . . could lever the treaty right into a factory trawler in Pomquet Harbour gathering the available harvest in preference to all non-aboriginal commercial or recreational fishermen. (This is indeed the position advanced by the intervener the Union of New Brunswick Indians.) This fear (or hope) is based on a misunderstanding of the narrow ambit and extent of the treaty right.

58   The recorded note of February 11, 1760 was that "there might be a Truckhouse established, for the furnishing them with <u>necessaries</u>" (emphasis added). What is contemplated therefore is not a right to trade generally for economic gain, but rather a right to trade for necessaries. The treaty right is a regulated right and can be contained by regulation within its proper limits.

59   The concept of "necessaries" is today equivalent to the concept of what Lambert

J.A., in *R. v. Van der Peet* (1993), 80 B.C.L.R. (2d) 75, at p. 126, described as a "moderate livelihood". Bare subsistence has thankfully receded over the last couple of centuries as an appropriate standard of life for aboriginals and non-aboriginals alike. A moderate livelihood includes such basics as "food, clothing and housing, supplemented by a few amenities", but not the accumulation of wealth (*Gladstone, supra,* at para. 165). It addresses day-to-day needs. This was the common intention in 1760. It is fair that it be given this interpretation today.

60   The distinction between a commercial right and a right to trade for necessaries or sustenance was discussed in *Gladstone, supra,* where Lamer C.J., speaking for the majority, held that the Heiltsuk of British Columbia have "an aboriginal right to sell herring spawn on kelp to an extent best described as commercial" (para. 28). This finding was based on the evidence that "tons" of the herring spawn on kelp was traded and that such trade was a central and defining feature of Heiltsuk society. McLachlin J., however, took a different view of the evidence, which she concluded supported a finding that the Heiltsuk derived only sustenance from the trade of the herring spawn on kelp. "Sustenance" provided a manageable limitation on what would otherwise be a free-standing commercial right. She wrote at para. 165:

> Despite the large quantities of herring spawn on kelp traditionally traded, the evidence does not indicate that the trade of herring spawn on kelp provided for the Heiltsuk anything more than basic sustenance. There is no evidence in this case that the Heiltsuk accumulated wealth which would exceed a sustenance lifestyle from the herring spawn on kelp fishery. [Emphasis added.]

In this case, equally, it is not suggested that Mi'kmaq trade historically generated "wealth which would exceed a sustenance lifestyle". Nor would anything more have been contemplated by the parties in 1760.

61   Catch limits that could reasonably be expected to produce a moderate livelihood for individual Mi'kmaq families at present-day standards can be established by regulation and enforced without violating the treaty right. In that case, the regulations would accommodate the treaty right. Such regulations would *not* constitute an infringement that would have to be justified under the *Badger* standard.

. . .

63   All of these regulations place the issuance of licences within the absolute discretion of the Minister. . . .

64   . . . there is nothing in these regulations which gives direction to the Minister to explain how she or he should exercise this discretionary authority in a manner which would respect the appellant's treaty rights. This Court has had the opportunity to review the effect of discretionary licensing schemes on aboriginal and treaty rights: *Badger,* . . . *R. v. Nikal,* . . . *R. v. Adams,* . . . and *R. v. Côté,* . . . The test for infringement under s. 35(1) of the *Constitution Act, 1982* was set out in *Sparrow,* . . .

Cory J. in *Badger, supra,* at para. 79, found that the test for infringement under s. 35(1) of the *Constitution Act, 1982* was the same for both aboriginal and treaty rights, and thus the words of Lamer C.J. in *Adams,* although in relation to the infringement of aboriginal rights, are equally applicable here. There was nothing at that time which provided the Crown officials with the "sufficient directives" necessary to ensure that the appellant's treaty rights would be respected. To paraphrase *Adams,* at para. 51, under the applicable regulatory regime, the appellant's exercise of his treaty right to fish and trade for sustenance was exercisable only at the absolute discretion of the Minister. Mi'kmaq treaty rights were not accommodated in the Regulations because, presumably, the Crown's position was, and continues to be, that no such treaty rights existed. In the circumstances, the purported regulatory prohibitions against fishing without a licence . . . do *prima facie* infringe the appellant's treaty rights under the Treaties of 1760-61 and are inoperative against the appellant unless justified under the *Badger* test.

65   Further, the appellant was charged with fishing during the close season with improper nets, contrary to s. 20 of the *Maritime Provinces Fishery Regulations.* Such a regulation is also a *prima facie* infringement, as noted by Cory J. in *Badger, supra,* at para. 90: "This Court has held on numerous occasions that there can be no limitation on the method, timing and extent of Indian hunting under a Treaty", apart, I would add, from a treaty limitation to that effect.

66   The appellant caught and sold the eels to support himself and his wife. Accordingly, the close season and the imposition of a discretionary licensing system would, if enforced, interfere with the appellant's treaty right to fish for trading purposes, and the ban on sales would, if enforced, infringe his right to trade for sustenance. In the absence of any justification of the regulatory prohibitions, the appellant is entitled to an acquittal.

Disposition

67   The constitutional question stated by the Chief Justice on February 9, 1998, as follows:

Are the prohibitions on catching and retaining fish without a licence, on fishing during the close time, and on the unlicensed sale of fish, contained in ss. 4(1)*(a)* and 20 of the *Maritime Provinces Fishery Regulations* and s. 35(2) of *the Fishery (General) Regulations,* inconsistent with the treaty rights of the appellant contained in the Mi'kmaq Treaties of 1760-61 and therefore of no force or effect or application to him, by virtue of ss. 35(1) and 52 of the *Constitution Act, 1982*?

should be answered in the affirmative. I would therefore allow the appeal and order an acquittal on all charges.

The reasons of Gonthier and McLachlin JJ. were delivered by

MCLACHLIN J. (dissenting)—

. . .

70   I conclude that the Treaties of 1760-61 created an exclusive trade and truckhouse regime which implicitly gave rise to a limited Mi'kmaq right to bring goods to British trade outlets so long as this regime was extant. The Treaties of 1760-61 granted neither a freestanding right to truckhouses nor a general underlying right to trade outside of the exclusive trade and truckhouse regime. The system of trade exclusivity and correlative British trading outlets died out in the 1780s and with it, the incidental right to bring goods to trade. There is therefore no existing right to trade in the Treaties of 1760-61 that exempts the appellant from the federal fisheries legislation. The charges against him stand. . . .

A.   *What Principles of Interpretation Apply to the Interpretation of the Treaty Trade Clause?*
78   This Court has set out the principles governing treaty interpretation on many occasions. They include the following:

1   Aboriginal treaties constitute a unique type of agreement and attract special principles of interpretation: *R. v. Sundown*, [1999] 1 S.C.R 393, at para. 24; *R. v. Badger*, [1996] 1 S.C.R. 771, at para. 78; *R. v. Sioui*, [1990] 1 S.C.R. 1025, at p. 1043; *Simon v. The Queen*, [1985] 2 S.C.R. 387, at p. 404. . . .

2   Treaties should be liberally construed and ambiguities or doubtful expressions should be resolved in favour of the aboriginal signatories: *Simon, supra*, at p. 402; *Sioui, supra*, at p. 1035; *Badger, supra*, at para. 52.

3   The goal of treaty interpretation is to choose from among the various possible interpretations of common intention the one which best reconciles the interests of both parties at the time the treaty was signed: *Sioui, supra*, at pp. 1068-69.

4   In searching for the common intention of the parties, the integrity and honour of the Crown is presumed: *Badger, supra*, at para. 41.

5   In determining the signatories' respective understanding and intentions, the court must be sensitive to the unique cultural and linguistic differences between the parties: *Badger, supra*, at paras. 52-54; *R. v. Horseman*, [1990] 1 S.C.R. 901, at p. 907.

6   The words of the treaty must be given the sense which they would naturally have held for the parties at the time: *Badger, supra*, at paras. 53 *et seq.; Nowegijick v. The Queen*, [1983] 1 S.C.R. 29, at p. 36.

7   A technical or contractual interpretation of treaty wording should be avoided: *Badger, supra; Horseman, supra; Nowegijick, supra.*

8   While construing the language generously, courts cannot alter the terms of the treaty by exceeding what "is possible on the language" or realistic: *Badger, supra*, at

para. 76; *Sioui, supra,* at p. 1069; *Horseman, supra,* at p. 908.

9   Treaty rights of aboriginal peoples must not be interpreted in a static or rigid way. They are not frozen at the date of signature. The interpreting court must update treaty rights to provide for their modern exercise. This involves determining what modern practices are reasonably incidental to the core treaty right in its modern context: *Sundown, supra,* at para. 32; *Simon, supra,* at p. 402.

79   Two specific issues of interpretation arise on this appeal. The answer to each is found in the foregoing summary of principles.

80   The first issue of interpretation arises from the Court of Appeal's apparent suggestion that peace treaties fall in a different category from land cession treaties for purposes of interpretation, with the result that, when interpreting peace treaties, there is no "presumption" that rights were granted to the aboriginal signatories in exchange for entering into the treaty. This raises the issue of whether it is useful to slot treaties into different categories, each with its own rules of interpretation. The principle that each treaty must be considered in its unique historical and cultural context suggests that this practice should be avoided.

81   The second issue of interpretation raised on this appeal is whether extrinsic evidence can be used in interpreting aboriginal treaties, absent ambiguity. Again, the principle that every treaty must be understood in its historical and cultural context suggests the answer must be yes. It is true that in *R. v. Horse,* [1988] 1 S.C.R. 187, at p. 201, this Court alluded with approval to the strict contract rule that extrinsic evidence is not admissible to construe a contract in the absence of ambiguity. However, subsequent decisions have made it clear that extrinsic evidence of the historic and cultural context of a treaty may be received absent ambiguity: *Sundown, supra,* at para. 25; *Badger, supra,* at para. 52. As Cory J. wrote in *Badger, supra,* at para. 52, courts interpreting treaties "must take into account the context in which the treaties were negotiated, concluded and committed to writing".

82   The fact that both the words of the treaty and its historic and cultural context must be considered suggests that it may be useful to approach the interpretation of a treaty in two steps. First, the words of the treaty clause at issue should be examined to determine their facial meaning, in so far as this can be ascertained, noting any patent ambiguities and misunderstandings that may have arisen from linguistic and cultural differences. This exercise will lead to one or more possible interpretations of the clause. As noted in *Badger, supra,* at para. 76, "the scope of treaty rights will be determined by their wording". The objective at this stage is to develop a preliminary, but not necessarily determinative, framework for the historical context inquiry, taking into account the need to avoid an unduly restrictive interpretation and the need to give effect to the principles of interpretation.

83   At the second step, the meaning or different meanings which have arisen from the wording of the treaty right must be considered against the treaty's historical and cul-

tural backdrop. A consideration of the historical background may suggest latent ambiguities or alternative interpretations not detected at first reading. Faced with a possible range of interpretations, courts must rely on the historical context to determine which comes closest to reflecting the parties' common intention. This determination requires choosing "from among the various possible interpretations of the common intention the one which best reconciles" the parties' interests: *Sioui, supra,* at p. 1069. Finally, if the court identifies a particular right which was intended to pass from generation to generation, the historical context may assist the court in determining the modern counterpart of that right: *Simon, supra,* at pp. 402-3; *Sundown, supra,* at paras. 30 and 33.

84   In the case on appeal, the trial judge heard 40 days of trial, the testimony of three expert witnesses, and was presented with over 400 documents. . . .

The trial judge's review of the historical context, the cultural differences between the parties, their different methods of communication, and the pre-treaty negotiations, led him to conclude that there was no misunderstanding or lack of agreement between the British and the Mi'kmaq that trade under the treaties was to be carried out in accordance with the terms of the trade clause. Having come to this conclusion, the trial judge turned again to the historical context to interpret the content of such terms, in accordance with the parties' common intention. In my opinion, the trial judge's approach to the interpretation of the Treaties of 1760-61 is in keeping with the principles governing treaty interpretation. With the greatest respect for the contrary view of my colleague, Justice Binnie, I find no basis for error in the trial judge's approach.

B.   *Do the Treaties of 1760-61 Grant a General Right to Trade?*
. . .

The clause is short, the words simple. The Mi'kmaq covenant that they will "<u>not</u> traffick, barter or Exchange any Commodities in any manner <u>but</u> with [British agents]" (emphasis added). The core of this clause is the obligation on the Mi'kmaq to trade only with the British. Ancillary to this is the implied promise that the British will establish truckhouses where the Mi'kmaq can trade. These words do not, on their face, confer a general right to trade.

88   The next question is whether the historic and cultural context in which the treaties were made establishes a general right to trade, having due regard for the need to interpret treaty rights generously. I will deal first with the linguistic and cultural differences between the parties, then with the historical record generally.

(2)   Cultural and Linguistic Considerations
89   The trial judge found that there was no misunderstanding or lack of agreement between the British and the Mi'kmaq that trade under the treaties was to be carried out in accordance with the terms of the trade clause, and that the Mi'kmaq understood those terms. He addressed and discounted the possibility that the French-speaking Mi'kmaq might not have understood the English treaty terms. The record amply supports this conclusion. French missionaries, long allied with the Mi'kmaq, were em-

ployed by the British as interpreters in the treaty negotiations. In the course of the negotiations, the Mi'kmaq were referred to an earlier treaty entered into by the Maliseet and Passamaquody, containing a similar trade clause in French. Some of the Mi'kmaq appeared to have acquired English; the records speak of Paul Laurent of LaHave, a Mi'kmaq Sakamow and one of the first signatories, as speaking English. More generally, by the time the Treaties of 1760-61 were entered into, the record suggests that the Mi'kmaq had developed an understanding of the importance of the written word to the British in treaty-making and had a sufficiently sophisticated knowledge of the treaty-making process to compare and discern the differences between treaties. The trial judge was amply justified in concluding that the Mi'kmaq understood the treaty process as well as the particular terms of the treaties they were signing. There is nothing in the linguistic or cultural differences between the parties to suggest that the words of the trade clause were not fully understood or appreciated by the Mi'kmaq.

(3) The Historical Context and the Scope of the Trade Clause
90 After a meticulous review of the historical evidence, the trial judge concluded that: (1) the Treaties of 1760-61 were primarily peace treaties, cast against the background of both a long struggle between the British and the French in which the Mi'kmaq were allied with the French, and over a decade of intermittent hostilities between the British and the Mi'kmaq; (2) the French defeat and withdrawal from Nova Scotia left the Mi'kmaq to co-exist with the British without the presence of their former ally and supplier; (3) the Mi'kmaq were accustomed to and in some cases dependent on trade for firearms, gunpowder, food and European trade goods; and (4) the British wanted peace and a safe environment for settlers and, despite recent victories, did not feel completely secure in Nova Scotia.

91 Considering the wording of the trade clause in this historical context, the trial judge concluded that it was not within the common intention of the parties that the treaties granted a general right to trade. He found that at the time of entering the treaties, the Mi'kmaq wanted to secure peace and continuing access to European trade goods. He described the Mi'kmaq concerns at the time as very focussed and immediate. The British, for their part, wanted peace in the region to ensure the safety of their settlers. While the British were willing to support the costly truckhouse system to secure peace, they did not want the Mi'kmaq to become a long-term burden on the public treasury. To this end, the trial judge found that the British wanted the Mi'kmaq to continue their traditional way of life. The trial judge found that the interpretation of the treaty trade clause which best reconciled the intentions of both parties was that the trade clause imposed an obligation on the Mi'kmaq to trade only at British truckhouses or with licensed traders, as well as a correlative obligation on the British to provide the Mi'kmaq with such trading outlets so long as this restriction on Mi'kmaq trade existed. This correlative obligation on the British gave rise to a limited Mi'kmaq "right to bring" goods to trade at these outlets. When the British ceased to provide trading outlets to the Mi'kmaq, the restriction on their trade fell as did the limited "right to bring" which arose out of the system of mutual obligations.

92 Although trade was central to the Treaties of 1760-61, it cannot be doubted that

achieving and securing peace was the preeminent objective of both parties in entering into the treaties. . . .

93   The desire to establish a secure and successful peace led each party to make significant concessions. The Mi'kmaq accepted that forging a peaceful relationship with the British was essential to ensuring continued access to European trade goods and to their continued security in the region. To this end, the Mi'kmaq agreed to limit their autonomy by trading only with the British and ceasing all trading relations with the French. Agreeing to restricted trade at truckhouses made the limit on Mi'kmaq autonomy more palatable as truckhouses were recognized as vehicles for stable trade at guaranteed and favourable terms. . . .

96   To achieve the mutually desired objective of peace, both parties agreed to make certain concessions. The Mi'kmaq agreed to forgo their trading autonomy and the general trading rights they possessed as British subjects, and to abide by the treaty trade regime. The British, in exchange, undertook to provide the Mi'kmaq with stable trading outlets where European goods were provided at favourable terms while the exclusive trade regime existed. This is the core of what the parties intended. The wording of the trade clause, taken in its linguistic, cultural and historical context, permits no other conclusion. Both the Mi'kmaq and the British understood that the "right to bring" goods to trade was a limited right contingent on the existence of a system of exclusive trade and truckhouses. On the historical record, neither the Mi'kmaq nor the British intended or understood the treaty trade clause as creating a general right to trade.

97   The parties' pre-treaty negotiations and post-treaty conduct point to the same conclusion. I turn first to the pre-treaty negotiations. British negotiations with the Mi'kmaq took place against the background of earlier negotiations with the Maliseet and Passamaquody on February 11, 1760. These negotiations led to the treaty of February 23, 1760, the first of the 1760-61 Treaties. When Mi'kmaq representatives came to negotiate peace with the British 8 days later on February 29, 1760, they were informed of the treaty entered into by the Maliseet and Passamaquody and agreed to make peace on the same conditions. . . .

98   The pre-treaty negotiations between the British and the Maliseet and the Passamaquody, indicate that the aboriginal leaders requested truckhouses in response to their accommodation of the British desire for restricted trade. The negotiations also indicate that the British agreed to furnish truckhouses where necessary to ensure that the Maliseet and the Passamaquody could continue to acquire commodities and necessities through trade. The negotiations highlight the concessions that both the aboriginal and the British signatories made in order to secure the mutually desired objective of peace. The negotiations also indicate that both parties understood that the treaties granted a specific, and limited, right to bring goods to truckhouses to trade.

99   This finding is confirmed by the post-treaty conduct of the Mi'kmaq and the British. Neither party's conduct is consistent with an expectation that the treaty granted the Mi'kmaq any trade right except the implied "right to bring" incidental to their

obligation to trade exclusively with the British. Soon after the treaties were entered into, the British stopped insisting that the Mi'kmaq trade only with them. The British replaced the expensive truckhouses with licensed traders in 1762. The system of licensed traders, in turn, died out by the 1780s. Mi'kmaq adherence to the exclusive trade and truckhouse regime was also ambiguous. Records exist of Mi'kmaq trade with the French on the islands of St. Pierre and Miquelon in 1763 and again in 1767: *Upton, supra,* at pp. 64-65. . . .

104 I conclude that the trial judge did not err—indeed was manifestly correct—in his interpretation of the historical record and the limited nature of the treaty right that this suggests.

. . .

106 In summary, a review of the wording, the historical record, the pre-treaty negotiations between the British and the Maliseet and Passamaquody, as well as the post-treaty conduct of the British and the Mi'kmaq, support the trial judge's conclusion that the treaty trade clause granted only a limited "right to bring" trade goods to truckhouses, a right that ended with the obligation to trade only with the British on which it was premised. The trial judge's conclusion that the treaties granted no general trade right must be confirmed.

C.   *Do the Treaties of 1760-61 Grant a Right to Government Trading Outlets?*
. . .

114 Based on the wording of the treaties and an extensive review of the historical evidence, the trial judge concluded that the only trade right conferred by the treaties was a "right to bring" goods to truckhouses that terminated with the demise of the exclusive trading and truckhouse regime. This led to the conclusion that no Crown breach was established and therefore no accommodation or justification required. The record amply supports this conclusion, and the trial judge made no error of legal principle. I see no basis upon which this Court can interfere.

VI. Justification
115 Having concluded that the Treaties of 1760-61 confer no general trade right, I need not consider the arguments specifically relating to justification. . . .

VII. Conclusion
116 There is no existing right to trade in the Treaties of 1760-61 that exempts the appellant from the federal fisheries regulations. It follows that I would dismiss the appeal. . . .

Appendix III

• • • • • •

Marshall No. 2 (Edited)

R. v. Marshall, (*Marshall No. 2*) [1999] 3 S.C.R. 533 (Rehearing application refused), Lamer C.J. and L'Heureux-Dubé, Gonthier, McLachlin, Iacobucci and Binnie JJ., November 17, 1999.

The following is the judgment delivered by

1   THE COURT—The intervener, the West Nova Fishermen's Coalition (the "Coalition"), applies for a rehearing to have the Court address the regulatory authority of the Government of Canada over the east coast fisheries together with a new trial to allow the Crown to justify for conservation or other purposes the licensing and closed season restriction on the exercise of the appellant's treaty right, and for an order that the Court's judgment, dated September 17, 1999, [1999] 3 S.C.R. 456, be stayed in the meantime. The application is opposed by the Crown, the appellant Marshall and the other interveners.

2   Those opposing the motion object in different ways that the Coalition's motion rests on a series of misconceptions about what the September 17, 1999 majority judgment decided and what it did not decide. These objections are well founded. The Court did not hold that the Mi'kmaq treaty right cannot be regulated or that the Mi'kmaq are guaranteed an open season in the fisheries. Justification for conservation or other purposes is a separate and distinct issue at the trial of one of these prosecutions. It is up to the Crown to decide whether or not it wishes to support the applicability of government regulations when prosecuting an accused who claims to be exercising an aboriginal or treaty right.

3   The Attorney General of Canada, in opposing the Coalition's motion, acknowledges that the Crown did not lead any evidence at trial or make any argument on the appeal that the licensing and closed season regulations which restricted the exercise of the treaty right were justified in relation to the eel fishery. Accordingly, the issue whether these restrictions could have been justified in this case formed no part of the Court's majority judgment of September 17, 1999, and the constitutional question posed in this prosecution was answered on that basis. . . .

5   The Coalition argues that the native and non-native fishery should be subject to the same regulations. In fact, as pointed out in the September 17, 1999 majority judg-

ment, natives and non-natives *were* subject to the unilateral regulatory authority of successive governments from 1760-61 to 1982. Until adoption of the *Constitution Act, 1982,* the appellant would clearly have been subject to regulations under the federal *Fisheries Act* and predecessor enactments in the same way and to the same extent as members of the applicant Coalition unless given a regulatory exemption as a matter of government policy.

6   As further pointed out in the September 17, 1999 majority judgment, the framers of the Constitution caused existing aboriginal and treaty rights to be entrenched in s. 35 of the *Constitution Act, 1982.* This gave constitutional status to rights that were previously vulnerable to unilateral extinguishment. The constitutional language necessarily included the 1760-61 treaties, and did not, on its face, refer expressly to a power to regulate. Section 35(1) simply says that "[t]he existing aboriginal and treaty rights of the aboriginal peoples of Canada are hereby recognized and affirmed". In subsequent cases, some aboriginal peoples argued that, as no regulatory restrictions on their rights were expressed in plain language in the Constitution, none could be imposed except by constitutional amendment. On the other hand, some of the Attorneys General argued that as aboriginal and treaty rights had always been vulnerable to unilateral regulation and extinguishment by government, this vulnerability was itself part of the rights now entrenched in s. 35 of the *Constitution Act, 1982.* In a series of important decisions commencing with *R. v. Sparrow,* [1990] 1 S.C.R. 1075, which arose in the context of the west coast fishery, this Court affirmed that s. 35 aboriginal and treaty rights are subject to regulation, provided such regulation is shown by the Crown to be justified on conservation or other grounds of public importance. A series of tests to establish such justification was laid out. These cases were referred to in the September 17, 1999 majority judgment, but the applicable principles were not elaborated because justification was not an issue which the Crown chose to make part of this particular prosecution, and therefore neither the Crown nor the defence had made submissions respecting the government's continuing powers of regulation. The Coalition recognizes that it is raising a new issue. It submits "that it is plain in the Reasons for Judgment, and in the earlier decisions of the Provincial Court of Nova Scotia at trial and of the Nova Scotia Court of Appeal on initial appeal, that that issue [of regulatory justification] has been neither considered nor decided". . . .

No Stay of Judgment

8   The appellant, like any other accused who is found to be not guilty, is ordinarily entitled to an immediate acquittal, not a judgment that is suspended while the government considers the wider implications of an unsuccessful prosecution. The Attorney General of Canada did not at the hearing of this appeal, and does not now in its response to the Coalition's motion, apply for a stay of the effect of the Court's recognition and affirmation of the Mi'kmaq treaty right. Should such an application be made, the Court will hear argument on whether it has the jurisdiction to grant such a stay, and if so, whether it ought to do so in this case.

Status of the West Nova Fishermen's Coalition

9   Those in opposition challenge the status of the Coalition to bring this application.

It is argued that the Coalition, being an intervener, does not have the rights of a party to ask for a rehearing. . . . While it would only be in exceptional circumstances that the Court would entertain an intervener's application for a rehearing, the extended definition of "party" in s. 1 of the Rules gives the Court the jurisdiction to do so. Not only are there no such exceptional circumstances here, but also the Coalition's motion violates the basis on which interveners are permitted to participate in an appeal in the first place, which is that interveners accept the record as defined by the Crown and the defence. Moreover, in so far as the Coalition's questions are capable of being answered on the trial record in this case, the responses are already evident in the September 17, 1999 majority judgment and the prior decisions of this Court therein referred to. . . .

10   The Coalition requests a rehearing on the following issues:

1   Whether the Appellant is entitled to have been acquitted on a charge of unlicensed sale of fish, contrary to s. 35(2) of the *Fishery (General) Regulations,* in the absence of a new (or further) trial on the issue of whether that Regulation is or can be justified by the government of Canada;

2   Whether the Appellant is entitled to have been acquitted on a charge of out-of-season fishing, contrary to Item 2 of Schedule III of the *Maritime Provinces Fishery Regulations,* in the absence of a new (or further) trial on the issue of whether those Regulations are or can be justified by the government of Canada;

3   Whether the government of Canada has power to regulate the exercise by Mi'kmaq persons, including the Appellant, of their treaty right to fish through the imposition of licensing requirements;

4   Whether the government of Canada has power to regulate the exercise by Mi'kmaq persons, including the Appellant, of their treaty right to fish through the imposition of closed seasons;

5   In any event, what is the scope of regulatory power possessed by the government of Canada for purposes of regulating the treaty right; and

6   . . . pursuant to section 27 of the *Rules of the Supreme Court of Canada,* [requests] an Order that [the Court's] judgment pronounced herein on the 17th day of September, 1999 be stayed pending disposition of the rehearing of the appeal, if ordered.

11   These questions, together with the Coalition's request for a stay of judgment, reflect a basic misunderstanding of the scope of the Court's majority reasons for judgment dated September 17, 1999. As stated, this was a prosecution of a private citizen. It required the Court to determine whether certain precise charges relating to the appellant's participation in the eel fishery could be sustained. The majority judgment of September 17, 1999 was limited to the issues necessary to dispose of the appellant's guilt or innocence.

12   An order suspending the effect of a judgment of this Court is infrequently granted, especially where (as here) the parties have not requested such an order. This was not a reference to determine the general validity of legislative and regulatory provisions, as was the case, for example, in *Reference re Manitoba Language Rights,* [1985] 1 S.C.R. 721, at p. 780, where the Court suspended its declaration of invalidity of Manitoba enactments until "the expiry of the minimum period required for translation, re-enactment, printing and publishing". Nor was this a case where the Court was asked to grant declaratory relief with respect to the invalidity of statutory provisions, as in *M. v. H.,* [1999] 2 S.C.R. 3, . . .

13   Here the Crown elected to test the treaty issue by way of a prosecution, which is governed by a different set of rules than is a reference or a declaratory action. This appeal was directed solely to the issue whether the Crown had proven the appellant guilty as charged. . . .

14   As stated in para. 56 of the September 17, 1999 majority judgment, the treaty right was "to continue to obtain necessaries through hunting and fishing by trading the products of those traditional activities subject to restrictions that can be justified under the *Badger* test" (emphasis added). . . . The Crown, as stated, did not offer any evidence or argument justifying the licensing and closed season restrictions (referred to in the statute and regulations as a "close time") on the appellant's exercise of the collective treaty right, such as (for example) a need to conserve and protect the eel population. The eel population may not in fact require protection from commercial exploitation. Such was the assertion of the Native Council of Nova Scotia in opposition to the Coalition's motion: . . .

. . . The majority judgment delivered on September 17, 1999, therefore directed the acquittal of the appellant on the evidence brought against him. The issue of justification was not before the Court and no judgment was made about whether or not such restrictions could have been justified in relation to the eel fishery had the Crown led evidence and argument to support their applicability.

Grounds on Which the Coalition Seeks a Rehearing
1.   *Whether the Appellant is entitled to have been acquitted on a charge of unlicensed sale of fish, contrary to s. 35(2) of the Fishery (General) Regulations, in the absence of a new (or further) trial on the issue of whether that Regulation is or can be justified by the government of Canada.*

15   The appellant, as any other citizen facing a prosecution, is entitled to know in a timely way the case he has to meet, and to be afforded the opportunity to answer it. The Coalition seeks a new trial on a new issue. The September 17, 1999 majority decision specifically noted at para. 4 that the treaty right

. . . was always subject to regulation. The Crown does not suggest that the regulations in question accommodate the treaty right. The Crown's case is that no such treaty right exists. Further, no argument was made that the treaty right was extinguished prior to [enactment of the *Constitution Act, 1982*], and no justification was offered by the Crown for the several prohibitions at issue in this case. [Emphasis added.]

. . . As stated, the Crown here opposes a rehearing and opposes a new trial. The issues of concern to the Coalition largely relate to the lobster fishery, not the eel fishery, and, if necessary, can be raised and decided in future cases that involve the specifics of the lobster fishery. It is up to the Crown to initiate enforcement action in the lobster and other fisheries if and when it chooses to do so.

2.   *Whether the Appellant is entitled to have been acquitted on a charge of out-of-season fishing, contrary to Item 2 of Schedule III of the Maritime Provinces Fishery Regulations, in the absence of a new (or further) trial on the issue of whether those Regulations are or can be justified by the government of Canada.*

16   The Coalition argues that a rehearing and a further trial are necessary because of "uncertainty" about the authority of the government to manage the fisheries. The Attorney General of Canada, acting on behalf of the federal government which regulates the fisheries, opposes the Coalition's position. . . .

18   The September 17, 1999 majority judgment further pointed out that the accused will be required to demonstrate (as the appellant did here) that the regulatory regime significantly restricts the exercise of the treaty right. The majority judgment concluded on this point, at para. 64, that:

> In the circumstances, the purported regulatory prohibitions against fishing without a licence (*Maritime Provinces Fishery Regulations,* s. 4(1)(*a*)) and of selling eels without a licence (*Fishery (General) Regulations,* s. 35(2)) do *prima facie* infringe the appellant's treaty rights under the Treaties of 1760-61 and are inoperative against the appellant under the *Badger* test. [Emphasis added.]

19   At the end of the day, it is always open to the Minister (as it was here) to seek to justify the limitation on the treaty right because of the need to conserve the resource in question or for other compelling and substantial public objectives, as discussed below. Equally, it will be open to an accused in future cases to try to show that the treaty right was intended in 1760 by *both* sides to include access to resources other than fish, wildlife and traditionally gathered things such as fruits and berries. The word "gathering" in the September 17, 1999 majority judgment was used in connection with the types of the resources traditionally "gathered" in an aboriginal economy and which were thus reasonably in the contemplation of the parties to the 1760-61 treaties. While treaty rights are capable of evolution within limits, as discussed below, their subject matter (absent a new agreement) cannot be wholly transformed. Certain unjustified assumptions are made in this regard by the Native Council of Nova Scotia on this motion about "the effect of the economic treaty right on forestry, minerals and natural gas deposits offshore". The Union of New Brunswick Indians also suggested on this motion a need to "negotiate an integrated approach dealing with all resources coming

within the purview of fishing, hunting and gathering which includes harvesting from the sea, the forests and the land". This extended interpretation of "gathering" is not dealt with in the September 17, 1999 majority judgment, and negotiations with respect to such resources as logging, minerals or offshore natural gas deposits would go beyond the subject matter of this appeal.

20   The September 17, 1999 majority judgment did not rule that the appellant had established a treaty right "to gather" anything and everything physically capable of being gathered. The issues were much narrower and the ruling was much narrower. No evidence was drawn to our attention, nor was any argument made in the course of this appeal, that trade in logging or minerals, or the exploitation of off-shore natural gas deposits, was in the contemplation of either or both parties to the 1760 treaty; nor was the argument made that exploitation of such resources could be considered a logical evolution of treaty rights to fish and wildlife or to the type of things traditionally "gathered" by the Mi'kmaq in a 1760 aboriginal lifestyle. It is of course open to native communities to assert broader treaty rights in that regard, but if so, the basis for such a claim will have to be established in proceedings where the issue is squarely raised on proper historical evidence, as was done in this case in relation to fish and wildlife. Other resources were simply not addressed by the parties, and therefore not addressed by the Court in its September 17, 1999 majority judgment. As acknowledged by the Union of New Brunswick Indians in opposition to the Coalition's motion, "there are cases wending their way through the lower courts dealing specifically with some of these potential issues such as cutting timber on Crown lands".

21   The fact the Crown elected not to try to justify a closed season on the eel fishery at issue in this case cannot be generalized, as the Coalition's question implies, to a conclusion that closed seasons can never be imposed as part of the government's regulation of the Mi'kmaq limited commercial "right to fish". A "closed season" is clearly a potentially available management tool, but its application to treaty rights will have to be justified for conservation or other purposes. In the absence of such justification, an accused who establishes a treaty right is ordinarily allowed to exercise it. As suggested in the expert evidence filed on this motion by the Union of New Brunswick Indians, the establishment of a closed season may raise very different conservation and other issues in the eel fishery than it does in relation to other species such as salmon, crab, cod or lobster, or for that matter, to moose and other wildlife. The complexities and techniques of fish and wildlife management vary from species to species and restrictions will likely have to be justified on a species-by-species basis. Evidence supporting closure of the wild salmon fishery is not necessarily transferable to justify closure of an eel fishery.

22   Resource conservation and management and allocation of the permissible catch inevitably raise matters of considerable complexity both for Mi'kmaq peoples who seek to work for a living under the protection of the treaty right, and for governments who seek to justify the regulation of that treaty right. The factual context, as this case shows, is of great importance, and the merits of the government's justification may vary from resource to resource, species to species, community to community and time

to time. As this and other courts have pointed out on many occasions, the process of accommodation of the treaty right may best be resolved by consultation and negotiation of a modern agreement for participation in specified resources by the Mi'kmaq rather than by litigation. La Forest J. emphasized in *Delgamuukw v. British Columbia*, [1997] 3 S.C.R. 1010 (a case cited in the September 17, 1999 majority decision), at para. 207:

> On a final note, I wish to emphasize that the best approach in these types of cases is a process of negotiation and reconciliation that properly considers the complex and competing interests at stake.

23   The various governmental, aboriginal and other interests are not, of course, obliged to reach an agreement. In the absence of a mutually satisfactory solution, the courts will resolve the points of conflict as they arise case by case. The decision in this particular prosecution is authority only for the matters adjudicated upon. The acquittal ought not to be set aside to allow the Coalition to address new issues that were neither raised by the parties nor determined by the Court in the September 17, 1999 majority judgment.

3.   *Whether the government of Canada has power to regulate the exercise by Mi'kmaq persons, including the Appellant, of their treaty right to fish through the imposition of licensing requirements.*

24   The government's power to regulate the treaty right is repeatedly affirmed in the September 17, 1999 majority judgment. In addition to the reference at para. 4 of the majority decision, already mentioned, that the treaty right "was always subject to regulation", the majority judgment further stated, at para. 7:

> In my view, the treaty rights are limited to securing "necessaries" (which I construe in the modern context, as equivalent to a moderate livelihood), and do not extend to the open-ended accumulation of wealth. The rights thus construed, however, are, in my opinion, treaty rights within the meaning of s. 35 of the *Constitution Act, 1982,* and are subject to regulations that can be justified under the *Badger* test. . . . [Emphasis added.]

. . . At para. 58, the limited nature of the right was reiterated:

> What is contemplated therefore is not a right to trade generally for economic gain, but rather a right to trade for necessaries. The treaty right is a regulated right and can be contained by regulation within its proper limits. [Emphasis added.]

At para. 64, the majority judgment again referred to regulation permitted by the *Badger* test. The Court was thus most explicit in confirming the regulatory authority of the federal and provincial governments within their respective legislative fields to regulate the exercise of the treaty right subject to the constitutional requirement that restraints on the exercise of the treaty right have to be justified on the basis of conservation or other compelling and substantial public objectives, discussed below.

25   With all due respect to the Coalition, the government's general regulatory power is clearly affirmed. It is difficult to believe that further repetition of this fundamental point after a rehearing would add anything of significance to what is already stated in the September 17, 1999 majority judgment.

26   As for the specific matter of licences, the conclusion of the majority judgment was *not* that licensing schemes as such are invalid, but that the imposition of a licensing restriction on the appellant's exercise of the treaty right had not been justified for conservation or other public purposes. The Court majority stated at para. 64:

> . . . under the applicable regulatory regime, the appellant's exercise of his treaty right to fish and trade for sustenance was exercisable only at the absolute discretion of the Minister. Mi'kmaq treaty rights were not accommodated in the Regulations because, presumably, the Crown's position was, and continues to be, that no such treaty rights existed. In the circumstances, the purported regulatory prohibitions . . . are inoperative against the appellant <u>unless justified under the *Badger* test</u>. [Emphasis added.]

27   Although no evidence or argument was put forward to justify the licensing requirement in this case, a majority of the Court nevertheless referred at para. 64 of its September 17, 1999 decision to *R. v. Nikal,* . . . where Cory J., for the Court, dealt with a licensing issue as follows, at paras. 91 and 92:

> With respect to licensing, the appellant [aboriginal accused] takes the position that once his rights have been established, anything which affects or interferes with the exercise of those rights, no matter how insignificant, constitutes a *prima facie* infringement. It is said that a licence by its very existence is an infringement of the aboriginal right since it infers that government permission is needed to exercise the right and that the appellant is not free to follow his own or his band's discretion in exercising that right.

> This position cannot be correct. It has frequently been said that rights do not exist in a vacuum, and that the rights of one individual or group are necessarily limited by the rights of another. The ability to exercise personal or group rights is necessarily limited by the rights of others. The government must ultimately be able to determine and direct the way in which these rights should interact. Absolute freedom in the exercise of even a *Charter* or constitutionally guaranteed aboriginal right has never been accepted, nor was it intended. Section 1 of the *Canadian Charter of Rights and Freedoms* is perhaps the prime example of this principle. Absolute freedom without any restriction necessarily infers a freedom to live without any laws. Such a concept is not acceptable in our society.

28   The justification for a licensing requirement depends on facts. The Crown in this case declined to offer evidence or argument to support the imposition of a licensing

requirement in relation to the small-scale commercial eel fishery in which the appellant participated.

4.   *Whether the government of Canada has power to regulate the exercise by Mi'kmaq persons, including the Appellant, of their treaty right to fish through the imposition of closed seasons.*

29   The regulatory device of a closed season is at least in part directed at conservation of the resource. Conservation has always been recognized to be a justification of paramount importance to limit the exercise of treaty and aboriginal rights in the decisions of this Court cited in the majority decision of September 17, 1999, including *Sparrow, supra,* and *Badger, supra.* As acknowledged by the Native Council of Nova Scotia in opposition to the Coalition's motion, "[c]onservation is clearly a first priority and the Aboriginal peoples accept this". Conservation, where necessary, may require the complete shutdown of a hunt or a fishery for aboriginal and non-aboriginal alike.

30   In this case, the prosecution of the appellant was directed to a "closed season" in the eel fishery which the Crown did not try to justify, and that is the precise context in which the majority decision of September 17, 1999 is to be understood. No useful purpose would be served for those like the Coalition who are interested in justifying a closed season in the lobster fishery if a rehearing or a new trial were ordered in this case, which related only to the closed season in the eel fishery.

5.   *In any event, what is the scope of regulatory power possessed by the government of Canada for purposes of regulating the treaty right?*

31   On the face of it, this question is not raised by the subject matter of the appeal, nor is it capable of being answered on the factual record. As framed, it is so broad as to be incapable of a detailed response. In effect, the Coalition seeks to transform a prosecution on specific facts into a general reference seeking an advisory opinion of the Court on a broad range of regulatory issues related to the east coast fisheries. As was explained in *Reference re Secession of Quebec,* [1998] 2 S.C.R. 217, the Court's jurisdiction to give advisory opinions is exceptional and can be invoked only by the Governor in Council under s. 53 of the *Supreme Court Act,* R.S.C., 1985, c. S-26. In this instance, the Governor in Council has not sought an advisory opinion from the Court and the Attorney General of Canada opposes the Coalition's attempt to initiate what she calls a "private reference".

32   Mention has already been made of "the *Badger* test" by which governments may justify restrictions on the exercise of treaty rights. The Court in *Badger* extended to treaties the justificatory standard developed for aboriginal rights in *Sparrow, supra.* Cory J. set out the test, in *Badger, supra,* at para. 97 . . .

33   The majority judgment of September 17, 1999 did not put in doubt the validity of the *Fisheries Act* or any of its provisions. What it said, in para. 66, was that, "the close season and the imposition of a discretionary licensing system would, if enforced, in-

terfere with the appellant's treaty right to fish for trading purposes, and the ban on sales would, if enforced, infringe his right to trade for sustenance. In the absence of any justification of the regulatory prohibitions, the appellant is entitled to an acquittal" (emphasis added). Section 43 of the Act sets out the basis of a very broad regulatory authority over the fisheries which may extend to the native fishery where justification is shown:

. . .

(Pursuant to this regulatory power, the Governor in Council had, in fact, adopted the *Aboriginal Communal Fishing Licences Regulations,* discussed below.) Although s. 7(1) of the *Fisheries Act* purports to grant the Minister an "absolute discretion" to issue or not to issue leases and licences, this discretion must be read together with the authority of the Governor in Council under s. 43(f) to make regulations "respecting the issue, suspension and cancellation of licences and leases". Specific criteria must be established for the exercise by the Minister of his or her discretion to grant or refuse licences in a manner that recognizes and accommodates the existence of an aboriginal or treaty right. In *R. v. Adams,* [1996] 3 S.C.R. 101, also cited in the September 17, 1999 majority judgment, the Chief Justice stated as follows at para. 54:

> In light of the Crown's unique fiduciary obligations towards aboriginal peoples, Parliament may not simply adopt an unstructured discretionary administrative regime which risks infringing aboriginal rights in a substantial number of applications in the absence of some explicit guidance. If a statute confers an administrative discretion which may carry significant consequences for the exercise of an aboriginal right, the statute or its delegate regulations must outline specific criteria for the granting or refusal of that discretion which seek to accommodate the existence of aboriginal rights. In the absence of such specific guidance, the statute will fail to provide representatives of the Crown with sufficient directives to fulfil their fiduciary duties, and the statute will be found to represent an infringement of aboriginal rights under the *Sparrow* test. [Emphasis added.]

While *Adams* dealt with an aboriginal right, the same principle applies to treaty rights.

34 The *Aboriginal Communal Fishing Licences Regulations,* SOR/93-332, referred to in the September 17, 1999 majority judgment, deal with the food fishery. These regulations provide specific authority to impose conditions where justified respecting the species and quantities of fish that are permitted to be taken or transported; the locations and times at which landing of fish is permitted; the method to be used for the landing of fish and the methods by which the quantity of the fish is to be determined; the information that a designated person or the master of a designated vessel is to report to the Minister or a person specified by the licence holder, prior to commencement of fishing; the locations and times of inspections of the contents of the hold and the procedure to be used in conducting those inspections; the maximum number of persons or vessels that may be designated to carry on fishing and related activities; the maximum number of designated persons who may fish at any one time; the type, size and quantity of fishing gear that may be used by a designated person; and the disposi-

tion of fish caught under the authority of the licence. The Governor in Council has the power to amend the *Aboriginal Communal Fishing Licences Regulations* to accommodate a limited commercial fishery as described in the September 17, 1999 majority judgment in addition to the food fishery.

35 Despite the limitations on the Court's ability in a prosecution to address broader issues not at issue between the Crown and the defence, the majority judgment of September 17, 1999 nevertheless referred to the Court's principal pronouncements on the various grounds on which the exercise of treaty rights may be regulated. These include the following grounds:

36 (a) *The treaty right itself is a limited right.* The September 17, 1999 majority judgment referred to the "narrow ambit and extent of the treaty right" (para. 57). In its written argument, the Coalition says that the only regulatory method specified in that judgment was a limit on the quantities of fish required to satisfy the Mi'kmaq need for necessaries. This is not so. What the majority judgment said is that the Mi'kmaq treaty right does not extend *beyond* the quantities required to satisfy the need for necessaries. The Court stated at para. 61 of the September 17, 1999 majority judgment:

> Catch limits that could reasonably be expected to produce a moderate livelihood for individual Mi'kmaq families at present-day standards can be established by regulation and enforced without violating the treaty right. In that case, the regulations would accommodate the treaty right. Such regulations would *not* constitute an infringement that would have to be justified under the *Badger* standard. [Underlining added; italics in original.]

37 In other words, regulations that do no more than reasonably define the Mi'kmaq treaty right in terms that can be administered by the regulator and understood by the Mi'kmaq community that holds the treaty rights do not impair the exercise of the treaty right and therefore do not have to meet the *Badger* standard of justification.

38 Other limitations apparent in the September 17, 1999 majority judgment include the local nature of the treaties, the communal nature of a treaty right, and the fact it was only hunting and fishing resources to which access was affirmed, together with traditionally gathered things like wild fruit and berries. With regard to the Coalition's concern about the fishing rights of its members, para. 38 of the September 17, 1999 majority judgment noted the trial judge's finding that the Mi'kmaq had been fishing to trade with non-natives for over 200 years prior to the 1760-61 treaties. The 1760-61 treaty rights were thus from their inception enjoyed alongside the commercial and recreational fishery of non-natives. Paragraph 42 of the September 17, 1999 majority judgment recognized that, unlike the scarce fisheries resources of today, the view in 1760 was that the fisheries were of "limitless proportions". . . .

The Mi'kmaq treaty right to participate in the largely unregulated commercial fishery of 1760 has evolved into a treaty right to participate in the largely regulated commercial fishery of the 1990s. The notion of equitable sharing seems to be endorsed by the Coalition, which refers in its written argument on the motion to "the equal importance of the fishing industry to both Mi'kmaq and non-Mi'kmaq persons". In its Reply, the Coalition says that it is engaged in discussions "with representatives of the Acadia and Bear River Bands in southwestern Nova Scotia and takes pride that those discussions have been productive and that there is reason to hope that they will lead to harmonious and mutually beneficial participation in the commercial lobster fishery by members of those Bands". Equally, the Mi'kmaq treaty right to hunt and trade in game is not now, any more than it was in 1760, a *commercial* hunt that must be satisfied before non-natives have access to the same resources for recreational or commercial purposes. The emphasis in 1999, as it was in 1760, is on assuring the Mi'kmaq equitable access to identified resources for the purpose of earning a moderate living. In this respect, a treaty right differs from an aboriginal right which in its origin, by definition, was *exclusively* exercised by aboriginal people prior to contact with Europeans.

39   Only those regulatory limits that take the Mi'kmaq catch *below* the quantities reasonably expected to produce a moderate livelihood or other limitations that are not inherent in the limited nature of the treaty right itself have to be justified according to the *Badger* test.

40   (b) *The paramount regulatory objective is the conservation of the resource. This responsibility is placed squarely on the Minister and not on the aboriginal or non-aboriginal users of the resource.* The September 17, 1999 majority decision referred to *Sparrow, supra,* which affirmed the government's paramount authority to act in the interests of conservation. This principle was repeated in *R. v. Gladstone, . . . Nikal, . . . Adams, . . . R. v. Côté, . . .* and *Delgamuukw, . . .* all of which were referred to in the September 17, 1999 majority judgment.

41   (c) *The Minister's authority extends to other compelling and substantial public objectives which may include economic and regional fairness, and recognition of the historical reliance upon, and participation in, the fishery by non-aboriginal groups.* The Minister's regulatory authority is not limited to conservation. This was recognized in the submission of the appellant Marshall in opposition to the Coalition's motion. He acknowledges that "it is clear that limits may be imposed to conserve the species/stock being exploited and to protect public safety". Counsel for the appellant Marshall goes on to say: "Likewise, Aboriginal harvesting preferences, together with non-Aboriginal regional/community dependencies, may be taken into account in devising regulatory schemes" (emphasis added). In *Sparrow, supra,* at p. 1119, the Court said "We would not wish to set out an exhaustive list of the factors to be considered in the assessment of justification." It is for the Crown to propose what controls are justified for the management of the resource, and why they are justified. In *Gladstone, supra* (cited at para. 57 of the September 17, 1999 majority judgment), the Chief Justice commented on the differences between a native *food* fishery and a native *commercial* fishery, . . . at para. 75 . . .

. . . The aboriginal right at issue in *Gladstone, supra,* was by definition exercised exclusively by aboriginal people prior to contact with Europeans. As stated, no such exclusivity ever attached to the treaty right at issue in this case. Although we note the

acknowledgement of the appellant Marshall that "non-Aboriginal regional/commu-
nity dependencies ... may be taken into account in devising regulatory schemes", and
the statements in *Gladstone, supra,* which support this view, the Court again empha-
sizes that the specifics of any particular regulatory regime were not and are not before
us for decision.

42   In the case of any treaty right which may be exercised on a commercial scale, the
natives constitute only one group of participants, and regard for the interest of the
non-natives, as stated in *Gladstone, supra,* may be shown in the right circumstances to
be entirely legitimate. Proportionality is an important factor. In asking for a rehearing,
the Coalition stated that it is the lobster fishery "in which the Applicant's members are
principally engaged and in which, since release of the Reasons for Judgment, contro-
versy as to exercise of the treaty right has most seriously arisen". In response, the
affidavit evidence of Dr. Gerard Hare, a fisheries biologist of some 30 years' experience, was filed. The correctness of Dr. Hare's evidence was not contested in reply by
the Coalition. Dr. Hare estimated that the non-native lobster fishery in Atlantic Canada,
excluding Newfoundland, sets about 1,885,000 traps in inshore waters each year and
"[t]o put the situation in perspective, the recent Aboriginal commercial fisheries appear to be minuscule in comparison". It would be significant if it were established that
the combined aboriginal food and limited commercial fishery constitute only a "minuscule" percentage of the non-aboriginal commercial catch of a particular species,
such as lobster, bearing in mind, however, that a fishery that is "minuscule" on a
provincial or regional basis could nevertheless raise conservation issues on a local
level if it were concentrated in vulnerable fishing grounds.

43   (d) *Aboriginal people are entitled to be consulted about limitations on the exercise of treaty and aboriginal rights.* The Court has emphasized the importance in the
justification context of consultations with aboriginal peoples. Reference has already
been made to the rule in *Sparrow, supra,* at p. 1114, repeated in *Badger, supra,* at para.
97, that:

> The special trust relationship and the responsibility of the government
> vis-à-vis aboriginals must be the first consideration in determining whether
> the legislation or action in question can be justified.

The special trust relationship includes the right of the treaty beneficiaries to be
consulted about restrictions on their rights, although, as stated in *Delgamuukw, supra,*
at para. 168:

> The nature and scope of the duty of consultation will vary with the circum-
> stances.

This variation may reflect such factors as the seriousness and duration of the
proposed restriction, and whether or not the Minister is required to act in response to
unforeseen or urgent circumstances. As stated, if the consultation does not produce an
agreement, the adequacy of the justification of the government's initiative will have to
be litigated in the courts.

44   (e) *The Minister has available for regulatory purposes the full range of resource management tools and techniques, provided their use to limit the exercise of a treaty right can be justified.* If the Crown establishes that the limitations on the treaty right are imposed for a pressing and substantial public purpose, after appropriate consultation with the aboriginal community, and go no further than is required, the same techniques of resource conservation and management as are used to control the non-native fishery may be held to be justified. Equally, however, the concerns and proposals of the native communities must be taken into account, and this might lead to different techniques of conservation and management in respect of the exercise of the treaty right.

45   In its written argument on this appeal, the Coalition also argued that no treaty right should "operate to involuntarily displace any non-aboriginal existing participant in any commercial fishery", and that "neither the authors of the Constitution nor the judiciary which interprets it are the appropriate persons to mandate who shall and shall not have access to the commercial fisheries". The first argument amounts to saying that aboriginal and treaty rights should be recognized only to the extent that such recognition would not occasion disruption or inconvenience to non-aboriginal people. According to this submission, if a treaty right would be disruptive, its existence should be denied or the treaty right should be declared inoperative. This is not a legal principle. It is a political argument. What is more, it is a political argument that was expressly rejected by the political leadership when it decided to include s. 35 in the *Constitution Act, 1982.* The democratically elected framers of the *Constitution Act, 1982* provided in s. 35 that "[t]he existing aboriginal and treaty rights of the aboriginal peoples of Canada are hereby recognized *and affirmed*" (emphasis added). It is the obligation of the courts to give effect to that national commitment. No useful purpose would be served by a rehearing of this appeal to revisit such fundamental and incontrovertible principles. . . .

46   At no stage of this appeal, either before or after September 17, 1999, has any government requested a stay or suspension of judgment. The Coalition asks for the stay based on its theory that the ruling created broad gaps in the regulatory scheme, but for the reasons already explained, its contention appears to be based on a misconception of what was decided on September 17, 1999. The appellant should not have his acquittal kept in jeopardy while issues which are much broader than the specifics of his prosecution are litigated. The request for a stay of the acquittal directed on September 17, 1999, is therefore denied.

A Stay of the Broader Effect of the September 17, 1999 Majority Judgment
47   In the event the respondent Attorney General of Canada or the intervener Attorney General for New Brunswick should determine that it is in the public interest to apply for a stay of the effect of the Court's recognition and affirmation of the Mi'kmaq treaty right in its September 17, 1999 majority judgment, while leaving in place the acquittal of the appellant, the Court will entertain argument on whether it has the jurisdiction to grant such a stay, and if so, whether it ought to do so in this case.

. . .

48   The Coalition's motion is dismissed with costs.

Index

Constitutional amendments and confer-
ences 42–3
Consultation 59, 71, 80–6, 101, 127, 129,
134, 141–2, 165–6; First Nations can-
not frustrate process of 83–4
Cree 66
Cree-Naskapi (of Quebec) Act 99–100
Criminal Code of Canada 77
Crown Lands Act (Nova Scotia) 91, 148
Crown Lands and Forests Act (New
Brunswick) 89, 146

Department of Fisheries and Oceans 69,
124, 144–5, 150–9, 161
Department of Indian Affairs and Northern Development 38–9, 153, 157–8

Education Act (New Brunswick) 42
Environmental Assessment Act (British
Columbia) 84
Excise Tax Act (Canada) 148
Existing rights 57
Evidence of Aboriginal rights 112–19,
136–7, 143, 145, 149, 166; extrinsic
108, 112–16, 118; oral 65, 75–6, 108,
113, 166
Extinguishment: of Aboriginal rights 27,
131–2; of Aboriginal title 25, 27, 29,
36, 131–2; of treaty rights 41, 52–3,
55–6, 60, 64

Federal government response to Burnt
Church crisis 149–61
Federal legislation: effect on Aboriginal
and treaty rights 46–8, 50–4, 131
Fiduciary duty of the Crown 63, 74–5,
101, 106, 137, 160
Fish as a resource 96, 159–60. *See also*
Aboriginal rights; Treaty rights
Fisheries Act (Canada) 50, 52, 56, 61, 63,
104–5, 107, 109, 125, 127
Fishery (General) Regulations 105
Forestry 79, 102, 123, 139, 163
Gambling/Gaming 77
Gas 77, 123
Gitksan 66

Government: authority to regulate Aboriginal rights 95, 111, 121–5, 135,
137–8, 141–2, 149, 160, 164, 167;
balancing interests 49, 81, 102–3, 124,
130, 133–5, 141–2, 159, 161; consultation requirements for 82, 120, 129,
134–5, 142; and duty of procedural
fairness 81, 135
Gwich'in Final Agreement (1992) 97

Honour of the Crown 51, 53, 64, 104, 106,
117, 134, 136–40, 160, 165
Huron Indians 55–6

Indian Act (1868) 37–8
Indian Act (1876) 38
Indian Act, R.S.C. 1985, c. I-5 37–42, 44,
51, 54–5, 67, 97–8, 104, 146; amend-
ments to 38–9; s.18(1) (reserve cre-
ation) 32; ss.37–41 74; s.77(1) 44; s.87
98; s.88 37, 39–42, 51, 54–5, 87, 131
Indian Brook Band, Nova Scotia 54, 143–
4, 149–56
Indian title. *See* Aboriginal title
"Indianness" 40, 132
Injunctive relief test 144
Inuvialuit Final Agreement (1984) 97

James Bay and Northern Quebec Agreement (1975) 97, 100
Justification of infringements of Aboriginal and treaty rights 40, 46–8, 58–9,
64–5, 79–80, 110–11, 116, 122–3,
125, 128, 134–5, 138–9, 141–2, 154,
158, 162–3, 166–7; and conservation
47, 59, 122, 135, 138–9, 141; and re-
gional/community dependence 158;
and substantial public interests 122,
130, 135, 138, 141. *See also Badger*
justification test; *Sparrow* justification
test

Lennox Island (P.E.I.) 32
Liberal approach to treaty interpretation
50–2, 55, 57, 64, 66, 101, 109, 112–
13, 117–18, 120, 141, 164, 166

About the Author

Thomas Isaac practises law in Vancouver, British Columbia, with McCarthy Tétrault LLP. His advises clients on a wide array of public-policy issues, government relations, negotiations, Aboriginal legal issues, and corporate law. Isaac has extensive national experience advising mining, oil and gas, and other resource companies and provincial, municipal, territorial, and First Nations governments in public policy and Aboriginal matters. He is a former chief treaty negotiator for the Province of British Columbia and was assistant deputy minister in the Northwest Territories cabinet office responsible for establishing Nunavut. Isaac has taught Aboriginal, constitutional, and business law at a number of universities in Canada and has been a contributing editor to the *Canadian Native Law Reporter* since 1992. He is the author of *Aboriginal Law: Cases, Materials, and Commentary* (first and second editions), along with two other books and numerous articles on Aboriginal issues in various legal and social science journals. Isaac holds bachelor and masters degrees in both political science and law. He is a member of the International Mining Professionals Society and the Law Societies of British Columbia and New Brunswick.